THE ECONOMICS
OF
POVERTY AND
DISCRIMINATION

Fourth Edition

THE ECONOMICS OF POVERTY AND DISCRIMINATION

BRADLEY R. SCHILLER

American University

PRENTICE-HALL, INC., *Englewood Cliffs, NJ 07632*

Library of Congress Cataloging in Publication Data

SCHILLER, BRADLEY R. (date)
  The economics of poverty and discrimination.

  Includes bibliographies and index.
  1. Poor—United States. 2 Poverty. 3. Discrimination
—United States. 4. Economic assistance, Domestic—United
States. I. Title.
HC110.P6S27 1984   305.5'69'0973   84-3455
ISBN 0-13-232034-7

Editorial/production supervision and interior design: Maureen Wilson
Cover design: Ben Santora
Manufacturing buyer: Ed O'Dougherty

Printed in the United States of America

10 9 8 7 6 5 4

ISBN 0-13-232034-7   01

PRENTICE-HALL INTERNATIONAL, INC., *London*
PRENTICE-HALL OF AUSTRALIA PTY. LIMITED, *Sydney*
EDITORA PRENTICE-HALL DO BRASIL, LTDA., *Rio de Janeiro*
PRENTICE-HALL CANADA INC., *Toronto*
PRENTICE-HALL OF INDIA PRIVATE LIMITED, *New Delhi*
PRENTICE-HALL OF JAPAN, INC., *Tokyo*
PRENTICE-HALL OF SOUTHEAST ASIA PTE. LTD., *Singapore*
WHITEHALL BOOKS LIMITED, *Wellington, New Zealand*

Contents

Preface

At first glance, the subjects of poverty and discrimination appear to have changed very little in the last few years. According to Census Bureau estimates, over 30 million Americans were poor in 1983, about the same number counted as poor in 1967. In the intervening years, expenditures on welfare, education, and social services grew steadily, although always accompanied by intense debate. And although the names of the programs keep changing, the clamor for "welfare reform" and more effective employment and social services continues. Every year the poor and their advocates demand more, while millions of taxpayers say welfare is already too generous.

The same sensation of timelessness is easily experienced on the subject of discrimination. Minority children are still segregated in our schools. Minority and women workers still suffer higher unemployment and lower incomes. Meanwhile, the U.S. Supreme Court is still trying to decide the limits of "affirmative action" and mandatory school busing.

But appearances are deceptive. The constancy of the official poverty count, for example, masks an intense controversy about the dimensions of poverty in America. Many people no longer believe official poverty estimates. Indeed, some critics argue that the War on Poverty has been won. They say that the income *not* counted by the Census Bureau (e.g., food stamps, public housing) is enough to pull most "poor" people out of poverty. The true size of the poverty population may be only 6 million, not the 30 million counted by the Census. If true, this would appear to justify a major cutback in public antipoverty programs. The Reagan Administration was sufficiently convinced to draw a distinction between "poor" people, the "truly needy," and those "morally eligible" for welfare services.

The debate on discrimination has intensified as well. Ten years ago, discrimination was discussed in terms of black vs. white. Today, other minority groups and women also demand their fair share of schools, jobs, and income. Moreover, they have compelled the government and the private sector to begin responding to their demands. In addition, the Supreme Court is now grappling with the limits to "reverse discrimination" and "comparable worth" (both remedies), not the legality of initial discrimination (the problem).

This fourth edition tries to convey these important developments in poverty and discrimination. As in earlier editions, this book offers an initial statement of the problem, a detailed analysis of possible causes, and a review of present and potential policies. Also as in earlier editions, the book provides no quick and easy solutions to either poverty or discrimination. Instead, the complexity of these socio-political-economic problems is emphasized. What emerges, hopefully, is a multidimensional view of both the problems and alternative policy responses.

In pursuit of a multidimensional view of poverty and discrimination, it must be recognized that neither phenomenon is purely economic. While the title of the book is intended to convey a particular perspective on the discussion, it is not meant to imply a strict disciplinary exclusiveness. On the contrary, frequent—and often extended—explorations are made into other disciplines, most notably sociology. These will be most apparent when the cultural and racial aspects of poverty are considered.

Finally, it must be clear from the outset that poverty and discrimination are related, but separate, concerns. Not all poor people are victims of discrimination. Nor are all victims of discrimination poor. Hence, we must recognize that the elimination of either poverty or discrimination does not imply the elimination of the other. While antidiscrimination and antipoverty policies may be mutually supportive, they are only rarely identical.

The ultimate objective of this book is to lay the foundations for a clearer understanding of poverty and discrimination and for a keener perspective on related public policy. Until we know why people are poor, or what kinds of programs are effective in combatting poverty and discrimination, we cannot expect these problems to disappear.

BRADLEY R. SCHILLER

1 The Nature of Poverty

Most Americans have little contact with poverty. Moreover, most people no longer regard poverty as a very serious social problem, much less an inevitable one. Despite recurrent recessions, plant closings, and occasionally high unemployment, most American families continue to enjoy a living standard far removed from poverty. With that distance, the conviction that poverty no longer exists has spread.

Nevertheless, there are millions of Americans who remain inadequately fed, clothed, and housed. As a nation we also continue to spend billions of dollars on welfare benefits, education, training programs, and other forms of help trying to eliminate poverty. We do so for at least two reasons. One is a genuine humanitarian concern for the plight of people who cannot afford a decent standard of living. The other motive is more selfish. Poverty is indelibly linked to higher taxes, more crime, and, on occasion, civil disorder. We attempt to reduce these social ills by trying to eliminate poverty.

Whatever the motivation for antipoverty efforts, they will not succeed unless two basic questions are addressed. First, why, despite our efforts, are so many Americans still poor? Second, what policies will eliminate their impoverishment?

In seeking to answer these questions, we must recognize their interdependence. What we believe to be the dimensions and causes of poverty will influence the policies we pursue. If we believe, for example, that people are poor because they cannot find decent jobs, our antipoverty efforts are likely to focus on the creation of more and better jobs. On the other hand, if we believe that people are poor simply because they are lazy, we are likely to provide fewer jobs and services.

Our perceptions influence not only our policy decisions but also our ultimate success or failure in eliminating poverty. If people cannot find decent jobs because they lack basic skills, then the provision of more and better jobs will not eliminate much poverty. In this case, misperceptions of the causes of poverty would result in an expensive failure for antipoverty policy. Hence, it is important that our public antipoverty policies be based on informed perceptions of the nature and causes of poverty.

Different historical phases of antipoverty activity in America illustrate this interdependence of causal perspectives and policy prescriptions. In colonial times poverty was viewed as a curse on those of disreputable character. Impoverishment was seen as the companion to and punishment for vice. Accordingly, early antipoverty prescriptions focused on religious training, corporal punishment (to drive out sin), and physical expulsion. Very little was done to help the poor become more self-sufficient or even to alleviate their suffering.

It was not until the depression of the 1890s that many people seriously began to question the proposition that poverty resulted from sin and slovenliness. The march of unemployed and poor men—Coxey's Army—on Washington, D.C., in 1894 helped stimulate fresh perspectives on the origins of poverty. But it was not until 15 million Americans simultaneously experienced unemployment in the depths of the Great Depression that a really new perspective on poverty took hold. Only when millions of otherwise responsible and industrious individuals fell abruptly into joblessness and poverty did the American public begin to view poverty as being outside the control of the individual. Awareness grew that poverty might be the consequence of social and economic forces rather than of immorality and vice.

From one point of view, our experience with depressions and poverty may have been too brief. With the passage of time and the return to prosperity, poverty lost its middle-class constituency, and people became less generous toward the poor. When everyone else is prospering, poverty becomes suspect. In good times, most observers again question the ambition, motivation, ability, and the entire cultural orientation of the poor—particularly those receiving welfare benefits. An editorial from the Tulsa, Oklahoma, *Tribune* typifies the residual hostilities and resentments that persist.

Relief is gradually becoming an honorable career in America. It is a pretty fair life, if you have neither conscience nor pride. The politicians will weep for you. The state will give a mother bonus for her illegitimate children, and if she neglects them sufficiently she can save enough of her AFDC payments to keep herself and her boyfriend in wine and gin.[1]

A more recent Gallup poll of the general population reflects the same undercurrent of hostility to people dependent on public assistance. Asked to

[1]Quoted in Edgar May, *The Wasted Americans* (New York: Harper & Row, 1964), p. 7

guess what proportion of welfare recipients are collecting more than they are entitled to, 36 percent of the population guessed that at least half were "cheaters."[2] An NBC poll showed that only 30 percent of the American public believe welfare recipients really need help.[3] Yet, most Americans still report that they favor help for the poor!

The implication of these conflicting views is that although poor people do warrant assistance, once they receive it they somehow become unworthy. As Professor John Tropman has observed, most Americans view acceptance of welfare as tantamount to "giving up." Welfare implies a lack of independence and individualism. Accordingly, those who accept welfare deserve punishment in the form of hostility and stigma.

Current American attitudes toward the poor, then, are best described as ambivalent. "On the one hand, government and individuals alike decry poverty and devise programs geared to eradicate or eliminate it. On the other hand, the poor are disliked and perhaps feared."[4] The disquieting suspicion that external social and economic forces are at the root of poverty continues to stir the public conscience. At the same time, however, the egocentric conviction that the poor are less deserving still lingers. Only as unemployment rates reach crisis proportions—as in the early 1980s—does the former perspective clearly gather significant strength. Even then, however, President Reagan was careful to draw a distinction between the "truly needy" and those who could get by if they wanted to.

Against this background of uncertainty about the dimensions and causes of poverty, it is not surprising that public policy is often contradictory and ineffective. Until we reach a consensus on the dimensions of the problem, we cannot muster the necessary political support for public action. Where the causes of poverty remain the subject of intense debate, we cannot expect our efforts to meet with success. Accordingly, a serious effort to eliminate poverty must begin with certain fundamentals. We must first decide precisely what we mean by "poor." Then we must determine how many persons fall into this category and why they are there.

POVERTY AND INEQUALITY

It is useful to begin a discussion of poverty with a broader view of the distribution of incomes. We all know that incomes are not distributed equally, that some people have less while others have more. The problem we confront is to determine how *much* less distinguishes a person as being "poor."

Figure 1.1 provides a quick summary of the actual distribution of income in

[2]Gallup survey of May 1979

[3]NBC News Poll of August 1977

[4]John E. Tropman, "The Image of Public Welfare: Reality or Projection?" *Public Welfare*, Winter 1977.

FIGURE 1.1   The Frequency Distribution of Family Incomes, 1982

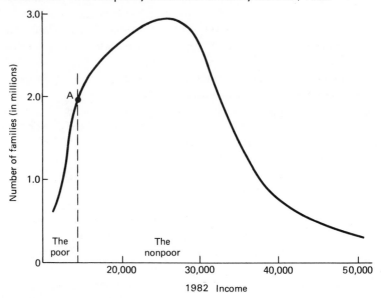

Source: Approximated from the U.S. Bureau of the Census: *Money Income and Poverty Status in 1982 of Families, and Persons in the United States: 1982* (Washington, DC: Government Printing Office, January 1983).

the United States. In 1982, the *median* income of American families was $23,400. But not every family received $23,400. On the contrary, the bell-shaped curve in Figure 1.1 indicates that although many families had incomes at or near the median (the top part of the bell), many families had incomes significantly higher or lower than $23,400 (the lower "tails" of the bell). Table 1.1 provides a closer look at the distribution. Over 10 percent of all families enjoyed an income

TABLE 1.1   THE INCOME DISTRIBUTION, 1982

	FAMILIES	
INCOME	NUMBER (IN THOUSANDS)	PERCENT
$50,000 and over	6,692	10.9
35,000–49,999	9,823	16.0
25,000–34,999	11,972	19.5
20,000–24,999	7,551	12.3
15,000–19,999	7,429	12.1
10,000–14,999	7,613	12.4
Under $10,000	10,314	16.8
In poverty	(7,512)	(12.2)
Total	61,393	100.0

Source: U.S. Bureau of the Census.

in excess of $50,000 in 1982. At the same time, more than one out of six families received less than $10,000, many of them much less.

If all incomes were equal, the frequency distribution depicted in Figure 1.1 would narrow to a vertical line, positioned at the average (or mean) income level. But clearly, we are a long way from such complete equality. As a result many people below the average—as well as a good many above it—feel that they are "poor," especially in comparison to others. Our initial task is to provide a sounder basis for defining poverty, in other words, to identify a level of income—like point A in Figure 1.1—that distinguishes those who are poor from those who aren't. We start the search with only the conviction that somewhere along the far left side of the graph there are families who are truly poor.

ECONOMIC DEFINITIONS OF POVERTY

Despite all the time that has been spent on poverty research, no consensus has been reached on the appropriate location for point A. That is to say, we have not yet agreed on what we mean by the term *poverty*.

It is facile and perhaps satisfying to reply that poverty is simply a lack of money. Of course, such a response is essentially correct; poverty *does* mean a scarcity of money. When we examine this definition more carefully, however, we must recognize a certain vagueness about the nature of poverty. Exactly what is meant by a *lack of money*? Do we mean no money, no income, no assets, and no credit, that is, a complete and devastating inability to acquire the basics of life? Or do we mean simply a shortage of cash? And if we mean one or all of these criteria, how do we measure and define them? Do we speak of a scarcity of money with reference to certain goods we think should or must be obtained, or do we mean scarcity relative to the amount of money, assets, income, or credit that others have? Even if we agree that poverty is, in essence, a lack of economic resources, there is room for a great deal of ambiguity and discussion.

The Absolute Approach

To achieve a workable and acceptable definition of poverty, we may begin by noting that there are two basic economic approaches to the concept of poverty. The first of these is the absolute approach, which deems some particular amount of goods and services as essential to an individual's or a family's welfare. Those who do not possess the economic resources to obtain these goods and services are considered poor. In the least humanitarian strain of the absolute approach this bundle of economic goods and services consists of the minimum caloric intake essential to human existence, and perhaps some form of shelter. Additional frills are tacked onto this basic diet according to the generosity of the analyst.

This, of course, is the fundamental problem with the absolute definition of poverty. Once the bare-bones, life-sustaining minimum caloric diet has been exceeded, there is no agreement as to how many additional frills can be included in the definitional bundle of basic goods and services. In the 1890s no one felt particularly poor if he did not possess electric lights. Yet, today a family without electricity will most likely be considered poor. So we include a provision for electricity in our minimum poverty-defining budget. But consensus is far more difficult to achieve on a table lamp, much less on a television, a car, or a six-pack of beer. How many of these items will we include in a poor family's budget? Our answer will determine where to draw the poverty line.

The differences of opinion on this subject are illustrated by the continuing controversy over "minimum" needs. Public opinion polls indicated that people felt $15,392 per year was the minimum amount of income a family of four "needed" in 1982. Yet, the official (government) definition of poverty in 1982 was an income of less than $9,862. Even more extreme, the state of Texas determined the basic needs of a family of four to be $2,412 a year. And Mississippi paid a welfare family of four with no other income source a mere $1,440.

These differences serve to focus attention on two basic issues, namely: Who should determine the basic needs of individuals? And on what basis is that determination to be made? Quite obviously, each person's conception of what a family "needs" will be conditioned by his or her own economic position. A millionaire might regard $50,000 a year as abject poverty while others might view it as an impossible dream. Likewise, people who have been unable to pay the rent, buy groceries, or find a job will have sharper perspectives on poverty than the typical middle-class family.[5] Faced with these conflicting perspectives, some observers have suggested an alternative approach to defining poverty, one that depends on *relative* standards.

The Relative Approach

As a practical matter, the absolute approach of defining poverty is vague and subject to the views of those formulating the yardstick. The relative approach is simply more explicit about this subjectivity. In essence, it states that a person is poor when his or her income is significantly less than the average income of the population. For example, we might say that a person or family with less than one-half of the average income is poor. By defining poverty in these terms, we not only avoid the need to define absolute needs, but also put more emphasis on the (in)equality of incomes. This broader perspective under-

[5]A technique for using subjective views of minimal needs to develop poverty lines is presented in Theo Goedhart, et al., "The Poverty Line: Concept and Measurement," *Journal of Human Resources*, Fall 1977; and discussed further by Constantine Kapsalis, "Poverty Lines: An Alternative Method of Estimation," in the same journal, Summer 1981.

scores the relationship between our views of poverty and our perspectives on the "fairness" of the entire distribution of incomes.

There are just as many relative measures of poverty as there are absolute ones. Perhaps the most extreme version of relative measures is one that defines poverty as the low end of the income distribution; for example, anyone in the lowest fifth (or tenth, or third) of the distribution is regarded as poor. From this perspective, poverty will persist as long as inequality does: If the frequency distribution depicted in Figure 1.1 were to move to the right—thus making everyone better off—point A would move along with the curve.

Table 1.2 illustrates the basic distinction between absolute and relative definitions of poverty in another way. Note, for example, that 1.6 percent of all American families earned less than $1,000 in 1970, 4.6 percent less than $2,000, and so forth. Only 4.6 percent of American families earned more than $25,000. Note also that incomes were much lower in the 1935 to 1936 period, even after adjusting for inflation (expressing amounts in 1970 dollar values). In the middle of the Depression 13.4 percent of the population earned less than $1,000, and nearly a third survived with less than $2,000 per year.

Suppose we wanted to compare the number of Americans who were poor in 1970 with the number who were poor in 1936. Franklin Roosevelt spoke of one-third of the nation as being "ill-housed, ill-clad, ill-nourished." Apparently he regarded an income of about $2,000 as a threshold of poverty (see Table 1.2). By Roosevelt's definition, only 4.6 percent of the American population was poor in 1970. From an historical perspective, then, we could conclude that the incidence of poverty in the United States had declined markedly over a period of thirty years.

But what would we conclude about the course of poverty between 1936 and 1970 if we had instead applied the relative concept of poverty to the comparison? If we consistently regard the lowest fifth of the American income distribution as poor, then by definition we would find that 20 percent of the population was poor in 1936 and continued to be so in 1970.

This example illustrates the basic weaknesses of the relative measure of poverty. First, it perpetuates poverty in the statistical sense that some fixed proportion of the population is always regarded as poor. Poverty will always exist if the lowest fifth of the income distribution is regarded as poor. Second, a relative measure of poverty alone says nothing about the quality of life for the people at the bottom of the income distribution. Yet we want to know not only how many people are in poverty but also how desperate their situation is. In a similar vein, we may want to know how much money poor families need to reach an acceptable standard of living.

An improved measure of relative poverty, which has been suggested by Victor Fuchs, meets at least the first objection to relative definitions of poverty. By his definition, those with incomes less than half of the national median are poor. In 1970, for example, the median family income was just under $10,000

TABLE 1.2 CUMULATIVE FAMILY INCOME DISTRIBUTION, 1970 AND 1935-1936

Income in 1970 dollars	$1,000	$2,000	$3,000	$4,000	$5,000	$10,000	$15,000	$25,000
Percentage of families with incomes less than specified amount								
in 1970	1.6	4.6	8.9	13.9	19.1	50.9	77.7	95.4
in 1935-36	13.4	31.3	47.3	65.3	77.8	94.8	—	—

Source: U.S. Bureau of the Census.

(see Table 1.2). Thus, according to the "Fuchs point," families with less than $5,000 (half of the median) should have been considered poor. The advantage of the Fuchs point over simpler relative definitions is that it distinguishes the elimination of poverty from the elimination of inequality. Whereas the simpler relative definition precludes the elimination of poverty until *complete* equality of incomes is attained, the Fuchs point envisions the elimination of poverty occurring with a *reduction* in inequality, that is, a *narrowing* of income differences (and thus a narrower distribution for Figure 1.1).

There is nothing sacred, of course, about the use of one-half the median as a relative standard of poverty; we could just as easily have chosen to define poverty in relative terms as one-fourth, one-third, or three-sixteenths of the median income. That is, there is as much subjectivity involved in defining the Fuchs point as there is in defining absolute "minimum" standards of poverty. In reality, one's choice of an appropriate Fuchs point is likely to be influenced by the absolute standard of living implied, just as the choice of an absolute standard is likely to be affected by the degree of inequality and the general standards of living we observe.

Professor Morton Paglin of Portland State University has raised another troubling issue. With *whom*, he asks, should we compare our incomes? A young family with children has different needs and income sources than an older couple living in retirement. Should both households be treated equally when computing the median income? Or should relative incomes be measured only in comparison with families of similar size and age? In the former case, older couples and single-parent households will be most likely to appear "poor." By the latter standard, however, more equal proportions of each population subgroup would be classified as poor.

In view of the conflicting measures of poverty, it is tempting to abandon the search for a poverty line. But this is neither necessary nor appropriate. We need an acceptable definition of poverty in order to identify people we desire to help and to measure our success in helping them. The search for a poverty line is analogous to the search for highway speed limits. No one really believes that all speeds in excess of 55 miles per hour are somehow dangerous and all speeds less than 55 miles an hour are somehow safe; the realities of highway driving are much more complex. Yet, we use 55 miles per hour as a convenient gauge of highway safety. The same is true of our poverty line. On the continuum of misery and human happiness, we cannot pretend that there is some point below which people are unhappy or poor and above which people are content. But, like highway speed limits, we do need a cutoff point—the poverty line.

In searching for the poverty line, we cannot conclude that one approach to defining poverty is inherently better than the other, or even maintain a rigid distinction between them. Instead, we will simply note that the contrast between relative and absolute measures of poverty highlights a basic policy issue. Is our primary policy concern with the misery of those who command low incomes, or are we concerned with the unequal distribution of incomes? Though income distribution and poverty are intrinsically related, they can be approached separately. Because absolute definitions of poverty maintain this distinction—and because they are the official basis for government policy—we shall utilize them throughout the remainder of the book. Thus, we allow for the possibility of eliminating poverty without altering the relative distribution of incomes, a goal that could be achieved by making *everyone* better off. But we also recognize that the direct redistribution of incomes from rich to poor could speed the elimination of poverty and might be a goal in itself.

NONECONOMIC MEASURES OF POVERTY

The distinction between absolute and relative measures of poverty does not exhaust the list of potential definitions. To some observers poverty is just as much a state of mind as it is a state of one's pocketbook. In this most subjective of views a person is not poor unless he or she *feels* poor. The Kentucky backwoodsman is sometimes seen not as impoverished but as enjoying the rich benefits of a bountiful and uncluttered natural world. He is not to be pitied, but rather idealized. To lift him out of financial destitution would be to corrupt him.

Although Henry Thoreau forcefully expressed this distinction between monetary and spiritual richness, his views are not easily translated into statistical or policymaking terms. Short of surveying all destitute persons as to their spiritual contentment and materialistic anxieties, Thoreau's distinction permits no census of the poor. His perspective merits reflection, but does not provide an adequate guide to policy formulation. Accordingly, we are led to use other criteria for identifying the poor and to conclude from their political agitation that the poor are not wholly content.

Recent observers from other social disciplines have construed similar definitions of modern poverty. Generally they focus on the hopes, expectations, and aspirations—the entire "culture" in some cases—of those without material means. To these observers, poverty is a lack of money, a lack of spirit, a lack of hope for a better life. Poverty is thus understood to be complete material and spiritual deprivation. Although these concepts have considerable merit in their own right, they are not easily observed, much less quantified. They may contribute to an understanding of poverty, but they add little to its definition or measurement. They are also likely to create more disagreement on poverty measures than already exists. Accordingly, we will rely on economic and strictly observable criteria in defining and measuring poverty.

THE OFFICIAL POVERTY INDEX

As noted above, the government has chosen to use the absolute approach to defining poverty. Naturally, this has required the government to identify the minimum amount of money required to sustain a family, a minimum estimated to be $9,862 for a family of four in 1982. But before we look at just who is poor according to this definition, or what conditions give rise to such poverty, we should first take a closer look at how that figure was obtained. One of the problems with not being poor is that it is difficult to comprehend just what it means to be poor. Hopefully, a short review of our current definition of poverty will help increase that comprehension.

The Concept of Minimum Needs

In order to state that a specific amount of money income is required to keep a family out of poverty, one must have a firm notion of just what that much money will buy. That is, the identification of a poverty measure denominated in dollars logically begins with a standard of living denominated in "essential" goods and services. That task is not easy, particularly in view of the very different opinions people have about just what goods and services are essential. But let us suppose that we really could be coldly scientific and single out such goods.

We may begin to assemble an inventory of "minimum needs" by determining the absolutely basic ingredients of human subsistence; presumably everyone will agree that our poverty measure should include at least these components. Such a list will include minimum food, clothing, shelter, and fuel requirements as determined by appropriate experts. To this list of basic minimums we may choose to include means of transportation, some recreation, and whatever additional goods and services we deem appropriate, if not absolutely essential. The sum total of our efforts, assuming consensus can be achieved, will be a shopping list of what we consider to be basic goods and services. Those persons who cannot obtain all the items on our list will be considered poor, those who can as not poor.

Suppose for the moment that nutritionists, physiologists, and other assorted scientific experts could actually detail the minimum subsistence requirements we have outlined. Such a list might be like the one in Table 1.3. Note that each functional requirement is expressed in its generic measure. To this list of social and biological minimums we might add additional food, clothing, or entertainment, depending on our sense of generosity. In this way we could construct a complete specification of what we deem to be the minimum acceptable (or poverty) standard of living.

But consider carefully the list we have compiled. To begin with, how are we to translate 2,471 calories into more familiar staples, such as peanuts, bananas, and chewing gum? As anyone who has ever dieted well knows, there are an infinite number of ways in which a person can consume the requisite number of calories. Or consider the clothing requirement. The specification "4 pounds" tells us nothing at all about the appropriate type of clothing or even whether we

TABLE 1.3   HYPOTHETICAL MINIMUM HUMAN NEEDS

CATEGORY	AMOUNT
Minimum food requirements	2,471 calories per day
Minimum fuel requirements	37 kilowatt-hours
Minimum shelter requirements	60 board feet
Minimum clothing requirements	4 pounds
Minimum transportation requirements	7 miles

should shop at Saks Fifth Avenue or a Salvation Army store. Similar problems arise with every item on our list.

As if this vagueness of detail were not a serious enough problem, let us return to the generic specifications. Though there is some conceptual foundation for speaking of "minimum" food, shelter, clothing, or fuel requirements, there is admittedly no firm basis for specifying what these minimums are. People do survive on varying amounts of calories; the warming and protective value of clothing cannot be adequately gauged in pounds; and the need for shelter varies enormously. Consequently, any claim to scientific precision, even in the generic specifications of our poverty standard, is pretentious and misplaced.

While the specification of a poverty standard is an imprecise endeavor, it is not necessarily useless. The achievement of consensus about the components of a poverty standard may be a formidable task, although not necessarily impossible. If we can achieve some sort of reasonable compromise, our basic objective of specification will have been attained.

We return, then, to our position that an absolute standard of poverty can be defined in terms of a shopping list of goods and services. Poverty is thus understood as the inability to obtain the goods and services sufficient to meet socially defined minimum needs. Momentarily sidestepping the issue of specification, our only remaining conceptual problem is to consolidate that list of goods and services into more convenient and observable units.

Units of Measure

In a market economy the ability of an individual to obtain needed goods and services is determined by his *purchasing power*. The producers and sellers of goods require some form of payment before they willingly yield up their wares. Accordingly, we may be able to simplify our poverty standard by expressing that measure, not in terms of a list of necessary goods and services but instead in terms of the purchasing power required to obtain those same goods and services. This simplification will greatly enhance the usefulness of our measure, as we will be able to inquire merely whether a person has a specific amount of purchasing power rather than a cumbersome list of essential commodities.

The obvious and familiar measure of purchasing power in a market economy is money, so it should come as no surprise that we express our poverty standard in dollars and cents. The necessary conversion requires that we price all the goods and services in our list, then add their prices up to determine the amount of money involved. That total is our gauge of poverty, for it represents command over the goods and services we have specified.

Not only is such a summary measure convenient, but it also facilitates the compromise that produced the standard itself. Suppose, for example, that Mr. Blixen believes that 1,437 calories and 1.57 pounds of clothing are the absolute daily minimum needs of one person. You, on the other hand, contend that 2,113 calories and 0.86 pound of clothing are necessary (a difference equivalent to giving up your shirt for a banana split). Given your respective resolutions, you and Mr. Blixen are unlikely to reach a compromise on the generic specifications of minimum needs. However, what if current market prices indicate that your "needs" require $4.37 to fulfill, while Mr. Blixen's budget is $4.35 per day. In *monetary* terms, it is obvious that you are not far away from a potential compromise and that agreement on the *generic* components of a minimum budget might be postponed indefinitely.

While we do need the food, shelter, and other items on our shopping list daily, it is not necessary to have the right amount of cash every day. Shopping each day for the minimum requirements of shelter, fuel, clothing, and food would be extraordinarily inconvenient, if not downright impossible. Our real interest lies in ascertaining that a person has an adequate flow of cash so that he or she can acquire the basic necessities as the need arises. Hence, our poverty standard will incorporate the basic needs of an individual for some particular span of time and will be expressed in terms of the amount of money needed during that period of time to make the required purchases. Whether that individual then elects to shop monthly, weekly, or daily is immaterial.

The best single indicator of a person's purchasing power over a period of time is *income*. Income is the flow of cash to a person over time, and thus it represents what he or she will have available to acquire goods and services. But here, too, there are complications. Income is not the sole determinant of purchasing power. Two other factors, assets and credit, can render a person's command over goods and services much larger than his or her current income. Where credit is available, goods and services can, in effect, be borrowed. No current income is necessary, just a promise to make repayment when time and circumstances permit (or when the creditors demand).

A similar situation holds true with assets. Here again, a person may acquire goods and services without an income, in effect by trading one good for another. In the most common instance, a person may sell a particular asset to acquire a desired commodity. Or he or she may trade the asset for the commodity or even combine the features of credit and wealth at a nearby pawnshop.

Finally, many people obtain goods and services *directly* without payment of cash or even a promise to pay (credit). In the last ten years or so, the government has assumed an increasing responsibility for providing basic goods and services to people, especially if they have insufficient income or assets. Food stamps, for example, allow one to "buy" groceries with coupons ("stamps") rather than money. Food-stamp recipients, therefore, need less cash income to achieve any particular "minimum" standard. Likewise, families that live in public housing or receive free medical care enjoy a standard of living higher than their money income suggests. Money incomes have become a less reliable index of living standards, especially at the low end of the income distribution.[6]

Despite these limitations, money incomes are the single best index of a family's living standard, and it is the yardstick the government uses for measuring poverty. We will first look at the official poverty index, then reexamine some of its limitations.

Poverty Thresholds

We are now in a position to identify what may be called a *poverty* line. We have established the process by which that line may be formulated; all that remains is to apply the process. But lest we become too complacent about our theoretical achievements, it should be noted that a nearly identical procedure was formulated at least as early as 1890. At that time Charles Booth, an English sociologist, estimated the goods and services necessary to maintain a family in what he called a "state of chronic want." He then priced those commodities and concluded that a weekly income of approximately twenty-four shillings or less was necessary to achieve the condition he described. At about the same time American economists estimated that from $400 to $600 per year was necessary to attain this condition in the United States.

Since Booth's time our standards of living have grown enormously. The number of proposed poverty lines has grown also, each varying with the circumstances of the time and the perspectives of the architect. While it is not necessary to review the history of those poverty lines, each of which had significance in its own time, it is of interest to examine two of the most important formulations.

The CEA Line

In 1963, the President's Council of Economic Advisers (CEA) officially sanctioned a poverty line of $3,000 per annum for a typical American family.

---

[6]In-kind income is not limited to poor families; middle-class families benefit from subsidized public schools, job-related fringe benefits, special tax advantages, and an array of other noncash ("in-kind") forms of income. If all in-kind benefits were added up—not just those the poor receive—the poor might actually appear relatively worse off than their money incomes imply. The rapid *growth* of in-kind benefits for the poor in recent years—not necessarily their aggregate share—is what complicates poverty measures.

While their effort was an important step in the development of poverty statistics and policy, we shall see that their estimate had serious faults.

The rationale behind the Council's poverty line estimate was similar to that which we have already outlined. The Council accepted the notion that food requirements constitute the foundation of any poverty budget. Accordingly, they set out to determine the minimum nutritional requirements of a typical American family. These requirements had been estimated by the Department of Agriculture for the Social Security Administration, which was already developing a poverty measure. The estimates indicated that three minimally adequate meals a day would cost the typical family of two adults and two children exactly $2.736 a day. Now, the very precision of that nutrition estimate makes it suspect. We have already suggested the difficulties inherent in specifying minimum nutrition requirements, converting those requirements into real commodities, and pricing those goods in the market. To pretend that this process could yield an estimate as precise as $2.736 a day is to strain one's credibility.

The Council adopted a more pragmatic approach to arrive at the *total* budget for a poor family. You will recall that the frills added to a starvation diet were the prime source of arbitrariness in the budgetary process. Some people said ice cream was essential, others insisted on beer and pretzels. These problems were circumvented by simply observing how much money low-income families actually spend on such frills. Consumer studies indicated that such families spend approximately two-thirds of their incomes on nonfood items—commodities like clothing, shelter, fuel, and goods that might be considered as less than essential to human subsistence. Using this observation as a benchmark, the Council then multiplied their basic food budget by three to determine how much total income a poor family needs. The results of their calculation are depicted in Table 1.4. The Council then rounded off the total budget estimate to the $3,000 figure. Using this measure, the Council found that there were 33.4 million poverty-stricken persons in America in 1963.

Michael Harrington once warned us "not to allow statistical quibbling to obscure the huge, enormous, and intolerable fact of poverty in America."[7] This is a warning we must take seriously, especially when millions of families may be involved. Accordingly, we would do well to overlook some of the imperfections in the Council's estimation procedures and concentrate on the mass of poverty they identified. Whether the "true" size of the poverty population in 1963 was then 33 million, 33.5 million, or even 35.23 million would not seem to be of much consequence.

TABLE 1.4   THE CEA POVERTY BUDGET, 1963

Food budget	$2.736 per day × 365 days = $ 998.64
Nonfood budget	2 × food budget = 1,997.28
	Total budget = $2,995.92

[7]Michael Harrington, *The Other America* (New York: The Macmillan Company, 1962), p. 10.

But one glaring error in the Council's estimation procedure prevents us from accepting their results. To appreciate the nature of the Council's error, let us look at three families from the 1963 income distribution:

The husband in Family 1 is thirty-seven years old and supports six children and a pregnant wife on his income of $3,200 a year.

Family 2 consists of a soon-to-be-retired couple, both in their mid-sixties. The wife does not work and the husband's earnings amount to $2,800 per year. They own their home, having made the final mortgage payment last Christmas.

Family 3 consists of a struggling graduate student, his working wife, and their three-month-old child. They both work at the college carryout store in their spare time. Their combined earnings, including overtime and tips, amounts to $2,400 a year.

How did these three families place in the Council's census of poor Americans? Family 1, consisting of eight and one-half persons, was officially classified as nonpoor. Families 2 and 3 were counted as poor, as their incomes were under the $3,000 limit. But how many people would be willing to accept the Council's classification of these families? Family 1 is clearly desperate, while Family 2 is living a quiet and perhaps comfortable life. Our graduate-student family is not exactly affluent, but they are not desperate on $200 a month.

The source of the Council's error should be obvious at this point. The Council calculated a poverty budget for a *typical* family of two adults and two children. But not all families consist of four persons, nor do all four-person families have consistently "typical" needs. As our illustration has made clear, the Council's definition of a poverty line must *at a minimum* be adjusted for varying family size. A further refinement should take into account gross differences in family needs even among families of the same size.

The SSA Index

These basic refinements of the Council's poverty line were undertaken by Mollie Orshansky of the Social Security Administration (SSA). She first adjusted for family size, then for varying family needs based on whether or not the family lived on a farm, whether the family was headed by a man or woman, and how many children there were. Using these four variables, she identified 124 family types and meticulously calculated an appropriate poverty budget for each one. And while Ms. Orshansky's estimates were not faultless, they represented a significant improvement over earlier estimation attempts.

For the "typical" family of four identified by the Council of Economic Advisers, the SSA poverty budget and the Council's own budget were very similar. The SSA adjustments, however, counted many more large families and fewer smaller families as poor due to different family needs. Our earlier examples illustrate the difference. Ms. Orshansky found that Family 3, the struggling graduate student and his wife and child, needed only $2,275 for a minimum budget. Hence, they were not counted as poor under the SSA Index. Family 2, the soon-to-be-retired couple, required a minimum of only $1,855 and was living quite comfortably on their income. Family 1, however, with eight persons, needed at least $5,100 per year to meet essential needs and was classified as poor by the Social Security Administration index.

The Current Poverty Index

Despite the considerable sophistication of the 1963 Social Security Administration poverty index, it was not presented as either perfect or static. It was recognized that, as prices and our standards of living continued to rise, the SSA poverty lines would require repeated upward adjustments. Over time our concept of what is essential to modern-day living will be enlarged, and the necessary ingredients will also cost more.

The official poverty index now in use has been revised to account for the rising prices of goods and services, but not for our steadily increasing standard of living. According to Ms. Orshansky's earlier calculations, an average family of two adults and two children required a minimum of $3,130 in 1963. In 1982, after nineteen years of inflation, that index stood at $9,862. We are saying that it cost $9,862 in 1982 to buy those goods and services that cost $3,130 in 1963. The increased dollar amount of our definition does not imply in any way an increased standard of living for the poor. It adjusts only for rising prices.[8] If we wanted to increase the standard of living of those whom we define as poor—and not many affluent persons are so inclined—then we would have to raise the index by more than the inflation adjustment, that is, to a figure higher than $9,862.

A current poverty line that adjusts only for changing prices leaves the standard of living of the poor unchanged. But the income and living standards of the rest of the population will continue to advance as the American economy grows. Hence, poverty lines adjusted only for inflation imply a growing disparity between the status of the poor and that of the rest of the population. Like any *absolute* poverty line, the official poverty thresholds imply increasing *relative* poverty over time.

Despite the limitations of current poverty line adjustments, we will adhere to present standards. Accordingly, a 1982 income of less than $9,862 will qualify a family of four for inclusion in our head count of the poor. The application of this standard to other family sizes is summarized in Table 1.5.

Enumeration of the persons below either the 1963 or the updated poverty

[8]Because of continuing inflation in 1983 and 1984, the poverty line for a family of four exceeded $11,000 in 1984. Here again, the higher dollar amount reflects only higher prices, not an improved standard of living for the poor.

TABLE 1.5 POVERTY STANDARDS, 1982

SIZE OF FAMILY	POVERTY STANDARD
One member	$ 4,901
Two members	6,281
Three members	7,693
Four members	9,862
Five members	11,684
Six members	13,207
Seven members	15,036
Eight members	16,719
Nine or more members	19,698

Source: U.S. Bureau of the Census.

index is a simple and straightforward task and will be undertaken in Chapter 2. Unfortunately, the clinical nature of the statistical operation tends to impress the observer very little with the real impoverishment that the numbers represent. Consequently, it is worthwhile to dwell for a few moments on the standard of living that a poverty budget implies.

The austerity of the poverty budget was well described by B. Seebohm Rowntree, an English sociologist, in 1901. The essence of his description is still valid today:

A family, living upon the scale allowed for in this estimate, must never spend a penny on railway fare or omnibus. They must never go into the country unless they walk. They must never purchase a half-penny newspaper or spend a penny to buy a ticket for a popular concert. They must write no letters to absent children, for they cannot afford to pay the postage. They must never contribute anything to their church or chapel, or give any help to a neighbor which costs them money. They cannot save, nor can they join sick or Trade Union, because they cannot pay the necessary subscription. The children must have no pocket money for dolls, marbles, or sweets. The father must smoke no tobacco and must drink no beer. The mother must never buy any pretty clothes for herself or for her children, the character of the family wardrobe as for the family diet being governed by the regulation, "nothing must be bought but that which is absolutely necessary for the maintenance of physical health, and what is bought must be of the plainest and most economical description."[9]

___

[9]B. Seebohm Rowntree, *Poverty: A Study of Town Life* (London: Longmans, Green & Co. Ltd., 1901).

That Mr. Rowntree's description of poverty living remains appropriate can be seen by looking first at the food component of the current poverty budget for a family of four. Our $9,862 budget allows approximately $2.25 per person per day. That is $2.25 for breakfast, lunch, dinner, and any snacks—an amount less than what one lunch costs in most places. This means that the homemaker must plan, buy, and prepare a nutritious meal for her family of four for approximately three dollars. When even hamburger costs over two dollars a pound, it is devastatingly clear that this poverty family is not eating either very well or very much.[10] And if they have aspirations to eat out on occasion, their only hope is to save money by eating lots of hot dogs and boiled eggs at home.

You may respond that this is a gross exaggeration of how the poor live. You may even know of a poor person who eats steak. And in a sense you are right. We have described how a poor family would act if they spent only their food allowance on food. In fact, poor families do not follow our carefully budgeted allowances. They tend to forego other items and spend some of their nonfood allowance money on better and more palatable meals—maybe even an occasional beer to wash down the grits and pick up their spirits. And it is this process that comes closest to describing what it means to be poor. Every day a poor person or family must choose between an adequate diet of the most economic sort and some other necessity because there is never enough money to have both. Consequently, some of the poor eat steak and walk around with holes in their shoes.

It is interesting to contrast what is officially regarded as a poverty income to what Americans generally believe is required to make ends meet. A Gallup poll taken in 1982 asked a cross section of Americans: "What is the smallest amount of money a family of four (husband, wife, and two children) needs each week to get along in this community?" Their answers averaged out at $296 a week, or $15,392 a year. Quite clearly, most Americans do not believe that the poverty standard is enough, that is, that families really could get by for long on the government's definition of minimum needs. It is nevertheless true that poor families must find some way to cope. Indeed, most poor families command even less income than the official standard. In 1982, for example, the typical poor family had a cash income (including cash welfare benefits it received) of only $4,800.[11] For these families, even having the opportunity to choose between steak and shoes would seem like affluence.

If the prospect of existing for a short time on a poverty budget or less is not disquieting enough, consider the prospect of subsisting at that level into the indefinite future. A poor family must not only adjust to a subsistence budget but

---

[10]Since 1963, the Department of Agriculture has increased its estimate of a minimum food budget, based on revised nutritional requirements and changing food choices. This increased food budget would increase the poverty line; however, no official action has been taken.

[11]The total real income of many poor families is higher than this as a result of receiving noncash income (e.g., food stamps, Medicaid, housing subsidies); this is discussed in Chapters 2 and 12.

must also be prepared to remain at that standard of living. That is why a more affluent person cannot adequately grasp the significance of poverty by adopting a subsistence budget for a brief time. The affluent person knows that his experiment can and will be terminated shortly. The poor person possesses no such luxury. As was reported on a similar experiment by Tolstoy, "poverty is not the lack of things; it is the fear and the dread of want. That fear Tolstoy could not know."[12]

Let us then be clear about what our poverty index implies. The line we have drawn separating the poor from the nonpoor does not indicate what is enough—it only asserts with confidence what is too little. As Robert Hunter observed in 1904, "to live up to the standard . . . means no more than to have a sanitary dwelling and sufficient food and clothing to keep the body in working order."[13] Those who fall below the line are unquestionably poor by contemporary standards. Nevertheless, many of those who have incomes above our standard cannot be regarded as rich or even as moderately well-off. While we will concentrate our discussion on those persons we have defined as poor, we would do well to remember that there are a great many more people whose standard of living is only marginally higher than that of the poor.

FURTHER READING

COE, RICHARD. "The Poverty Line: Its Function and Limitations," *Public Welfare*, Winter 1978.

HARRINGTON, MICHAEL. *The Other America.* New York: The Macmillan Company, 1962.

HUNTER, ROBERT. *Poverty.* New York: The Macmillan Company, 1904.

KRISTOL, IRVING. "Taxes, Poverty, and Equality," *The Public Interest*, Fall 1974.

PAGLIN, MORTON. "The Measurement and Trend of Inequality: A Basic Revision," *American Economic Review*, September 1975.

PEN, JAN. *Income Distribution.* New York: Frederick A. Praeger, Inc., 1971, Ch. 3.

TREAS, JUDITH. "U.S. Income Stratification: Bringing Families Back In," *Sociology and Social Research*, May 1982.

U.S. CONGRESS, COMMITTEE ON WAYS AND MEANS. *Background Material on Poverty.* Washington, DC: Government Printing Office, October 18, 1983, Sections 1 and 7.

[12]Conversation quoted in Robert Hunter, *Poverty* (New York: The Macmillan Company, 1904), p. 1.

[13]*Ibid.*, p. 7.

The
Poor

Having established a workable measure of contemporary poverty, we are now in a position to proceed with a census of the poor. In doing so, we will consider several related questions. First, how many Americans have incomes below the official poverty standards? Second, who are the poor; do they have distinguishing characteristics (other than lack of income)? Have the number or characteristics of the poor changed over time? Finally, how long do people remain poor? Is poverty a permanent condition for some families or do families move in and out of poverty?

These questions are of more than merely academic interest. What we know about the extent of poverty helps to determine the interest and resources we devote to its elimination. If we were to discover that economic hardship affects only a few thousand individuals in the United States, antipoverty concerns probably would occupy a very low position on our scale of public priorities. On the other hand, if poverty were found to be the condition of a majority of Americans, we can suppose that its eradication would be of foremost public concern. What one considers a "large" or "small" poverty population is essentially a question of individual predilections, of course, but at least a specification of the number of poor persons will provide a common basis for discussion and policy planning.

Unfortunately, estimates of the size of the poverty population vary tremendously. A recent poll of college seniors elicited estimates ranging from 120,000 to over 60 million poor persons. Even experienced researchers argue about the true size of the poverty population. The official (Census Bureau) estimates of the poverty population exceed 30 million people. Many economists argue, however, that this figure grossly overestimates the amount of poverty in

America. Indeed, they claim poverty has virtually been eliminated in the United States. Clearly, agreement on the importance of America's poverty problems would be difficult to attain in the face of such diverse perspectives.

THE NUMBER OF POOR PEOPLE

The Official Poverty Count

We will begin our own census of the poor with official estimates of the poverty population. These are based on a comparison of a family's *cash* income to its estimated needs. As noted in Chapter 1, 34 million persons—one out of five Americans—were officially counted as poor in 1963. According to our definition of poverty, that is the number of persons whose cash income in 1963 was less than the minimum standard needed for their particular family size and type. This tremendous number of poor persons convinced President Kennedy and President Johnson to start a "war on poverty." As Michael Harrington observed at the time, the number of poor Americans was simply unconscionable.

Table 2.1 updates the official poverty count as of 1982. According to this table, the number of poor Americans was slightly larger in 1982 than it had been in 1963: Over 34 million persons were still officially poor in 1982. Although the poverty *rate* had declined—from 20 percent to 15 percent of the population—the number of poor people still appeared to be remarkably high.

Table 2.1 also indicates that the incidence of poverty varies enormously among population groups. For example, more whites experience poverty than blacks but in far smaller numbers than the relative size of the white population would suggest. Accordingly, we may say that blacks face a far greater likelihood (35.6 percent) of being poor, although blacks still comprise a minority of the poor. The same relationship applies to the aged population and, to a lesser extent, all children. We will discuss these inequities in later chapters.

TABLE 2.1   THE POVERTY POPULATION, 1982

GROUP	U.S. POPULATION	PERSONS IN POVERTY	POVERTY RATE (%)
All persons	229,320,000	34,398,000	15.0
White	195,975,000	23,517,000	12.0
Black	27,239,000	9,697,000	35.6
Aged persons*	25,692,000	3,751,000	14.6
Spanish origin	14,385,000	4,301,000	29.9
Children (under 18)	62,972,000	13,476,000	21.4

*Aged persons = 65 years and older.

Source: U.S. Bureau of the Census.

Figure 2.1 tracks the changes in the official poverty count that occurred between 1963 and the early 1980s. Throughout the 1960s the poverty population diminished rapidly. In the 1970s, however, the poverty population stopped declining and then started to increase. This reversal in the trend brought us back to the same sized poverty population of twenty years earlier.

Alternative Poverty Counts

Critics of official poverty estimates argue that our apparent failure to win the War on Poverty is an illusion. In reality, argues Professor Martin Anderson of Stanford's Hoover Institution, "The war on poverty has been won, except for perhaps a few mopping-up operations."[1] According to his reading of the data, there are only a few million people still poor in America.

FIGURE 2.1   Changes in the Official Poverty Count

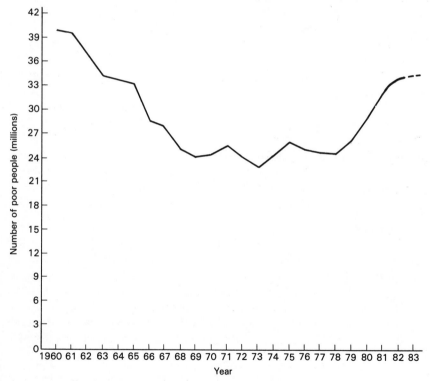

Source: U.S. Bureau of the Census.

[1]Martin Anderson, *Welfare* (Stanford, CA: Hoover Institution Press, 1978), p. 37.

The major deficiency of official poverty statistics is that they count only a family's *cash* means. Yet, all families receive some income "in-kind." Many low-income families, for example, receive food stamps, Medicaid or Medicare, or subsidized housing. Instead of giving poor families the cash needed to buy groceries, health care, or housing, the government provides these goods directly.[2] As a result, low-income families don't need as much cash income to maintain a given standard of living; in-kind transfers substitute for cash income.

The Census Bureau ignores all in-kind transfers when it counts the number of poor people. As a result, many of the people who are counted as "poor" may in fact have a total income (cash and transfers) that exceeds our poverty standards. In this case, official estimates exaggerate the size of the poverty population. If all in-kind transfers are added up, the overestimate appears to be substantial. Table 2.2 provides a quick summary of how in-kind benefits alter the poverty count. The first two columns show the official poverty counts and rates for 1979. By considering cash incomes only, the U.S. Census Bureau counted over 23 million poor Americans. Yet, nearly 4 million of these people received enough food stamps and housing assistance to raise their living standard above poverty levels. If these in-kind benefits were considered along with cash, only 19.9 million people would have been deemed poor. Were medical assistance (Medicaid, Medicare) also counted, even fewer Americans would have been regarded as poor.

Table 2.2 clearly documents the limitations of the official poverty count. By neglecting in-kind benefits, the Census Bureau ignores an important source of real income. In so doing, it exaggerates the official count of poor Americans.[3]

Although it is evident that the official poverty counts are exaggerated, the "corrected" estimates are subject to criticism as well. Not all in-kind transfers represent an improved standard of living. The amount of medical assistance a person receives, for example, depends on how sick one is. Accordingly, it isn't appropriate to regard a person as "nonpoor" just because he or she receives a lot of in-kind medical assistance (Medicaid or Medicare).

Latent Poverty   There is no agreement as yet about how many people move from poverty to nonpoverty as a result of in-kind transfers. All we can say with certainty is that official estimates of poverty are too high. Even after all appropriate adjustments, however, there are still millions of poor Americans. It is also important to recall that the official census of the poor takes place *after* the provision of government assistance. Remember that we are defining poverty in terms of a family's total cash income, relative to its needs. Part of this cash income is provided by the government, in the form of Social Security benefits,

---

[2]The in-kind transfers programs are described more fully in Chapter 12.

[3]See Morton Paglin, *Poverty and Transfers In-Kind* (Stanford, CA: Hoover Institution Press, 1979); Timothy M. Smeeding, "The Antipoverty Effectiveness of In-Kind Transfers," *Journal of Human Resources*, Summer 1977; and Congressional Budget Office, *Poverty Status of Families Under Alternative Definitions of Income* (Washington, DC: Government Printing Office, 1977).

TABLE 2.2 ALTERNATIVE POVERTY COUNTS, 1979 (numbers in thousands)

| | NUMBER (RATE) CONSIDERED TO BE POOR COUNTING . . . . | | | |
| | CASH INCOME ONLY | CASH PLUS FOOD AND HOUSING BENEFITS | CASH PLUS FOOD, HOUSING, AND MEDICAL CARE | |
			EXCLUDING INSTITUTIONAL CARE	INCLUDING INSTITUTIONAL CARE
All persons	23,623 (11.1)	19,933 (9.4)	14,023 (6.6)	13,634 (6.4)
Aged (over 65)	4,097 (14.7)	3,601 (12.9)	1,452 (5.2)	1,251 (4.5)
White	16,167 (8.6)	14,059 (7.5)	10,151 (5.4)	9,922 (5.3)
Black	7,456 (30.4)	5,874 (23.9)	3,872 (15.8)	3,712 (15.1)

Source: U.S. Bureau of the Census, *Alternative Methods for Valuing Selected In-Kind Transfer Benefits and Measuring Their Effect on Poverty* (Washington, DC: Government Printing Office, 1982), Table A.

public welfare assistance, or unemployment benefits. As a result, many families who would be poor in the absence of government assistance are not counted in our census; the "nonpoor" status of such families depends on continued public assistance. Charles Murray has called these people the *latent* poor; they would be poor in the absence of government help. The Congressional Budget Office estimates that the latent poverty population is twice as large as the official count, especially if Social Security benefits are included. From this perspective, America still has a very serious poverty problem.

We should also note that a reduction in poverty is not synonymous with a reduction in inequality. Because we use an absolute measure of poverty, it is possible for the entire distribution of incomes to shift to the right, leaving everyone better off, including some families who were formerly poor. This possibility is illustrated in Figure 2.2. In this case, relative incomes (the degree of inequality) remain virtually constant while absolute incomes rise. Hence, even if the number of people officially counted as poor were to diminish, that need not vitiate efforts to reduce inequality.

A final qualification to all poverty counts concerns the permanence of poverty. The numbers used to depict the size of the poverty population tell only part, perhaps only a small part, of the poverty story. They fail to tell us how malignant a disease poverty is, or how widespread the affliction is. To understand this failure, we must examine the concept of income mobility.

FIGURE 2.2　A Shifting Income Distribution

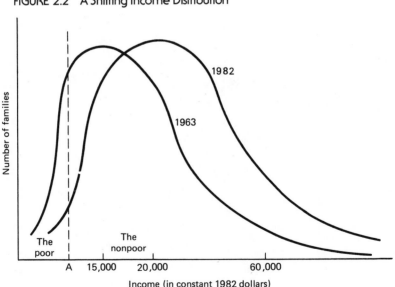

Income Mobility

Consider again the number of persons who were poor in 1963. Our total indicated approximately 34 million. The number itself is based on a statistical sample undertaken by the Census Bureau. Of course, there are problems with any estimate based on samples. The individuals sampled may not be representative; they may not be willing or able to tell the truth. But these are straightforward statistical problems, and we learn to solve them, or at least to live with them. They need not detain us here.

In evaluating our census of the poor, however, we must consider how much poverty qualifies a family for our statistical count. Must a family be in poverty all year long to be counted as "poor," or will more limited exposure to poverty suffice? Suppose, for example, that your family's income was $7,000 in 1963. You had one brother, your mother was a housewife, and your father was a plumber. Based on your father's income, we excluded your family from our count of the 1963 poverty population.

But suppose further that in August your father dislocated his wrist while bowling. He recovered but was not able to turn a wrench for the remainder of the year. Although he earned $250 a week during the first seven months of the year, his earnings dropped to zero after his accident. Because his accident was not work-related, your father was not eligible for medical insurance benefits. From that point on your family began to taste poverty. Your allowance disappeared, your mother was suddenly doing babysitting and ironing, the family vacation was canceled, and in the fall you and your brother had to drop out of school.

Regardless of whether your family recovers, we are faced with a serious conceptual and statistical problem. Should we restrict our census to those families who were poor throughout 1963, or do we want to include all families who experienced impoverishment at least part of the year? In the extreme, you might even want to include yourself as impoverished because you were out of money and hungry on Sunday night. In practice, we consider only *annual* income and needs, thus omitting from our poverty count many individuals and families who experience severe economic distress at least some of the time.

Our use of an annual accounting period also obscures another important problem: Incomes change from one year to the next. Some families who appear "poor" in one year may enjoy a comfortable income in the following year. Such families are probably less in need of public assistance and services than those families who are in poverty year after year.

Consider again the observed stability in the size of the "official" poverty population.[4] The number of poor people was 34 million in both 1963 and 1982. The numbers themselves do not tell us whether the people who were poor in 1982 are the same people who were poor nineteen years earlier. But it matters a

---

[4]Hereafter, all poverty statistics refer to the official Census Bureau estimates.

great deal whether poverty is a malignant affliction for some identifiable part of our population or if, instead, it is a communicable disease that strikes different families every year. The one situation implies, for example, the need for a lot of social work and family counseling, while the other argues for improved unemployment insurance.

Apparently, families do experience significant changes in income from one year to the next. By observing the same families over a period of seven years, Frank Levy (University of California–Berkeley) discovered that one-third of the nonaged families who were poor in 1967 were not poor in 1968. However, many families fall back into poverty in later years. Over the entire seven-year period (1967–73), Levy observed that

> Only 25 percent of the families who were poor in 1967 were nonpoor at least five of the subsequent six years.
>
> 30 percent of the 1967 poor families remained poor about half the time.
>
> 45 percent of the families who were poor in 1967 remained in poverty in almost all years.[5]

How completely one can distinguish between a "permanent" poverty population and a more "temporary" one is a basic policy concern. In later chapters we shall examine this issue more fully, seeking to identify those forces that distinguish one group of poor people from the other. In the remainder of this chapter, we will set the stage for this analysis by reviewing the characteristics of those people presently counted as poor.

CHARACTERISTICS OF THE POOR

While the statistics we have reviewed might justly support the statement that poverty in America is still of massive proportions, we must be cautious in our use of descriptive adjectives. The poverty that we have observed is certainly not like the mass poverty that still exists in most of the world today. Whatever the differences in the depth of deprivation experienced in earlier times and in other countries, an outstanding dissimilarity between modern American poverty and the poverty of India or Sicily is that, in America, to be poor is to be markedly distinguishable from the majority of the population.

If you lived in India, you would not have to make an effort to uncover the poor—they would be everywhere all the time. In America the situation is dramatically different. Except for an occasional panhandler on a downtown

[5]Frank Levy, "How Big Is the American Underclass?"(Berkeley, CA: University of California, 1976). Income mobility among a broader spectrum of individuals and families is described in James Morgan, et al., *Five Thousand American Families* (Ann Arbor, MI: Institute for Social Research, 1976); and Bradley R. Schiller, "Relative Earnings Mobility in the United States," *American Economic Review*, December 1977.

street, most of us never come into direct contact with the people we have enumerated in our census of the poor. The poor in America are a minority, albeit a sizable minority, and they are largely unseen and unheard by the affluent majority. As a consequence, very few of us know anything substantial about the characteristics of the poor—we rely instead on gross generalities and largely unfounded stereotypes.

We have already previewed some of the most salient characteristics of the poor in our census. In this section we continue that examination and attempt to deepen our familiarity with the 34 million poor individuals we have counted. The formulation of intelligent policies to combat poverty demands not only that we know how many persons are poor but also whether they are young or old, infirm or employed, and whether they live in Abbeville, Louisiana, or Winchester, Oregon.

A complete statistical profile of the poor would demand considerable effort and patience. In addition, such an array of statistics might smother any meaning the numbers might possess. Therefore, we will examine the composition of the poverty population only as it relates to three major and policy-relevant characteristics: age and family status; geography and residence; and labor force status. We will observe also the racial makeup within each category.

Age and Family Status

Michael Harrington has said that this is no country for old men—that our society is obsessed with youth and tries to ignore age.[6] Statistics on the number of aged poor confirm his observations. Figure 2.3 shows that the aged comprise a sizable minority of the poor. In 1982 they accounted for one-ninth of the poverty population, and one out of every seven aged persons was poor.[7]

Who are the aged poor? Approximately one-third are couples, many of whom own, or have an equity in, their own modest homes. The other two-thirds are primarily widows, some living in their own homes, but more often renting rooms in old hotels and apartment houses. They are just as likely to be found in metropolitan areas as in smaller cities and rural communities. Their income sources are few and consist primarily of public or private retirement payments, such as Social Security. Their savings are negligible.

Although the aged command the barest sort of material existence, poverty is not their only misfortune. Most of the aged poor live isolated, lonely lives and suffer chronic poor health. While we cannot hope to explain the American ethos that has led to the social deprivation of the aged, we should not ignore it.

The second population group depicted in Figure 2.3 refers to nonaged persons without children under the age of eighteen. Statistically they account

[6]Michael Harrington, *The Other America* (New York: The Macmillan Company, 1962), p. 10.
[7]We employ the term *aged* here to refer to persons over the age of sixty-five.

FIGURE 2.3   Age and Family Status of the Poor, 1982

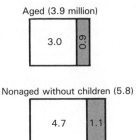

Aged (3.9 million)

3.0 | 0.9

Nonaged without children (5.8)

4.7 | 1.1

Families with children (21.1 million)

	Male-headed		Female-headed
8.5	2.1	5.4	5.1

Note: Shaded areas represent black population.

Source: U.S. Bureau of the Census.

for approximately 20 percent of the poor. Although these retired and soon-to-be-retired men and women are slightly younger than the aged poor, the social and material circumstances of the two groups are very similar; the only significant distinction is age. What is perhaps most disheartening about this subpopulation of the poor is that they have so much misery to look forward to. They have no tangible prospect for a better life; they simply get older and poorer.

The aged and aging poor, for whom there are few alternatives, represent failures of our politico-economic system. The existence of such clusters of poverty serves to underscore the importance of doing something about material deprivation while there is still a variety of remedies available.

An important reason for concentrating our attention on the younger generations of the poor is the sheer size of this group. As Figure 2.3 clearly indicates, families with children constitute the dominant subgroup of the poor population, accounting for approximately two-thirds of the American poor in 1982.

Contrary to popular belief, approximately half of the families in the younger poverty group have a male head-of-household (father). Nevertheless, families headed by females account for a sizable majority of the young black poor.

Of the 21 million people in the youngest poverty classification, over 12 million are children under eighteen years of age. Children alone comprise fully 40 percent of all poor persons in the United States. We might well reflect on how equitable such a distribution of poverty is and what kind of preparation for adulthood an impoverished childhood provides. Will poor children become poor adults? If so, we may confidently predict that poverty has a great future in this country.

Geography and Residence

In an increasingly urban nation, it is not surprising to find a high proportion of poor families in metropolitan areas.[8] In 1982 60 percent of the poor lived in metropolitan areas, most of them in the central city. In general, the residential distribution of poor families resembles the residential distribution of all families. However, there does exist a tendency for the poor to be overrepresented in large central cities and in rural areas and underrepresented in suburban communities (see Table 2.3).

The racial distribution of poverty among metropolitan and nonmetropolitan areas is very similar; that is, poor whites are just as likely as poor blacks to reside in metropolitan locations. However, a marked racial difference is apparent *within* metropolitan areas. While poor whites are likely to be found in either central cities or suburban communities, poor blacks are confined almost exclusively to the cities. It is important to note, though, that the high number of poor blacks in central cities is a result of the greater degree of urbanization among the black population rather than a higher likelihood of poverty in the cities. Indeed, a black person in a rural area is more likely to be poor than his counterpart in an urban metropolis (poverty rates of 42.3% and 33.5%, respectively).

Nonmetropolitan areas include smaller cities, rural communities, and farms. While nearly one-half of all the poor live in such localities, very few poor persons actually live on farms. Farm poverty is a serious problem in the sense that the incidence of poverty among farmers is very high (over 21 percent for whites and 51 percent for blacks), but because the entire U.S. farming population is relatively small, poor farmers constitute less than 3 percent of all the poor.

TABLE 2.3   RESIDENTIAL DISTRIBUTION OF THE POOR, 1982

	NUMBER (THOUSANDS)		POVERTY RATE (%)	
LOCATION	WHITE	BLACK	WHITE	BLACK
Entire U.S.	23,517	9,697	12.0	35.6
Metropolitan areas	13,563	6,897	10.4	33.5
In central cities	6,757	5,438	14.5	36.9
In suburban rings	6,806	1,460	8.1	25.0
Outside metropolitan areas	9,955	2,799	15.1	42.3
Farm	1,131	93	21.0	51.4

Source: U.S. Bureau of the Census.

[8]The term *metropolitan area* essentially refers to cities of at least 50,000 persons and their surrounding communities.

In this case we must distinguish between the incidence of poverty among a particular group and the prevalence of that group within the entire poverty population.

Because the economic resources and social conditions of different regions in the United States vary tremendously, it is important to know the geographical location of the poor. Slower economic growth or less opportunity in a region is likely to create a regional concentration of poor families and require special programs. Were the poor all concentrated in Appalachia, for example, particular antipoverty policies would be appropriate.

Outside the South, poverty is fairly proportionately distributed across the country for both whites and blacks (see Table 2.4). Thus, a person is as likely to be poor in New England as he is in the Corn Belt or in the West. In each of those areas, the incidence of poverty among whites is around 9 to 11 percent and around 25 to 33 percent for blacks. While there are fewer poor persons in the West than in the northeastern or north central states, that disparity conforms to general population patterns.

It is apparent from Table 2.4 that the South[9] contains a disproportionate number of poor persons. Less than a third of the total U.S. population lives in the South, but 40 percent of the poor reside there. This excess of poverty results not only from a high concentration of blacks in the South, but also from the fact that the South is simply poorer and less urban than any other region. A southern resident, regardless of his color, is more likely to be poor than his northern counterpart, and in both the North and the South, a black person is three times as likely to be poor as is a white person.

Labor Force Status

The geographic and family characteristics of the poor are important considerations in the formulation of antipoverty policies, but their primary value is to identify the potential of the poor to participate in national employment- and

TABLE 2.4   REGIONAL DISTRIBUTION OF THE POOR, 1982

REGION	NUMBER (THOUSANDS)		POVERTY RATE (%)	
	WHITE	BLACK	WHITE	BLACK
Northwest	4,666	1,523	10.8	31.6
North Central	5,527	2,050	10.6	39.8
South	8,297	5,487	13.4	37.6
West	5,027	636	13.0	23.9

Source: U.S. Bureau of the Census.

[9]The Census Bureau includes the following states in its definition of "South": Alabama, Arkansas, Delaware, District of Columbia, Florida, Georgia, Kentucky, Louisiana, Mississippi, Maryland, North Carolina, Oklahoma, South Carolina, Tennessee, Texas, Virginia, West Virginia.

income-generating policies. In a market economy the relationship of a person or his family to the labor market is the prime determinant of his income. Furthermore, society's willingness to provide for the poor is materially affected by whether the poor are thought to work or at least seek work. Accordingly, the last characteristic we shall observe is the labor force status of the poor.

To be "in the labor force" signifies that a person is either employed or actively seeking employment ("unemployed"). Also included in this category are persons who are temporarily not working because of illness, bad weather, vacation, or a labor-management dispute. All these people are regarded as idle only momentarily, with visible prospects of returning to work. Their regular work may be full-time or part-time (less than thirty-five hours per week), and it must be monetarily compensated. Hence, volunteer work is regarded as activity outside the labor force.

Being "out of the labor force" means essentially that a person does not fall into one of the foregoing categories. These persons are keeping house; attending school; unable to work because of age or disability; or, if otherwise able to work, are not actively seeking employment. The inactivity of the last group may result from a desire for leisure or the fact that employment prospects are too dim to merit job-hunting.

It is widely believed that the poor are essentially a lazy lot. While we will examine this contention in considerable detail in later chapters, Table 2.5 provides a preliminary perspective on the employment behavior of the poor. This table indicates what percentage of poor families worked at some time during the year. Nearly three out of four fathers of poor families worked in 1982. So did more than one out of three women who headed poverty families. Although these employment percentages are lower than those of nonpoor families, they still suggest substantial labor force participation. In later chapters

TABLE 2.5   WORK EXPERIENCE OF POVERTY POPULATION, 1982

	PERCENT WHO WORKED DURING 1982	
	POOR (%)	NONPOOR (%)
Families with children		
Male-headed		
White	77	94
Black	60	89
Female-headed		
White	42	89
Black	36	86
Aged persons		
Males	9	26
Females	5	12

Source: U.S. Bureau of the Census.

we will examine the reasons for these differences, as well as the reasons why many working families remain in poverty.

OVERVIEW

The statistical profiles of the preceding section are not intended to dull one's senses nor to obscure the many problems of the poor. Rather, they are offered as a backdrop to the analytical discussions that follow in later chapters. If any general impressions are possible, we might say that the statistical profiles of the poor are not markedly different from those of the rest of the population. For the most part, the poor population is a little older, more southern, blacker, and slightly less attached to the labor force than is the rest of society. Nevertheless, the poor, like the larger society, consist primarily of whites, of younger families with children, of urban dwellers, and of labor force participants. There do exist important distinguishing demographic characteristics, but they must not be allowed to conceal the basic similarities between the poor and nonpoor populations.

The demographic characteristics we have reviewed by no means provide a complete description of the poor. Among the more obvious omissions in our profile are education, family size, and health. These characteristics are discussed in later sections, where a more complete examination of the traits described above is also found. But our profiles are incomplete in another important sense. We deal in this book almost exclusively with measurable, or at least observable, phenomena. Thus, we may report how old, white, or employed the poor are, or whether they live in cities or suburbs. What we are unable to do is relate how oppressed, politically isolated, or hostile the poor may be. In *The Other America*, Michael Harrington argues that today's poor are "more isolated and politically powerless than ever before." Although we are not in a position to evaluate that statement, we must recognize that such forces may be critical considerations in the lives of the poor.

FURTHER READING

CONGRESSIONAL BUDGET OFFICE. *Poverty Status of Families Under Alternative Definitions of Income*. Washington, DC: Government Printing Office, 1977.

DANZIGER, SHELDON, and ROBERT PLOTNICK. *Has the War on Poverty Been Won?* New York: Academic Press, 1980.

MORGAN, JAMES, et al. *Five Thousand American Families.* Ann Arbor, MI: Institute for Social Research, 1976–1981.

MURRAY, CHARLES A. "The Two Wars Against Poverty," *The Public Interest,* Fall 1982.

PAGLIN, MORTON. "Poverty in the United States: A Reevaluation," *Policy Review,* Spring 1979.

PLOTNICK, ROBERT D., and FELICITY SKIDMORE. *Progress against Poverty: A Review of the 1964–1974 Decade.* New York: Academic Press, Inc., 1975.

SCHILLER, BRADLEY R. "Relative Earnings Mobility in the United States," *American Economic Review,* December 1977.

SMEEDING, TIMOTHY M. "The Antipoverty Effectiveness of In-Kind Transfers," *Journal of Human Resources,* Summer 1977.

U.S. BUREAU OF THE CENSUS. *Current Population Reports, Series P-60.* Washington, DC: Government Printing Office, periodic.

U.S. CONGRESS, COMMITTEE ON WAYS AND MEANS. *Background Material on Poverty.* Washington, DC: Government Printing Office, October 18, 1983. 1976–1981.

―――――. *Hearings on Poverty Rate Increase.* October-December 1983.

3
General Perspectives

Although there is much disagreement about the actual size of the poverty population, all estimates run into the millions. Hence, the existence of a substantial number of poor Americans must be accepted as fact. This fact leads to an entirely new question: Why are millions of Americans so poor?

The question of "why" is even more controversial than the question of "how many." Indeed, people generally approach the subject of causation from one of several extreme perspectives. From the first perspective, poverty is regarded as the natural result of individual defects in aspiration or ability. In colonial times, this perspective was aptly summarized by the puritanical Humane Society, which concluded that "by a just and inflexible law of Providence, misery is ordained to be the companion and punishment of vice." In more modern times, theories of sin and immorality have not fared well, and there now exists a general reluctance to ascribe to the laws of Providence the misery of the poor. Instead, we speak in terms of "motivation" or "work ethic": Poverty is thought to result from insufficient amounts of either. According to this view, modern poverty originates from Flawed Characters, much as in puritanical times. The Flawed Character argument comes in many forms. However, an essential ingredient in all such arguments is the assumption of pervasive opportunity. From this perspective, there are abundant opportunities for material advancement. Anyone who wants to escape poverty can do so. By implication, anyone who remains poor has not made the required effort.

The Flawed Character argument applies both to jobs and schools. In the labor market, people who do not find good jobs are assumed to lack sufficient initiative or diligence. To the extent that they are less able—as measured by education, skills, or ability tests—their disadvantage is to be explained by earlier lack of motivation in school. Individuals who do not work hard in school end up failing in the job market as well. Thus, the Flawed Character perspective sees individuals as in full control of their socioeconomic status.

An alternative explanation of poverty claims that impoverishment may result from forces beyond the control of the individual. According to this argument—the Restricted Opportunity argument—the poor are poor because they do not have adequate access to good schools, jobs, and income, because they are discriminated against on the basis of color, sex, or income class, and because they are not furnished with a fair share of government protection, subsidy, or services. In the face of these socially imposed constraints, no amount of work ethic or effort assures escape from poverty. A basic implication of this argument is that only the provision of improved opportunities—such as more and better jobs and improved access to quality education—would assure a reduction in the number of people we count as poor.

There is a third view of poverty that falls between these two extremes. This view—the Big Brother argument—blames the government for destroying incentives for stable families and economic self-sufficiency. From this perspective, poor people are not inherently flawed. Rather, the government perverts their perspectives and behavior through high taxes, welfare benefits, racial quotas, and other public policies. These policies, though intended to help the poor, actually destroy work incentives and create what George Gilder has called a "blight of dependency."[1]

The following eight chapters examine the substance of these different perspectives in great detail. But before proceeding to that examination, we should recognize some potential biases. The Flawed Character argument, for example, appeals directly to the psychological needs of the middle-class majority. If the poor are poor because of flawed characters, then the nonpoor must be nonpoor as a result of nonflawed characters. (Otherwise, how are we to explain the superior position of the latter class?) Hence, the Flawed Character argument implies a psychological pat on the back for the nonpoor. Adam Walinsky made note of this same phenomenon when he observed that ego satisfaction requires each of us to ascribe the status of "those above us" to luck and the status of "those below us" to character and ability.[2] Thus, the Flawed Character argument not only explains poverty, but explains and justifies the position and privileges of the nonpoor as well. To deny the Flawed Character argument is tantamount to questioning the status of the middle and upper classes.

Economic interests are also concealed in the Flawed Character argument. A basic implication of this argument is that society is already doing everything it can to help the poor, by providing the opportunities necessary for escape from poverty. This view is economically appealing as it implies fewer additional public expenditures, lower taxes, and the lack of any need to initiate structural

[1]George Gilder, *Wealth and Poverty* (New York: Basic Books, 1981), p. 12.
[2]Adam Walinsky, "Keeping the Poor in Their Place," *New Republic*, July 4, 1964.

changes in the way the economy functions. To the harassed taxpayer who equates higher taxes with more money for "the bums on welfare," the Flawed Character argument sounds very convincing.

The Restricted Opportunity argument likewise derives support from unspoken biases. Some people are simply convinced that society is to blame for *all* social ills, that individuals are forever innocent and blameless. As a consequence, they are not inclined to collect or even examine evidence that might fault individuals for their own plight. This type of bias is often referred to as "bleeding heart liberalism." Often, this liberalism may be buttressed by economic interests (e.g., university researchers and public employees who would benefit from expanded social programs and budgets)

The Big Brother argument also appeals to identifiable interests. The principal implication of the Big Brother view is that the government is trying too hard to take care of people's needs. By doing less, the government would foster greater private initiative and ultimately eliminate more poverty. In the process, of course, government spending and taxes would be reduced—a goal many people desire for its own sake. Also, if the government were to cut back on affirmative action and related activities, many white males and others would reap direct gains. Hence, there are political and economic interests wrapped up in the Big Brother argument that go beyond its antipoverty effectiveness.

Knowing our potential biases does not settle the controversy, of course, or even assure that we will remember them at the right times. But awareness of them may help engender just a bit more objectivity as we proceed through the details of our analysis. At least we know that the deck *may* be stacked before the game begins.

LABOR MARKET FOCUS

Our basic approach for identifying the true causes of poverty begins with a distinction between those who are in the labor force and those who are not. To be "in the labor force" means that a person is either employed or actively seeking a job. Obviously, such persons (and their families) are much more likely to be out of poverty, either now or in the near future. On the other hand, those individuals and families who do not participate in the labor force do not have access to a prime source of income—labor earnings—and are thus more likely to be represented among the poor.

It remains to be seen, of course, just why such people are out of the labor force—whether they are excluded by "flawed characters," "restricted opportunities," or "Big Brother." For example, the decision whether or not to search for a job—that is, whether or not to enter the labor force—may itself be influenced by the jobs available. If the probability of finding a job is very low (opportunities are restricted), the incentive to enter the labor force is negligible, and it is misleading to point to nonparticipation (flawed character) as an explanation for poverty. On the other hand, even abundant job opportunities may be economically unattractive because of high taxes or welfare benefits (Big Brother). As is true of so many other social problems, the interaction of different forces needs to be examined.

In view of the fact that poor people tend to shuttle back and forth between jobs, unemployment, and welfare, we must also take care not to regard our distinction between participants and nonparticipants as a rigid dichotomy. Nor can we assume that labor force participation alone is a ticket out of poverty. In 1982 over 50 percent of the families in poverty participated in the labor force at some point during the year. Moreover, over 1 million families were poor despite the presence of at least one person who worked full-time, all year long. Nearly as many families were poor despite having at least two family members working. Clearly, we must look more carefully at labor market dynamics to explain such widespread poverty.

The major causes of poverty for labor force participants may be classified into three types: human capital deficiencies, deficient demand for labor, and discrimination.

HUMAN CAPITAL DEFICIENCIES

Human capital refers to the bundle of skills and abilities that a person carries with him into the labor market. In general, the less human capital a worker possesses, the lower is his or her potential productivity on a job. Employers will be less eager to hire persons with little human capital and less willing to pay them high wages once they are employed; such decisions tend to leave many workers in poverty as a result of both unemployment and low wages.

The human capital a worker possesses is significantly determined by genetic endowments ("natural ability") and social environment. However, a person can increase his or her human capital by learning new skills. Education and training provide such opportunities, and a worker can effectively invest in his or her own human capital by pursuing them. The "dividends" from such an investment will typically include better jobs and higher pay in the future. Thus, a direct link between educational attainment and income should be apparent. And in fact it is. People with college educations are rarely found among the ranks of the poor, whereas people who fail to acquire as much as a high school diploma are all too often poor.

DEFICIENT DEMAND FOR LABOR

Having the "right" amount of human capital is itself no guarantee of job success, however. Human capital traits such as education merely define the supply characteristics of the labor force, and thus only begin to explain income status. It is equally important to examine the labor market forces that determine the demand for labor, and thus to ascertain the market value of specific human capital characteristics. To determine how much a person's productivity is "worth," we must know something about the market value of the goods or services he or she produces. This value will be determined by the interaction of market supply and demand forces.

The distinction between supply characteristics and market demand applies even to college graduates. If there is little market demand for the services of college graduates, the attainment of a diploma will add little to an individual's income. In the early 1960s, for example, there was a great demand for engineers, largely as a consequence of our attempts to beat the Russians to the moon. In response to this demand, the value of an engineering degree rose markedly, and thousands of college students eagerly switched majors. Widespread disillusionment set in later, however, when the increased supply of engineers entered the labor market and discovered that the space program and the derived demand for their particular skills had been reduced. The upshot of this little lesson in economics was higher unemployment and lower wages for engineers.

The sad saga of the engineers provides insights for other members of the labor force as well. When the aggregate demand for labor is low, an increased number of people are going to discover that their human capital is "deficient." During the exceptionally high unemployment that persisted throughout the 1930s—official unemployment rates rose as high as 25 percent and never fell below 10 percent during the decade—even Ph.D. degrees were inadequate stepping-stones to secure jobs and income. On the other hand, when the aggregate demand for labor is high, everyone's chances for a decent job and income are improved. Accordingly, we may say that the demand for labor is an important determinant of incomes and, more specifically, that a deficient demand for labor can be an important cause of poverty.

DISCRIMINATION

The third general set of causes are those related to discrimination, both in the schools and in the labor market. Minority groups, women, and the offspring of the poor are generally not given an equal chance to acquire the right set of human capital characteristics nor to use those characteristics in the labor market. As long as such institutional barriers remain, poverty may exist even in the presence of abundant human capital and a high demand for labor. Hence, race, sex, and class discrimination may have significant impact on both the distribution and the extent of poverty. As long as discrimination persists, we may predict that children of the poor, blacks, and families headed by women will dominate the ranks of the poverty population.

In terms of our earlier generalizations it is clear that those demographic forces that define a person's human capital are the focus of Flawed Character perspectives, while Restricted Opportunity arguments build on the notions of deficient demand for labor and the institutional barriers erected by discrimination.

The Big Brother argument helps explain the *appearance* of flawed characters and restricted opportunities. In trying to identify the relative importance of each explanation, it is important to distinguish between correlates of poverty and causes of poverty. Everyone agrees, for example, that poor people are generally less-educated than the rest of the population, that is, that low educational attainments are *correlated* with poverty. What is debated is the nature of the causal relation. On the one hand, low educational attainments may so constrain a person's productivity that he or she can never earn a decent income. On the other hand, there may not be enough good jobs to go around, with those available being parceled out according to educational attainments. In this case, it would be more reasonable to argue that deficient demand for labor is the *cause* of poverty, with educational attainments determining how that poverty is distributed among us.

The distinction between correlates and causes is perhaps even clearer in the case of race. As we noted in Chapter 2, blacks are much more likely to be poor than are whites; thus being black is correlated with poverty. But what is the *causal* relationship? Is it true, as some argue, that black individuals are so genetically or culturally handicapped that they simply cannot bring enough human capital to the market? Or is it more correct to suggest that a combination of deficient demand for labor and institutional barriers traps them in poverty? Obviously, the heart of the argument is over causes, not correlates.

In assessing the significance of any particular demographic, labor market, or institutional force, we will be interested in two dimensions of causation: With respect to each force, we will inquire as to its effect either on the *extent* or on the *distribution* of poverty. The extent of poverty refers to the particular people who are consigned to impoverishment. Some forces may influence the size of the poverty population without affecting the selection of individuals so included. Other forces may markedly affect the distribution, but not the total extent, of poverty. Therefore, we are asking what forces determine how many individuals will be poor and which determine who is to be included in that total.

4
Subemployment

We have already suggested that a deficient demand for labor may be a major cause of poverty. One symptom of that deficiency would be high unemployment rates. Another would be large numbers of potential workers outside the labor force, waiting for improved job opportunities to emerge. A third symptom would be large numbers of workers employed at jobs far beneath their actual capabilities. Together all these phenomena constitute subemployment, and can contribute significantly to the number of poor in America. These relationships between the demand for labor and the level of poverty are examined in this and the following chapter.

CAPITALIST IDEOLOGY

This assumption is wrong.

It is a basic tenet of capitalist ideology that an individual must contribute to the output of the economy in order to share in its output. Specifically, each person's share of total output should reflect his or her contribution to the production of that output. That contribution may result from actual work effort or from the productivity of other resources (land, capital) that an individual owns. In either case, individuals who aspire to higher incomes must work or save harder, thereby asserting a claim to more output. In such an economy, an individual choosing not to contribute to the production process may be denied a share of the goods produced.

In a purely competitive capitalist economy, it is clear that the unemployed will not eat, or at least they will not obtain sustenance by conventional routes. By the same token, among those who are employed, individual productivities will

42

determine how much and how well each person eats. In assessing the relationship between poverty and work we have to identify those who work and those who do not.

Labor Force Status

In examining work patterns, it is convenient to start by classifying people according to their labor force status. The labor force includes not only all people who are working for pay, but also people who are actively looking for jobs. Hence, both *employed* persons and *unemployed* persons are counted as labor force participants. *Non*participants are people who are neither working for pay nor actively seeking paid employment. In early 1983, there were 110 million participants in the U.S. labor force, of whom 99 million were employed and 11 million were unemployed. The rest of the population—120 million people— were *non*participants, neither working nor actively seeking paid employment.

Clearly, we do not enforce a rigid policy of "no work, no bread." On the contrary, we both support and encourage nonparticipation, for a variety of reasons. Millions of spouses choose to stay at home to care for children or households rather than seek paid employment outside the home. Then there are millions of children, many of whom are legally barred from employment. To this list we may add the aged, whom we often compel to retire; the infirm, who cannot work; and college students, whose productivity is assumed and deferred. Indeed, the number of people eating but not working exceeds the number of workers.

The link between labor force status and poverty seems to be very direct. In general, one would expect nonparticipants to be poor and participants not to be. But the relationship is not that simple.

SUBEMPLOYMENT AND POVERTY

The Nonparticipants

People not participating in the labor force must have an alternative source of support. For most nonparticipants, this support comes from their immediate families; they share the income of a relative who works. A good many other individuals are past traditional working ages and depend on retirement incomes, typically public (Social Security) or private pensions. But not all families are retired or contain a working member. These latter families are most likely to be poor. Indeed, the median income, including welfare, of families headed by men not participating in the labor force is less than $1,000 per month. Very few of these men are able to sustain their families far above the poverty line.

Why do these men fail to participate in the labor force? Is it because they prefer idleness and impoverishment, or because they are physically unable to work or locate a job? A 1967 U.S. Department of Labor study suggested that a good many such persons were "dreamers and drifters who were able to adjust both financially and psychologically to nonworker status." No data were available, however, to support that allegation. More recent studies have shown that very few men with family responsibilities desire to "dream and drift" rather than work. More likely, these nonparticipants are either sick or disabled.[1] A considerable number of others have not looked for jobs because they are convinced that no employment opportunities are presently available for them.

As we observed in Chapter 2, half of all poor families are headed by women. These women typically must fend for themselves to support their families. Yet, only one-third of the women who head poor families participate in the labor market in any given year.

The lower labor force participation of women who head poor families is most readily explained by their family responsibilities. A single-parent family simply does not have the capability to keep one parent at work and one at home. Moreover, the jobs available to poor women may not pay enough to provide for nonparental child care, even if the mother would prefer to work outside the home. As a result, the labor force participation of female heads of poor families is restricted by both family and economic forces.[2]

The phenomenon of nonparticipation is not a permanent state. Most so-called nonparticipants do work if and when they are able. As their physical condition, child-care arrangements, and/or the economic outlook improves, nonaged nonparticipants are most likely to resume their search for employment. Indeed, a salient characteristic of the poor is their extraordinarily high rate of mobility between different labor forces statuses. The poor are constantly moving in and out of the labor force and from employment to unemployment. A poor person out of the labor force one week may well be working or looking for a job the next week.[3]

To note that nonparticipation is likely to be a temporary condition is not tantamount to denying its causal importance for poverty. On the contrary, we have observed that nonparticipation is a condition that many poor heads-of-

---

[1]Disabilities are themselves not completely objective, however. Donald Parsons has shown that labor force withdrawal of prime-age males is related to the availability of disability benefit payments. See Donald O. Parsons, "The Decline in Male Labor Force Participation," *Journal of Political Economy*, February 1980. This issue is examined further in Chapter 12.

[2]The availability of welfare benefits also discourages labor force participation, as we shall demonstrate in Chapter 12. Because work outside the home necessarily reduces home production (e.g., child care, cooking, etc.), many single-parent families remain poor in a fundamental sense even if their market income exceeds the poverty standard (see Clair Vickery, "The Time-Poor: A New Look at Poverty," *Journal of Human Resources*, Winter 1977).

[3]In fact, there are six times as many prime-age men outside the labor force at some time during the year than there are outside the labor force all year long. Nonparticipation is obviously a temporary condition for the father of a poor family.

household experience. In later chapters we shall examine the causes of this nonparticipation in more detail.

The Unemployed

That unemployment, like nonparticipation, might lead to poverty is a chain of causation few people question. After all, to be unemployed means that one is out of work and actively seeking employment. Can we assert with confidence, then, that unemployment is a major cause of poverty?

Some seeds of doubt about this association between unemployment and poverty are sown by those who compare unemployment totals with the size of the poor population. In 1981, for example, there were an average of about 8.3 million persons unemployed, while there were nearly 32 million poor persons (see Table 4.1). Moreover, not all of the 8,273,000 unemployed were from poor families. From an aggregate perspective, unemployment thus appears to account for only a small fraction of poverty at best.

To compare the total number of people with the average number of unemployed is quite unfair, however. First, the poverty population includes not only heads-of-household but also their dependents. As the unemployment figures do not include dependents, the comparison is obviously unbalanced. Looking more closely at the figures in Table 4.1, we find that only 2,600,000 of the unemployed were nonaged heads-of-household. At the same time, there were only 6,213,000 nonaged poor *families*, and thus that many poor household heads. Accordingly, on this more detailed basis, it appears that unemployment may contribute to the low economic status of as many as 40 percent of all nonaged poor families.

The comparison between unemployed and poor heads-of-household suggests a markedly stronger relationship between poverty and unemployment than do simple comparisons of national averages. Yet even this adjustment is only the beginning of a serious analysis. Just as nonparticipation is likely to be a temporary condition for the poor male head-of-household, we must recognize that unemployment is likely to be a transitory state for most of the poor. There

TABLE 4.1   UNEMPLOYMENT AND POVERTY STATISTICS, 1981

GROUP	UNEMPLOYED	POOR
Average, all persons	8,273,000	31,822,000
Average, heads-of-household*	2,600,000	6,213,000
Number of heads-of-household who experience unemployment during year	10,400,000	1,699,000

*Figures for heads-of-household exclude aged population.

Source: U.S. Bureau of the Census and U.S. Department of Labor.

will be many more persons who *experience* unemployment during the year than there are unemployed at any given time. In fact, the turnover in the ranks of the unemployed approaches 300 percent. This means that nearly three times more persons experience unemployment during the year than are unemployed at any one time. In 1981, for example, over 23 million persons (of whom 10 million were household heads) experienced unemployment even though only 8.3 million (2.6 million household heads) were unemployed at any one time. Hence, there are more heads-of-household who experience unemployment than there are poor heads-of-household. On this basis unemployment begins to look like a dominant explanation of poverty.

Can we say, though, that all of these household heads who experience unemployment are poor? No, a great many of these unemployed persons enjoy incomes sufficiently high while working to stave off poverty when jobless. Others are fortunate enough to have other family members in the labor force who can provide alternative incomes. As a consequence, less than one-fifth of all families who experience unemployment have incomes below our poverty standard. The relationship varies markedly by family type, however, as Table 4.2 reveals. Single-parent families in particular are extremely likely to be poor if the household head experiences unemployment. The most vulnerable families are those headed by women; the poverty rate soars to 42.6 percent when the female head experiences any unemployment.

Although unemployment does not necessarily lead to poverty, it is apparent that joblessness afflicts many poor families. As Table 4.2 indicates, 17.7 percent of *all* families experiencing unemployment are poor. This amounts to 2.8 million *poor* families, or almost one-half of all poor families. Hence, we may conclude that one-half of all poor families experience direct income loss as a result of unemployment.[4]

The Process of Economic Deterioration   Just how unemployment leads to poverty is evident when the relationship is viewed over time. Whereas a few days or a week of unemployment will not significantly diminish a family's income, several weeks of joblessness will begin to undermine a family's economic foundations. Accordingly, we expect to see more and more people slip into poverty as the duration of unemployment status lengthens. This process is confirmed by Table 4.3, which portrays the various methods families use to meet expenses as the duration of unemployment increases.[5]

[4]The relationship between unemployment and economic hardship is also discussed by the National Commission on Employment and Unemployment Statistics in *Counting the Labor Force* (Washington, DC: Government Printing Office, 1979). The Commission's "hardship index" is discussed in Chapter 5.

[5]For a closer look at the experiences of people unemployed for an extended period of time, see Walter Nicholson and Walter Corson, "Experiences of Unemployment Insurance Recipients During the First Year After Exhausting Benefits" (Princeton, NJ: Mathematica Policy Research, Inc., 1976); also U.S. Congress, Committee on Energy and Commerce, *Health Benefits: Loss Due to Unemployment*, January 1983.

TABLE 4.2   POVERTY AMONG LABOR FORCE PARTICIPANTS BY FAMILY TYPE AND UNEMPLOYMENT EXPERIENCE

	POVERTY RATE OF HOUSEHOLDS WITH AT LEAST ONE LABOR FORCE PARTICIPANT AND	
	WITH NO MEMBER UNEMPLOYED DURING YEAR	WITH AT LEAST ONE MEMBER UNEMPLOYED DURING YEAR
All families	5.9%	17.7%
Two-parent families	4.0	10.6
Single-parent families		
Male headed	5.6	30.5
Female headed	18.5	42.6
Persons living alone	6.8	23.3

Source: Sylvia Lazos Terry, "Work Experience, Earnings, and Family Income in 1981," *Monthly Labor Review*, April 1983.

In Table 4.3, the income sources of short-term and long-term unemployed families are compared. It can be seen, for example, that among the short-term (up to twenty-six weeks!) unemployed, 49 percent of the families have savings from which to draw in order to meet their everyday living expenses. As the duration of unemployment surpasses twenty-seven weeks, however, the number of families with savings or available credit declines. As unemployment continues and families become more desperate, they begin to sell their homes, seek aid from friends, and, most striking of all, fall back on public or private charity.[6]

Discouraged Workers

While it is already clear that unemployment constitutes a direct and increasingly serious threat to a family's economic welfare, we have not yet completely described the dimensions of that threat. So far, we have considered only the immediate income loss to those families who suffer unemployment. There are indirect effects as well, however. The indirect effects further strengthen the causal link between unemployment and poverty and extend the resultant hardships to still more persons.

When unemployment rates are high in a particular area, job-seekers are apt to become increasingly frustrated in their efforts to secure employment. Jobs are scarce and available to only a select few. Faced with one employment rejection after another, job-seekers are likely to give up the search. This erosion of confidence was expressed by a young man who described his search for a job as follows:

[6] In early 1983 the average duration of unemployment for *all* the unemployed, poor and nonpoor, was twenty-one weeks.

I'll tell you, man, I go to Catholic Charities, to the youth center, down by the employment people—a couple of weeks ago I try to buy a job—I talk to social workers . . . you go from place to place, you know, and you get tired. I guess you get bored. Guys say no work, no nuthin', and then you say, "to hell with it. Let the job come to me."[7]

Not surprisingly, this young man is called a "discouraged worker." Because he no longer seeks work actively, he is not counted as among the unemployed; he belongs to the ranks of the nonparticipants previously discussed. Yet it is clear that the two categories are not wholly separable. The extent and likely duration of unemployment in an area has a significant effect on the size of the nonparticipating population. Accordingly, many discouraged workers must be counted among the casualties of unemployment.

No one knows the exact number of discouraged workers among the poor. We do know, though, that a household head cannot maintain both a discouraged status and a family for long. The family must eat, and the head of the household will be compelled to locate some work, any work, just to keep body and soul together.

Discouragement is not limited to household heads. In families with both a mother and a father present, high rates of unemployment are most likely to affect the mother's labor force participation. Where unemployment is prevalent, a wife's chances for employment are likely to be even smaller than her husband's. Hence, the family may decide that her job search is fruitless and that her productivity will be highest in the home. Unfortunately, in withdrawing from the labor force—giving up the search for paid employment—the wife markedly increases the family's chances of becoming poor. Working wives are one of the surest escape routes from poverty.

TABLE 4.3   METHODS USED BY FAMILIES TO MEET LIVING EXPENSES, BY DURATION OF UNEMPLOYMENT (Percent Distribution*)

METHOD	DURATION OF UNEMPLOYMENT	
	5 TO 25 WEEKS	27 WEEKS OR MORE
Used savings	49.1	39.9
Borrowed money	23.7	18.8
Moved to cheaper housing	8.8	12.0
Received help from friends	18.0	22.5
Received public or private charity	14.7	31.9

*Sum of percents is more than 100 because many families resorted to more than one method.

Source: Adapted from Stanley Lebergott, ed., *Men Without Work* (Englewood Cliffs, NJ: Prentice-Hall, Inc. 1964), p. 144.

[7]Quoted in Edgar May, *The Wasted Americans* (New York: Harper & Row, Publishers, 1964), p. 60.

Considerable statistical attention has been directed recently toward the phenomenon of discouraged workers. As a result, the U.S. Department of Labor estimated that in 1983 there were over 1.7 million persons at any time who wanted a job but were not looking for work because they felt their search would be in vain. A much larger number of people were out of the labor force for this reason at some time during the year. Two-thirds of these discouraged workers were women and most of the rest were teenage males or older men. What proportion of these individuals were from poor families we do not yet know, but the impact of this group on the size of the poverty population is potentially sizable.

Underemployment

Another indirect hardship resulting from high unemployment rates concerns the type and amount of work people undertake when jobs are scarce. As noted, the head of a low-income family, facing a dismal labor market, may have to accept whatever employment wages are available. The work may not fully utilize either his or her time or talents and is likely to be menial. But the person accepts the work as a temporary measure while waiting for better employment opportunities to emerge. A person who is in this situation is *underemployed.* That is, the person is at work (hence not unemployed) but not working to capacity. Commonly, the underemployed work full-time at menial jobs or part-time at any job, while seeking more or better employment. In 1981, the U.S. Department of Labor estimated that 14.6 million people were involuntarily employed on a part-time basis. Close to 10 million of these workers had seen their hours cut because of slack work; the rest had not been able to find full-time jobs. Millions more were underemployed because the full-time jobs they *had* located paid wages below their usual experience. At least a million persons were poor in 1981 as a direct consequence of such underemployment. Far more were poor because of the combination of underemployment *and* unemployment.

Subemployment

The phenomena of unemployment, discouragement, and underemployment combine to form the concept of *subemployment.* Taken as a whole, the distressing impact of subemployment on a family's finances is reasonably clear; very few families have enough economic resources to maintain themselves in the face of these forces for long. What is not so obvious is that the social foundation of the family, as well as its economic foundation, may suffer from the impact of these phenomena. Can we expect the father in a low-income family to gain self-respect or familial admiration as his employment prospects and income diminish? Do we anticipate a Charles Dickens kind of increased solidarity as the family begins to sink into impoverishment?

It is more reasonable to expect intrafamily tensions to mount along with economic distress. In fact, studies show that both divorce and child abuse increase when fathers are out of work. According to one study, children of unemployed fathers are three times as likely to be abused than children of employed fathers.[8] These kinds of effects are difficult to measure, but are potentially of greater social significance than lost wages alone.[9] In Chapter 7 we will take a closer look at some of these effects.

Tallying the Losses   As the list of direct and indirect consequences of unemployment grows, the crushing burden of a loose labor market on the economic status of the poor becomes apparent. The size of this burden can be approximated by asking how much income the poor have lost as a result of each form of subemployment. The total answer represents the amount of income the poor would have received had they been able to participate fully in the economy. The totals, presented in Table 4.4, are striking.

We have suggested that as many as 2,800,000 poor heads-of-household may have experienced direct unemployment in 1981. Given the typical wages of the working poor ($160 per week) and the typical duration of their unemployment (eighteen weeks), we may estimate the income loss to these families as approximately $2,880 per unemployed family. This is the amount of additional income these poor families would have received had they not experienced unemployment. Multiplying the number of affected families (2,800,000) by their average loss ($2,880) tells us that the poor as a group lost approximately $8 billion of potential income as a direct result of unemployment.

We estimate the number of poor persons out of the labor force in 1981 due to the erosion of confidence we term discouragement to be about 400,000 individuals, mostly wives and female heads-of-household. Because these individuals were out of work all year long, their implied loss is equal to their opportunity incomes, that is, the incomes they would have received if they had been able to get a job. For poor persons, we may approximate this figure as $5,000 per discouraged worker. Multiplying the number of affected families (400,000) by the average loss ($5,000) indicates that the poor were deprived of another $2 billion by labor market discouragement.

---

[8]This and other studies are reported in U.S. Congress, House Committee on Education and Labor, "Hearings on the Impact of Unemployment on Children and Families," January 31, 1983.

[9]We should also note that an involuntary change in status from employed to unemployed may have serious and long-term effects on a person's self-perception and social behavior. See D.D. and B.M. Braginsky, "Surplus People: Their Lost Faith in Self and System," *Psychology Today*, August 1975; and Harvey Brenner, "Estimating the Social Costs of National Economic Policy: Implications for Mental and Physical Health, and Criminal Aggression," a study prepared for the Joint Economic Committee, U.S. Congress (Washington, DC: Government Printing Office, 1976). Other researchers report that the anxieties that accompany unemployment reduce a person's life expectancy by as much as five years.

TABLE 4.4   APPROXIMATE LOSSES FROM SUBEMPLOYMENT

SOURCE OF LOSS	NUMBER OF POOR FAMILIES AFFECTED	AGGREGATE INCOME LOSS
Unemployment	2,800,000	$ 8 billion
Discouragement	400,000	2 billion
Underemployment	1,000,000	2 billion
Total	4,200,000	12 billion
Broken families	?	?

The third effect of high unemployment rates, namely underemployment, deprives about 1 million poor families, each losing on the order of $2,000 per year. Their losses are smaller because they are employed much of the time, but these losses still add up to a significant $2 billion for the poor population.

On the basis, then, of some rather conservative assumptions, we may conclude that at least 4 million poor families are financially stricken by subemployment in one form or another. The implied aggregate loss to the poor approached $12 billion in 1981, *enough money to move most of these families out of poverty*! If we include the number of families broken up as a result of subemployment, the total number of affected families would probably reach 70 percent of all nonaged poor families, or 60 percent of all poor families, including the aged. Given the enormity of this loss, we must conclude that subemployment is a direct, and perhaps the dominant, cause of poverty.

THE QUESTION OF CAUSATION

The tremendous significance of subemployment on the extent and depth of poverty is apparent. However, we have not really resolved the question of causation. The evidence we have reviewed only confirms that subemployment is a major correlate of poverty; it does not tell us how subemployment came about.

Do the Poor Really Try?

When we seek to explain why so much subemployment exists among the poor, we may fall back to our earlier distinction between the Flawed Character, Restricted Opportunity, and Big Brother perspectives. On the one hand, it may be the case that the poor are not serious or persistent enough in their job search activity. They may be unrealistic in their employment demands or simply too lazy to go out and secure available work. On the other hand, the subemployment of the poor may result from no fault of their own; perhaps it is simply a reflection of the fact that few decent jobs are presently available for them. A third possible explanation might take into account the work disincentives imposed by government programs, especially the prohibitions on working associated with receipt of unemployment or welfare benefits.

The first explanation is more convenient for the nonpoor and enjoys a distinct popularity. If the poor are unconcerned about their own welfare, then society's responsibility for their impoverishment is considerably reduced. Sociologist Nathan Glazer is among those who sense a certain irresponsibility on the part of the poor. He perceives that at "the heart of the crisis is a massive change in values which makes various kinds of work that used to support families undesirable to large numbers of potential workers today."[10] In other words, the jobs are there but the poor simply refuse to take them. Unfortunately, Glazer offers no evidence to support his allegation. However, a later attempt by a second observer in New York City yielded the following evidence:

> No one who rides the subways can fail to see the numerous ads for electrician's helpers (about $7,000 per year), subway patrolmen (around $8,000 per year), Office Temporaries, and Kelly Girls. The New York Telephone Company urges people to join them and be trained by them. No one who walks down Madison, Lexington, or Third Avenue will miss the signs for Help. No one who has had the misfortune of staying in a hospital recently, or even visiting one, is untroubled by the shortage of auxiliary and service personnel.... and any one who rides taxis with any frequency is aware of the number of taxis in the garage despite the industry's efforts to recruit additional drivers.... One of the fascinating statistics about New York City is that fewer persons were employed in domestic service in 1968 than in 1960. This is surely not the result of diminished demand but of a refusal to accept such employment.[11]

Despite this catalogue of apparent opportunities, there seems to be little evidence to support the notion that the poor are turning down abundant job offers. At the time Bernstein related her impressions (1970) there were about 5,000 standing job vacancies for unskilled workers in New York City. Confronting these vacancies were 139,000 unemployed individuals and over 200,000 heads-of-household receiving public assistance. In light of the enormous number of potential and actual job seekers, the number of available jobs for the poor is hardly significant. Even if a poor person desires to secure a dead-end job, his chances to do so hardly seem encouraging.

Another study in Washington, DC, compared the job vacancies advertised in the local Sunday paper (the *Washington Post*) with the number and charac-

---

[10]Nathan Glazer, "Beyond Income Maintenance," *The Public Interest*, Summer 1969, p. 120.
[11]Blanche Bernstein, "Welfare in New York City," *City Almanac*, February 1970, p. 6.

teristics of the poor people in the metropolitan area. At the time of the study, 36,400 people were officially counted as "unemployed," and 28,000 adults were receiving welfare payments. Yet, 3,028 job vacancies were listed in the paper, suggesting that many of the jobless could have found work if they really wanted to. Closer examination of the ads revealed a very different story, however. Most of the jobs required educational attainments or experience that poor people simply do not have. In all, only 354 of the job vacancies—12 percent—were jobs that poor people might get. Phone calls to the employers listing these jobs confirmed that nearly all of the job vacancies were filled, usually in a day or two.[12]

Despite evidence to the contrary, the conviction that the poor are shunning job vacancies persists. This conviction is reinforced by the observation that unemployment and welfare benefits often provide more income than could be obtained from low-wage employment. Big Brother effectively compels unemployment, it is argued, by confronting poor people with such alternatives. The specific nature of such work disincentives will be examined in later chapters. At this stage we will simply note that empirical studies show that the actual work reduction resulting from the availability of unemployment and welfare benefits is quite small, especially for male household heads.[13]

What is surprising, then, about the poor is not that they sometimes appear idle but that they exert so much energy trying to secure employment, despite limited job opportunities and work disincentives. We have already seen evidence of this activity in the high turnover rates among the employed and the attendant mobility of the poor between labor market statuses. Even the U.S. Department of Labor acknowledges that "policies aimed at reducing poverty should start from the premise that most poor people are already working unless barred from jobs by labor market or personal circumstances. Contrary to a widely held opinion, what the great majority of poor people need is not a stronger work ethic but added skills and more employment opportunities."[14] An earlier study by the Labor Department noted that the poor actively seek jobs, seek primarily lower skilled jobs, and have very low salary expectations.[15] The poor do not appear conspicuously indolent or unrealistic in their employment demands.

[12]Bradley R. Schiller, "Want Ads and Jobs for the Poor," *Manpower* (U.S. Department of Labor), January 1974.

[13]National Commission on Unemployment Compensation, *Unemployment Compensation: Studies and Research* (Washington, DC: Government Printing Office, July 1980); see also Chapter 12.

[14]U.S. Department of Labor, *Manpower Report of the President,* March 1970 (Washington, DC: Government Printing Office, 1970), p. 119.

[15]Robert Stein, "Work History, Attitudes and Income of the Unemployed," in Stanley Lebergott, ed., *Men Without Work* (Englewood Cliffs, NJ: Prentice-Hall, Inc., 1964), pp. 130–46; see also John Pucher and Bennett Harrison, "Reservation Wages, Unemployment and Earnings Expectations in Urban Labor Markets" (Cambridge, MA: Massachusetts Institute of Technology, 1975).

Where Are the Jobs?

If the poor are trying so hard to secure regular and decent employment, why are such jobs not available to them? If we favor the ethic that a person should work for his keep and the poor do try to find jobs, we must determine what obstacles impede the fulfillment of our ideological objectives and the economic needs of the poor.

To visualize the potential impact of labor market demand on unemployment and poverty rates, imagine that all potential workers could be ranked on the basis of their employability. That is, suppose that we could somehow assign everyone a relative position based on the amount of human capital they bring to the labor market. The most productive workers will be at the front of the line, the least productive at the back.

It seems reasonable to assume that employers will seek to hire the most productive workers first, and thus will start filling job vacancies from the front of the line. In many cases, of course, an employer will not be able to determine exactly who is the more or less productive job applicant. But he will try to approximate that distinction, perhaps with the aid of aptitude tests, school records, even racial and sexual prejudices. All we need to note at this point is that employers will tend to start making their selections at the front of the line and proceed toward the back.

The question that concerns us now is how far back in the line employers will go; that is, how many jobs will be available. Clearly, an individual's chances of getting a job depend not only on his or her position in line (supply characteristics) but also on how many workers employers decide to hire (demand characteristics). What we want to emphasize here is that deficiencies in demand can overwhelm supply characteristics, leaving otherwise qualified people among the ranks of the unemployed and poor.

The potential of demand fluctuations to overwhelm forces on the supply side of the picture is perhaps most apparent when we compare labor market conditions at different points in time. Consider the years 1977 and 1983, for example. The average unemployment rate in 1977 was 7 percent, meaning that 7 million people were out of work and searching for jobs. In early 1983, by contrast, the unemployment rate was 10.2 percent and nearly 11.5 million people were out on the streets at one time. Can anyone reasonably argue that the increased unemployment was due to deteriorating supply characteristics? Had our labor force grown less educated, less experienced, less motivated, less intelligent, or generally less able? Surely not. In fact, we would expect that the supply characteristics of the labor force *improve* with the passage of time, rendering such arguments almost ludicrous. Seen in this context, fluctuations in the demand for labor emerge as a primary cause of unemployment and, by implication, the level of poverty.

The relationship between fluctuations in demand and the extent of unemployment is illustrated in Figure 4.1. Note that we have arrayed all labor force participants according to their skills (human capital), with the most skilled at the top. As we suggested above, the distinction between those who are employed and those who are unemployed depends not on any absolute level of skill development, but on just how far down the line employers choose to go. In 1983 employers stopped far short of where they went in 1977, leaving millions of previously employable (and employed) workers on the jobless side of the line. Hence, we may conclude that the additional unemployment represented by the shaded area in the figure was due to a deficiency of demand in 1983.

Although deficiencies of demand clearly emerge as a major cause of unemployment and poverty, we cannot attribute *all* unemployment to demand forces. Instead, economists distinguish between four types of unemployment: frictional, seasonal, cyclical, and structural. *Frictional* unemployment arises when people move from one job to another with only a slight interval of time in between. People who are frictionally unemployed normally have visible job prospects and are simply in geographic or occupational transition. Likewise, people who are *seasonally* unemployed often face the sure prospect of renewed employment as the weather or season changes. This is not to say that their unemployment is not serious; we merely distinguish its sources from other types of unemployment.

Aggregate or *cyclical* unemployment is markedly different from the first two types of unemployment. Not only is the nature of later job prospects uncertain, but the causes of this type of unemployment are also distinct. Cyclical unemployment exists when there is less demand for labor in the economy than there is labor willingly available. In this situation, neither a change in the weather nor a change of residence is likely to create employment for the jobless.

FIGURE 4.1   The Impact of Deficient Demand

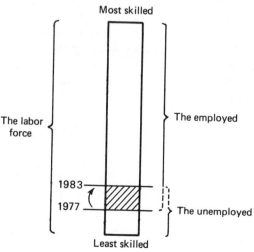

For this reason the jobless have no certain prospect of later employment. Instead, they must wait for an expansion of the demand for labor. This is the kind of unemployment depicted in Figure 4.1.

Structural unemployment is, in many respects, similar to cyclical unemployment. Here, however, the shortage of demand appears to be confined to only a few occupations or areas. While most people seem able to locate jobs, there may be a large number of pipe fitters, coal miners, or flight engineers seeking employment. There may be a large number of people out of work in the Texas Panhandle and Appalachia but relatively few in other areas of the country. Thus, it appears that localized or structural deficiencies in demand are more at fault than general demand shortages. The "dislocated worker" has become a popular symbol of such unemployment. Changing technology, trade patterns, and consumer demands have eliminated thousands of jobs in the steel, auto, and textile industries. As a result, many experienced workers have been forced to seek new jobs in other industries, occupations, or locations. In principle, this kind of structural unemployment looks less damaging than cyclical unemployment since an occupational or geographical move appears to hold promise of improved employment opportunities.

The purely structural character of structural unemployment can, however, be easily exaggerated. Can we maintain that the jobless situation of steelworkers and flight engineers is impervious to the state of demand in other occupations or areas? While it is reasonable to expect some hesitancy in moving across geographical or occupational boundaries, it is unrealistic to imagine that the speed and extent of such moves are not conditioned by employment opportunities. When good jobs exist in plentiful supply elsewhere, the structural character of structural unemployment is bound to erode. People will move and change occupations as alternative prospects merit. Even in Appalachia, an area often presumed to exist in economic isolation, unemployment rates follow national patterns. Accordingly, the apparent dimensions of structural unemployment are shaped in part by the state of aggregate demand and are subject to the social decisions which we have mentioned. As Paul Samuelson has noted, "the alleged hard core of the structurally unemployed is in fact a core made of ice and not of iron. The core of ice can be melted over a period of time by adequate effective demand, or it can be solidified from inadequate over-all demand."[16]

SUMMARY

A positive relationship between an individual's employment status and economic status is central to the American capitalist ethic. Accordingly, we are not surprised to discover that among those who work little or not at all, poverty is a

[16]Paul A. Samuelson, *Economics*, 8th ed. (New York: McGraw-Hill Book Company, 1967), p. 802.

relatively common occurrence. What is perhaps more noteworthy is the observation that the poor are integral members of the labor force and are constantly shifting from one labor force status to another. Therefore, we may conclude that millions of individuals are poor, not because they never work, but because they do not work as much or as often as others.

The work loss of the poor takes many forms. They may, at any given time, be out of the labor force, unemployed, or underemployed. These conditions are not independent but instead are related, in the market place, by the forces of aggregate demand. Together they constitute a condition of subemployment and may be costing the poor as much as $12 billion a year in lost income. Hence, subemployment appears to be a major cause of American poverty.

Finally, we have seen that the subemployment of the poor cannot be explained by their failure to seek employment. On the contrary, it appears that their subemployment is determined in large part by the decisions society makes regarding the utilization of economic resources. As long as the demand for labor is deficient, we must expect high unemployment rates and the resulting poverty.

Appendix:
Unemployment as a Social Goal

The deficiencies of aggregate demand that result in increased unemployment and poverty are not the consequence of unbridled market forces. Nor will the required expansion of demand emerge as the work of an "invisible hand" of the kind that Adam Smith described. On the contrary, the level of demand, and hence the level of aggregate unemployment, is now a widely recognized responsibility of government. Fiscal and monetary policies largely determine the number of available jobs. Because these policies are the outcome of conscious activity on the part of a federal administration and not autonomously formulated by an invisible hand, we may say that the level of unemployment is part of society's matrix of goals. Hence, the level of demand we seek and the means by which we achieve it are directly subject to the collective will, as expressed in the political process.[17]

Of course, no one consciously and forcefully promotes a high level of aggregate unemployment for the sheer sense of achievement or Satanic art. Were the level of demand our only social concern, then we could confidently anticipate that aggregate unemployment would disappear. But we must recognize that the goal of aggregate full employment competes with other social objectives for the limited attention and resources of the public. As a consequence, consciously, unthinkingly, or simply by default, a nonzero level of aggregate unemployment may become a social goal.

[17]For an introduction to the fiscal and monetary policies appropriate to the goal of full employment see Bradley R. Schiller, *The Economy Today*, 2nd ed. (New York: Random House, Inc., 1983).

The goal must often deemed in direct competition with full employment is that of price stability. It is widely believed that we cannot have both price stability and full employment at the same time. This implies that the pursuit of one objective necessarily means the abandonment of the other. Furthermore, because the potential destruction of currency and market functions that might accompany really serious inflation is widely feared, price stability is considered a foremost policy goal. As a consequence, some unemployment is tolerated as part of the cost of maintaining existing price levels.

The seriousness with which this trade-off is regarded by policymakers is evident in their actions. Upon taking office, President Carter initiated policies to reduce the rate of unemployment. As the unemployment rate dropped, however, prices began to rise more quickly. Carter responded by designating inflation "our top economic priority" and slowing the progress towards full employment.[18] President Reagan started out by promising both lower unemployment and less inflation, but quickly abandoned that course. Higher unemployment came to be accepted as the "necessary cost" of achieving less inflation.

THE PHILLIPS CURVE PROBLEM

President Reagan's willingness to tolerate high levels of unemployment was based on the historical relationship between inflation and unemployment. As Figure 4.2 suggests, lower rates of unemployment have generally been accompanied by higher rates of inflation. This tendency, first observed in England by A. W. Phillips (for whom the curve in Figure 4.2 is named), has been found to prevail in scores of countries. Accordingly, the Phillips curve not only summarizes a historical relationship between unemployment rates and inflation rates, but appears to offer policymakers a finite set of choices. As long as the curve is an accurate description of economic performance, then full employment and price stability are not attainable at the same time. Instead, some point on the curve, a distinct compromise between the two goals, must be selected as a policy target. And so it happens that some policymakers choose to sacrifice full employment in the hopes of achieving lower rates of inflation.

Although the Phillips curve appears to present policymakers with a finite set of trade-offs, we must not be too quick in rejecting the goal of full employment. At best, the Phillips curve is a *generalization* of historical experience; in fact, we have experienced scores of inflation–unemployment combinations that lie both above and below the curve depicted in Figure 4.2. Thus, it is certainly *possible* to achieve more desirable combinations of unemployment and inflation than the Phillips curve suggests.

The reasoning behind the Phillips curve is also suspect, resembling as it

[18]Council of Economic Advisers, *Economic Report of the President* (Washington, DC: Government Printing Office, 1979).

FIGURE 4.2   The Phillips Curve

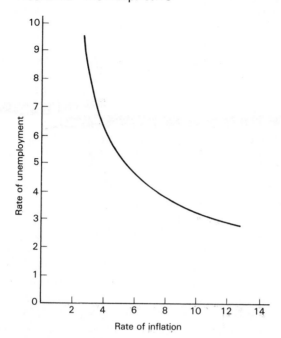

does certain structural unemployment arguments. Nearly everyone agrees that an expansion of aggregate demand is necessary to reduce high levels of unemployment. The proponents of the Phillips curve theory argue that comparatively few benefits of increased spending actually reach the unemployed, because they have the wrong skills, are too young or old, live in the wrong places, or are simply unaware of new opportunities. Accordingly, demands for new output are met by overworking existing employees rather than by hiring new workers. Wage rates, and then prices, go up while unemployment rates change little. The greater the effort to reduce unemployment, the faster the rate of inflation.

The argument for a trade-off between fuller employment and greater price stability has a solid empirical basis. However, the terms of the trade-off are not immutable. On the contrary, the Phillips curve shifted (moved) to the right many times in the 1970s, leading to both higher unemployment *and* higher inflation. It should be possible, then, to shift it to the left as well, permitting both less unemployment and less inflation. Indeed, both theory and practice suggest that the relationship between unemployment and inflation is more flexible than current attitudes and policy presume.

Even a fixed (unmovable) Phillips curve need not necessitate a permanent sacrifice. The element of time is important. Suppose, for example, that an increase in the demand for goods and services occurred. To satisfy this demand, producers will have to hire additional workers or employ their existing labor forces more fully. Other workers may not be immediately available, however, and they are likely to require training or orientation before they can contribute to output. As a result, producers probably will have to rely primarily on their existing workers for an initial expansion of output. Such reliance is expensive, however, as overtime wage rates are high; productivity is likely to decline with longer hours; and workers will feel in a better position to demand higher base wages. Producers will have a large and increasing incentive to locate and train new workers as expanded output continues. As time passes, producers will substitute new labor for overtime labor, thus reducing costs.

The labor market adjustment process described here implies that expansion of demand will, indeed, lead to higher prices but that the increased rate of inflation may be a temporary phenomenon. As new workers are absorbed into the production process, the pressure on prices may abate. What the Phillips curve may portray on an aggregate level is the rate of inflation necessary to evoke the required labor force adjustment. The curve should not necessarily be understood to mean that the same high rate of inflation will continue once the adjustment is made. Not only may the price rise be temporary, but it is an integral feature of the adjustment mechanism. Hence, we might be able to say that an 8 percent rate of inflation is necessary to reduce the unemployment rate from 6.0 to 5.5 percent, but we have no firm reason for anticipating continued high rates of inflation once the lower level of unemployment is reached.

High rates of inflation could continue, of course, but they would be the consequence of actions other than the initial effort to reduce employment. Inflationary *expectations* are often the source of continued wage–price escalation. When people see prices rising, they may come to expect inflation to continue. Prodded by such expectations, they may themselves demand higher wages and prices, thereby making inflation more permanent.

To the extent that structural factors or expectations create a trade-off between unemployment and inflation, attaining full employment is obviously more difficult. This does not mean, however, that we are stuck with any particular trade-off. Policies that reduce structural bottlenecks or restrain inflationary expectations can *shift* the Phillips curve to the left. In so doing, they make it less costly (in terms of inflation) to reach the goal of full employment.

If, for example, the move toward full employment is slowed by the fact that unemployed workers possess skills in small demand or live in the wrong areas, further expansion of demand might be channeled more specifically in their direction. The *pattern* of demand, both occupationally and geographically, will affect the speed of adjustment and, thus, the dynamic trade-off. Accordingly, there is no unchangeable relationship of inflation to unemployment. The relationship depends on the capability and determination of policymakers to alter the pattern of demand as they expand it.

A similar qualification to the Phillips curve emerges when we consider the phenomenon of racial discrimination in the labor market. Even when employers are reluctant to hire black workers, their reluctance will not be impervious to economic forces. An unassisted market adjustment thus implies that more and more racial barriers will be eliminated as the economic incentive for recruiting new and able workers increases. By the same token, the extent and strength of discrimination are among the forces that determine the dynamic trade-off between unemployment and inflation. The government's efforts to overcome or circumvent discrimination can lead to different trade-offs. Again, there is no necessary or fixed relationship between inflation and unemployment.

The upshot of these considerations is that a fixed rate of inflation is not associated with any given level of unemployment or with efforts to reduce unemployment by any given amount. Policymakers have a variety of options available to effectuate an improved trade-off between inflation and unemployment. By changing the pattern of demand or improving the function of the labor market, policymakers can achieve lower rates of unemployment with little pressure on prices. To formulate the goal of price stability as an alternative to fuller employment is to ignore other options and rob the poor.

FURTHER READING

COUNCIL OF ECONOMIC ADVISERS. *Economic Report of the President*, Washington, DC: Government Printing Office, annual.

FINEGAN, T. ADRICH, "Should Discouraged Workers Be Counted as Unemployed?" *Challenge*, November/December 1978.

FISH, MARY, "Income Inequality and Employment," U.S. Department of Labor, R & D Monograph 66, 1978.

GARRATY, JOHN A. *Unemployment in History: Economic Thought and Public Policy*. New York: Harper & Row, 1978.

NATIONAL COMMISSION ON EMPLOYMENT AND UNEMPLOYMENT STATISTICS. *Counting the Labor Force*. Washington, DC: Government Printing Office, 1979.

TAGGART, ROBERT. *The Welfare Consequences of Labor Market Problems*. Kalamazoo, MI: Upjohn Institute, 1982.

"THE STRUCTURE OF LABOR MARKETS: DIVERSE VIEWS (A SYMPOSIUM)," *Challenge*, May/June 1978.

U.S. DEPARTMENT OF LABOR, *Employment and Training Report of the President*. Washington, DC: Government Printing Office, annual.

The Working Poor

If deficient demand for labor and the resultant unemployment is a major cause of poverty, we should be able to eliminate most poverty by providing everyone with a job. According to this reasoning, employment emerges as a sure route to at least some economic security. This route, however, is not so certain. We know, for example, that many poor people whom we think of as "unemployed" do work a great deal. In fact, a salient characteristic of the subemployed poor is that they are repeatedly engaged in part-time or part-year work. Hence, we can quickly reject the naive assumption that employment automatically lifts a person out of poverty.

A slightly more sophisticated view of the relationship between employment and poverty would suggest that the attainment of economic security depends not just on whether one works but also on how much one works. By and large, economic security is reserved for those individuals and their families who work full-time throughout the year. In this chapter, we examine this expectation in greater detail. In so doing, we focus on those individuals who fail to meet our expectations—the working poor.

WORK EXPERIENCE AND POVERTY

The expectation that increased employment improves one's chances of escaping poverty is fully supported by available data. As Figure 5.1 shows, there is a distinct inverse relationship between the number of weeks a household head works and the likelihood of poverty. As the duration of employment increases,

FIGURE 5.1   Poverty and Employment, 1981

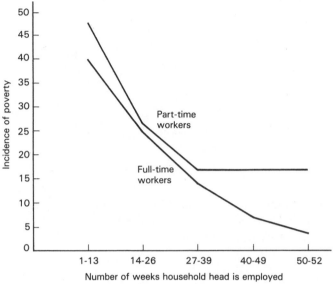

Source: U.S. Bureau of the Census.

the incidence of poverty progressively drops. Among household heads who typically work full-time (thirty five hours per week), those who are employed less than half the year have a one out of three chance of being poor. By contrast, household heads who work full-time all year round have a one in thirty chance of being poor.

The same relationship between the duration of employment and poverty is true for part-time workers, as Figure 5.1 also indicates. The only difference is that the incidence of poverty does not continue to drop beyond twenty-six weeks of work. This is due to the fact that most of the part-time workers are female heads-of-household, who have large family responsibilities and few income sources.

The relationships depicted in Figure 5.1 are likely to instill the comfortable feeling that there are few full-time, year-round workers among the poor. But this impression is dispelled quickly when the numbers are examined more closely. Because year-round workers in the economy vastly outnumber part-year workers, the incidence rates do not adequately reflect the work experience of the poor. Once again, numbers and proportions convey very different impressions.

Table 5.1 summarizes the work experience of the poor in absolute numbers. It shows that there are 1.2 million poor families whose heads work full-time all year round. Another 287,000 poor family heads work part-time all year round. In fact, the number of poor year-round workers nearly equals the number of

TABLE 5.1   WORK EXPERIENCE OF THE POOR (HEADS-OF-HOUSEHOLD), 1981

WEEKS WORKED	FULL-TIME WORKERS	PART-TIME WORKERS	TOTAL
50–52	1,200,000	287,000	1,487,000
40–49	261,000	103,000	364,000
27–39	291,000	143,000	434,000
14–26	430,000	175,000	605,000
1–13	357,000	288,000	585,000
Total, 1–52 weeks	2,539,000	996,000	3,476,000
Did not work	—	—	

Source: U.S. Bureau of the Census.

poor part-year workers. From another perspective, we may observe that one-fifth of *all* poor families are headed by a year-round worker, while one-fourth of the nonaged poor families are so headed. In short, extensive work effort and experience is characteristic of the poor.

THE HARD-WORKING POOR

If we include the dependents of these household heads in our calculations we find that there are over 5 million persons in families headed by individuals who worked all year round at full-time jobs. Why, we may ask, are so many people poor if their families work so much? Doesn't the existence of this paradox violate the very same principles that comprise our capitalist ideology? If we cannot guarantee economic security to those individuals who contribute their maximum work effort, what sort of admonitions or incentives can be directed to those who work less?

We may entertain two general explanations for the status of the hard-working poor. The most obvious suggestion is that their wages are unusually low. At poverty wages, very few people can work hard enough or long enough to attain economic security. But low wages are not the only possible explanation for the plight of the working poor. Poverty refers to the relationship between a family's income and its needs. Thus, it might also be the case that the poor simply have above-average needs, due to either larger families or special expenses, for example, medical bills. In this situation, even standard wages would tend to leave the family financially destitute. The distinction between income and needs is vital for policy concerns. The one situation implies the need for labor market intervention of some kind, while the second implies the need to address nonmarket phenomena, such as family planning or health insurance.

To the extent that the poor have larger families, they require higher wages.

The full-time working head of a family of four required wages of $4.50 per hour in 1981 to attain our poverty standards. The head of a five-person family needed $5.30 an hour to reach the same level, while families of six required $6. Still larger families would have to command over $7 an hour to maintain a poverty budget. With average blue-collar and clerical wages only slightly higher than this, it is clear that heads of large families will have to be fairly productive workers.

While it is obvious that the incidence of poverty will be aggravated by the wage requirements of larger families, it does not follow that the poor are impoverished because of above-average needs. We still must inquire whether the hard-working poor command wages high enough to support even an average (four-person) family. If they do not, then the above-average needs of larger families deepen rather than explain their poverty.

Poor Wages

There is abundant evidence that the hard-working poor do not command wages high enough to assure economic security for an average-size family or, for that matter, for any family. Very few full-time working poor earn as much as $5 an hour, and virtually none earns more than $6 an hour. On the contrary, the typical wage of a poor head-of-household who works all year round at a full-time job is between $3.50 and $4 an hour.

Working long hours all year and still remaining in poverty must be tremendously frustrating, and yet many of these families supply even more work effort. Among poor families with full-time working heads, close to half send other family members into the labor market also. Not only is the head of the family unable to provide financial security as a result of his or her own efforts, but even the contribution of working spouses and children still leaves many families in poverty.

The total incomes of families with full-time working heads are given in Table 5.2. Note that these incomes include not only the full-time earnings of the head-of-household, but also the earnings of any other family members who work, plus any income from other sources (including welfare). When viewed from this perspective, it is evident that the wages of poor workers are extremely limited. Especially disheartening is the high concentration of working families with incomes of less than $6,000 per year.

The hard-working poor are not the only workers to command low wages. While the poor are slightly more visible than other low-wage workers, nearly 13 million workers earned hourly wages of less than $4 as recently as 1982; over a million of these earned less than $3 an hour. Although increases in nominal wages since 1982 have reduced the number of people earning such low wages (exact figures are not available), in 1982 there were still over 4 million *year-round, full-time workers* earning less than $10,000 a year and many part-

TABLE 5.2   INCOMES OF THE WORKING POOR (TOTAL INCOME OF FAMILIES WHOSE HEAD WORKED FULL-TIME YEAR ROUND), 1981

TOTAL INCOME	PERCENT OF FAMILIES
Under $2,000	23
$2,000–3,999	7
$4,000–5,999	16
$6,000–7,999	22
$8,000 or more	32
Total	100
Number of families	1,200,000

Source: U.S. Bureau of the Census.

time workers earning still less. Accordingly, we can conclude that low-wage workers are still in abundance. What keeps these persons out of poverty is the fact that they have slightly smaller families or none at all, or keep more family members in the labor force for longer periods of time. Many are also dependents of workers commanding more substantial incomes. Nonetheless, these workers are not very far removed from poverty; they and their families have incomes very close to our poverty standards. In the best of circumstances, they are referred to as the near-poor. In less favorable times they become part of the poverty population.

Poor Jobs

If there is any moral to be gleaned from the foregoing figures, perhaps it is this: A poor janitor who works hard stands a very good chance of becoming a hard-working poor janitor. There seems to be little prospect of economic security for the poor as a result of their own efforts. Too many people earn too little money. Elliot Liebow has summarized the prospects for the working poor:

> . . . the man does not have any reasonable expectation that, however bad it is, his job will lead to better things. Menial jobs are not, by and large, the starting point of a track system which leads to even better jobs for those who are able and willing to do them. The busboy or dishwasher in a restaurant is not on a job track which, if negotiated skillfully, leads to chef or manager of the restaurant. The busboy or dishwasher who works hard becomes, simply, a hard-working busboy or dishwasher. Neither hard work nor perseverance can conceivably carry the janitor to a sit-down job in the office building he cleans up.[1]

[1] Elliot Liebow, *Tally's Corner: A Study of Negro Streetcorner Men* (Boston: Little, Brown and Company, 1967), p. 63.

Not all the poor, of course, are janitors. Most middle-class persons, in fact, probably think of janitors as low-income workers, but not poor. More likely to come to mind—if we admit the poor work at all—are bellboys, busboys, and nonunionized street cleaners, plus a small army of aged farmers and stooping sharecroppers. Once again, however, the preconception departs considerably from the reality of everyday poverty. The working poor are likely to be found in all broad occupational categories. Table 5.3 depicts the actual occupational distribution of the poor. While it is true that nearly 30 percent of all farmers and farm workers are poor, these two occupations account for less than one-sixth of the jobs held by the poor; as many poor work as operatives or service workers. Even white-collar jobs do not guarantee financial security, as more than 800,000 people depicted in the table testify.

It is just as easy to overstate the occupational status of the poor as it is to understate it. The occupational profile of Table 5.3 includes very broad employment categories and may lead to erroneous impressions. While there are 168,000 poor professional and technical workers, there are very few poor scientists, dentists, or even college professors among them. More likely to be poor within that occupational classification are hospital technicians, recreation and social workers, and evangelist healers. Similarly, in other occupational categories, the poor tend to hold the least desirable, most marginal kinds of jobs. They are dishwashers, loggers, theater ushers, porters, tailors, shoe repairmen, and laundry workers. Accordingly, while it is true that the working poor are distributed throughout the labor market and in all industries, they will always be found in the lowest-ranking, least noticeable jobs. They constitute what might be called a phantom labor force.

TABLE 5.3 OCCUPATIONS OF THE POOR (HEADS-OF-HOUSEHOLD), 1981

OCCUPATION	NUMBER OF PERSONS
Professional and technical	168,000
Managers, officials, and proprietors	258,000
Clerical workers	322,000
Sales workers	115,000
Craftsmen and foremen	481,000
Operatives	484,000
Private household workers	94,000
Other service workers	694,000
Unskilled laborers	256,000
Farmers and farm managers	327,000
Farm laborers and foremen	138,000
Total	3,876,000

Source: U.S. Bureau of the Census.

The Significance of Secondary Workers

We have already drawn attention to the fact that poor families often send wives and other family members into the labor force to supplement the low wages of the family head. These secondary workers contribute a great deal to family incomes and often help lift the family above the poverty standard. In fact, these secondary workers are often the only available bridge between poverty and near-poverty. Poor families, however, are often prevented from sending secondary workers into the job market by the presence of young children in the household. Younger children tend to keep their mothers out of the labor market, and younger families have fewer older children available for part-time work. Consequently, a major distinction between poor families and near-poor families is that the former are slightly younger and less likely to contain secondary workers. One implication of this distinction is that many of the near-poor passed through poverty in the natural course of family development. Later chapters will consider how and why they return.

A Hardship Index

The President's Commission on Employment and Unemployment Statistics attempted to summarize the effects of low wages, secondary workers, and repeated unemployment on low-wage workers and their families. To do so, the Commission formulated an index of "economic hardship," which relates a worker's earnings to his or her family income. A person is counted as a "hardship" case if he or she (1) participates in the labor force at least forty weeks during the year, (2) earns less than the poverty threshold, and (3) is a member of a household whose total income is less than twice the poverty standard. The hardship index thus encompasses all the working poor, many of the subemployed poor, and many others who are close to our standards of minimal need—despite extensive labor force participation. The Commission counted over 7.5 million such persons in 1976. From this perspective, labor market participation is clearly no assurance of nonpoverty status.

WHY ARE WAGES SO LOW?

While poverty and employment might seem incompatible, there is no shortage of available explanations for the low wages of the working poor. Predominant among these are that the poor are undereducated, inexperienced, underskilled, geographically handicapped, and trained in the wrong occupations. Abundant evidence exists to support each of these explanations, and we cannot deny their importance in holding down the wages of the poor. We must also recognize, however, that these explanations focus almost exclusively on the supply side of the labor market. They tell us what qualities an individual brings to the labor market but do not provide a complete explanation of why the worker is paid so little for them. To understand the process by which wages are determined, we must also ask what the demand side of the labor market looks like.

In the most general terms, we say that a worker's wages are determined by the contribution he or she makes to output, that is, by his or her marginal product. But what is it that makes the output of a pipe fitter less valuable than the output of an advertising executive? What differentiates the incomes of these two people is not the physical output that each produces, but rather the value that society attaches to their products. If society suddenly became disenchanted with the wares of advertising executives and found increased value in fitted pipes, the incomes of pipe fitters would exceed those of advertising executives, regardless of their respective physical outputs. By the same reasoning, if society were to attach more value to the kinds of output that the poor can and do produce, we could expect the incomes of the working poor to rise.

The notion that the extent and structure of demand are significant determinants of the wages of the poor does not constitute a revolution in economic thinking. On the contrary, economists have long taken credit for the discovery that prices, and thus wages, are determined by the interaction of supply and demand. In the realm of policy formulation, however, the impact of the demand side of the market on the economic position of the poor is easily neglected. Doing so ignores tremendous potential for eliminating poverty.

During the 1940s, there was a tendency for wage rates and incomes at the bottom of the occupational ladder to rise faster than those at the top. This was due to an upsurge in demand for unskilled, semiskilled, and operative kinds of labor needed for war production. The structure of demand since the 1940s, however, has primarily benefited workers with higher education and more technical expertise. Accordingly, we find the unskilled, semiskilled, and operative workers heavily represented among the poor. The distribution of wages and incomes is partly a reflection of collective social decisions regarding the merits of particular kinds of output. Sociopolitical decisions to expand the educational system, to arm for peace, and to explore the moon have all had a profound impact on the structure of demand for labor. Had we decided instead to dredge more rivers, to build more houses, or to clean up our cities, the extent and nature of poverty might now be markedly different. Without attempting to predict those changes here, we may at least take note of the fact that the poor now suffer from some of society's past and current labor utilization decisions and stand to benefit if and when society decides to place higher value on the available services of the poor.

SUMMARY

In Chapter 4, we observed that labor market forces have a substantial impact on the rate of employment for the poor. In particular, we observed that, in 1981 approximately 4 million poor families suffered income losses as a direct or indirect consequence of unemployment. We noted further that this unemployment was beyond the control of the poor and largely determined by labor market forces. We may add to that analysis now by observing that the level and structure of demand also helps determine what incomes the poor will command when they do work. Relatively low levels of aggregate demand will restrain all wages, while particularized demand shortages may, and do, depress the wages of the working poor.

We suggested earlier that about 70 percent of all nonaged poor families were affected by unemployment. We have now counted another 1.2 million poor families whose heads work full-time but whose wages are too low. Because these wages are themselves influenced by the same variables that determine unemployment rates, we may reasonably conclude that labor market forces are responsible for most of the poverty among nonaged families.

Appendix:
Dual Labor Markets
and the Trickle Down Theory

A major implication of the last two chapters is that the poor would benefit substantially from an expansion of aggregate demand—in particular, that the poor would benefit in the form of more jobs and higher wages, thus making possible their escape from poverty. But the link between aggregate demand expansion and the plight of the poor is not always apparent. Indeed, there are many observers who argue that the poor will benefit little—perhaps not at all—from traditional increases in demand; that they are largely excluded from the jobs and higher wages such expansions create. The purpose of this brief appendix is to examine more carefully the relationship between demand expansion and the status of the poor.

THE TRICKLE DOWN PERSPECTIVE

Rarely does the government use its fiscal and monetary powers to expand aggregate demand in a form that is designed to help the poor *directly*. Instead, demand is expanded for those goods and services deemed to be of intrinsic worth to society (say, transportation or weapons systems) with the underlying conviction (hope?) that the poor will share in the benefits of the *generalized* demand expansion that follows. The expectation is that some of the benefits of increased demand will ultimately "trickle down" to the poor.[2]

Will the trickle really occur? In what forms?

To evaluate the validity of the trickle down hypothesis, suppose that the federal government decides to build a moon shuttle capable of taxiing busloads of scientists and tourists back and forth to the moon. Obviously, such an undertaking would require the expenditure of tens of billions of dollars and the employment of highly skilled labor and capital equipment. The question is whether and how the poor folks back in the ghetto would benefit from this excursion into space.

It is possible, of course, that some of the poor would be employed directly in the moon shuttle program, say as grounds sweepers, gate attendants, or other low-skilled jobs. But the potential for such *direct job creation* is apt to be small. A far likelier source of jobs are the *multiplier effects* that will take place once the program gets under way. The aerospace workers will want to spend their increased incomes, and in so doing will add to the demand for more conventional goods and services, such as houses, hot dogs, beer, gardeners, and maids. As the production of these goods and services expands, more jobs and incomes will be created, thereby increasing the chances that some needy souls from the ranks of the poor will obtain better jobs and wages. Such multiplier effects will continue to reverberate through the economy as the income spent by the aerospace workers is passed from hand to hand.

Although multiplier effects provide the best hope of jobs and income for the folks in the ghetto, there are other ways in which the poor might benefit from the moon shuttle program. The people who obtain jobs directly in the moon shuttle program will probably vacate positions that offered lower wages or benefits, jobs which then are available to others, including the poor. Such *substitution effects* may continue all the way down the occupational ladder, ultimately resulting in job vacancies for the poor. In addition, employers faced with a sudden shortage of labor will have an economic incentive to *train* the poor and unskilled, thereby further enlarging the size of the trickle.

THE DUAL LABOR MARKET PERSPECTIVE

Although the trickle down hypothesis seems plausible enough (even if somewhat remote), not everyone shares the expectations it generates. In particular, it is argued that the poor do not really participate in the mainstream economy, and

---

[2]The expression "trickle down" was coined by W. H. Locke Anderson in "Trickling Down: The Relationship between Economic Growth and the Extent of Poverty among American Families," *Quarterly Journal of Economics*, November 1964, and has earlier origins in William Jennings Bryan's 1896 "Cross of Gold" speech in which he declared, "There are those who believe that, if you will only legislate to make the well-to-do prosperous, their prosperity will leak through on those below."

are excluded from the jobs and income that a moon shuttle program would create. In effect, it is argued, the poor participate in a separate and distinct labor market, a *secondary labor market*, which is distinguished from the mainstream or *primary labor market*. From the perspective of the dual labor market hypothesis an expansion of demand that occurs in the primary market—such as in a moon shuttle program—will not benefit workers in the secondary market.

A variety of barriers allegedly exclude the poor from the primary labor market, in effect creating the secondary market. Outright discrimination against minority groups or the poor, for example, would exclude the poor from the trickle. So, too, would recruiting practices that emphasized skill, experience, and stable work histories, prerequisites that the poor job-seeker can rarely satisfy. Institutional barriers like strong labor unions could have the same effect, especially if unions opted to maximize the earnings of their current members rather than to expand employment and union membership.

It is unlikely, of course, that these barriers would be so great as to exclude all poor job-seekers from the benefits created by a moon shuttle program (or any other form of demand expansion). It is much more reasonable to expect that *some* additional jobs and income will in fact trickle down, thereby reducing the number of people we count as poor. But the dual labor market hypothesis serves to remind us that the really critical issue is *how much* actually "trickles down." And it also suggests that public policy can be used to increase the size of that trickle by reducing the barriers that separate the poor from the jobs and incomes we create.

FURTHER READING

CAIN, GLEN G. "The Challenge of Segmented Labor Market Theories to Orthodox Theory: A Survey," *Journal of Economic Literature*, December 1976.

DOERINGER, PETER, and MICHAEL PIORE. "Unemployment and the 'Dual Labor Market,'" *The Public Interest*, Winter 1975.

GARFINKEL, IRWIN, and ROBERT HAVEMAN. "Earnings Capacity, Economic Status, and Poverty," *Journal of Human Resources*, Winter 1977.

GORDON, DAVID. *Theories of Poverty and Underemployment*. Lexington, MA: D. C. Heath and Company, 1972.

HARRISON, BENNETT. "How American Households Mix Work and Welfare," *Challenge*, May/June 1978.

HIRSCH, BARRY T. "Poverty and Economic Growth: Has Trickle Down Petered Out," *Economic Inquiry*, January 1980.

LEVITAN, SAR, and ROBERT TAGGART. *Employment and Earnings Inadequacy: A New Social Indicator.* Baltimore, MD: Johns Hopkins University Press, 1974.

THORNTON, J. R., R. J. AGNELLO, and C. R. LINK, "Poverty and Economic Growth: Trickle Down Peters Out," *Economic Inquiry,* July 1978.

Age and Health

Although it is clear that deficiencies of aggregate demand explain much of the poverty we have observed, we cannot conclude that labor market forces are the sole explanation for poverty. As noted earlier, income-earning opportunities may be limited by supply-side characteristics as well, particularly human capital deficiencies. Government policies may also make available opportunities appear unattractive. The search for poverty causes must continue. This chapter examines the demographic characteristics of the poor and the potential such characteristics possess for explaining poverty. We have already counted among the poor 3,751,000 individuals over the age of 65.

The problem of poverty among the aged was significantly reduced between 1966 and 1974. This was largely due to two factors—overall economic growth and successful public efforts to improve the adequacy of retirement benefits. This trend stalled in the 1970s, however, and was even reversed for a few years as a result of economic stagnation and a slowdown in income transfers. Figure 6.1 provides poverty rates for groups under and over 65, illustrating this trend.

The overall decline in aged poverty since 1966 masks some serious inequalities among the aged. Over 70 percent of the aged poor are women, most of them living alone. Although fewer in number, older black women are especially likely to be poor, with a 43.5 percent poverty rate.

AGE

Our purpose in reexamining the situation of the aged poor is not to remind ourselves how desperate they are but to investigate the link between their age

FIGURE 6.1   Poverty Rates of Young and Elderly Populations, 1966–1981

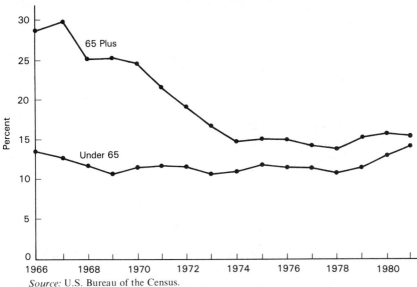

Source: U.S. Bureau of the Census.

and their economic status. What we seek to determine is whether there is something in the process of aging itself that leads to poverty.

The very size of the aged poor population creates a strong presumption that a causal link exists between age and poverty. Not only are 14 percent of the aged poor, but such individuals comprise one-ninth of the total poverty population. The economic problems of the aged will become increasingly important as the number of people living past the age of 65 continues to grow. Since 1900, the number of people living until age 65 has increased dramatically. In addition, the life expectancy of people *at age 65* has also increased. Life expectancy for people reaching 65 was about eleven years in 1900, now it is nearly twenty. Hence, there are far more aged people today and they are living longer. This is partly reflected in the overall increase in life expectancies. In 1900, life expectancy at birth was forty-nine years; today it is over seventy years.

This increase in the size of the older population is continuing. In fact, the post-World War II "baby boom" will become a "seniors' boom" in the early part of the twenty-first century. In the process, the number of aged persons will nearly double—from 25.5 million in 1980 to 51.4 million in the year 2020. And by 2030, the percentage of older people in the total U.S. population will also nearly double, from 11.3 percent to 21.1 percent.[1] Continuing discoveries in medical science may expand the aged population still further.

These considerations have led Michael Harrington to observe that "the

[1] President's Commission on Pension Policy, *Coming of Age: Toward a National Retirement Income Policy* (Washington, DC: Government Printing Office, 1981).

poverty of old age in America is rooted in a biological revolution."[2] We must take care, however, not to attribute to biology the economic ills of the aged. Changing fertility patterns and medical advances are responsible only for the fact that so many more people live to old age. They do not explain why so many of these people live in poverty. To understand more fully the forces that lead to economic destitution, we begin by reviewing the sources of support that the aged command.

Sources of Economic Support

The most obvious constraint on the incomes of the aged is the fact that so few older individuals remain in the labor force. Only one-fourth of all aged couples have at least one member in the labor force. Among aged individuals living alone (mostly women) labor force participation is even lower—about 12 percent. Accordingly, earnings from employment account for less than one-fifth of the incomes of the aged and provide little income at that. The poor among the aged are even less likely to work (see Table 2.5), and this absence of employment income is a major determinant of their economic status.

Low labor force participation among the aged reflects a continuing trend in American society. At the beginning of the century, more than two-thirds of all men over the age of 65 were in the labor force; today, only one out of five older men work. The reasons for this decline in labor force participation are many, but surely they do not include the increased physical requirements of labor or diminished health status of the aged. An increased desire for leisure, an abatement of the economic necessity to work, and a reduced demand for the skills of the aged are more likely to have contributed to the decline in labor force participation.

There is considerable evidence that many of the aged are involuntarily removed from the labor force because of forced retirement and prolonged unemployment. If an older worker is laid off for any reason (for example, plant shutdowns, production slowdowns, or forced retirement), he faces little chance of finding another job. He probably has developed highly specialized skills in a declining occupation. Moreover, because of his advanced age, other employers see little benefit in retraining him or redirecting his skills. Other employers also anticipate the increased costs of higher disability rates and imminent retirement. Simple economics weigh against the older job-seeker. Because his employment prospects are so unpromising the older job-seeker is likely to drop out of the labor force earlier than desired, eliminating a prospective income source. Of those older persons already "retired," over one-third report they were forced out

---

[2]Michael Harrington, *The Other America* (New York: The Macmillan Company, 1962), p. 102.

of their jobs. Nearly half of those older persons in poverty report forced retirements.[3]

There are alternatives to employment income, of course. Some of the most common substitutes are income from savings, assets, and various retirement plans. Generous provisions of these can help reduce the impact of lost employment income. Indeed, the availability of alternative sources of income could actually encourage retirement, with no implied loss of individual welfare. The question is: Are the aged adequately provided with nonemployment retirement income?

A potentially important source of income for the aged is the savings they accumulated during their working years. Unfortunately, such savings are typically inadequate. Because the aged live longer and retire earlier today, they must accumulate greater savings than they once did. The unfortunate but simple economic fact is that the longer one lives, the greater are the chances of destitution. A person's employment capabilities and opportunities disappear at the same time that their savings are depleted. Today's aged must command considerable assets and savings if they are to experience a comfortable retirement.

At present, the aged poor clearly do not possess such savings and therefore suffer after retirement. Many of the nonpoor aged do not fare much better, either. A 1979 survey indicated that only half of all aged families hold at least $100 in a savings account. The average value of an aged family's total assets is only about $15,000, with most of this value in home ownership. The average value of liquid assets (that is, assets that can be readily sold or converted into cash) of aged families averages much less. In fact, one out of five aged households possesses no liquid assets; half have liquid assets of less than $3,000.[4] Therefore, accumulated savings provide little antipoverty protection. There is also abundant evidence that the near-aged (people 55 to 65 years old) have no greater savings. It appears, then, that today's aged poor are only a small percentage of the number that will be poor in years to come.

Two more questions arise with regard to the savings of the aged: First, did the aged ever possess enough resources to save for old age? And second, did they save what resources they had? The distinction is important for policy purposes because many observers still believe it is necessary to distinguish the deserving poor from the undeserving poor, even among the aged. From this perspective, an impoverished older individual may simply be suffering the consequences of an earlier decision to make merry while the sun was shining.

There is no evidence that the aged poor enjoyed especially lascivious or

[3]National Council on Aging, *The Myth and Reality of Aging in America* (Washington, DC: National Council on Aging, 1977), p. 87. Workers in the age group 55–64 foresee these problems: A 1981 Harris poll showed 73 percent favored greater availability of part-time work after "retirement."

[4]Joseph Friedman and Jane Sjogren, "Assets of the Elderly as They Retire," *Social Security Bulletin*, January 1981.

spendthrift lives. A University of Michigan study suggests that the aged poor had never earned enough income to provide for a comfortable living either before or after retirement. Among those aged poor whose incomes were known, over 40 percent had never earned as much as $2,000 per year. One observer of these statistics concluded that "the misery of their old age is simply the conclusion to life of misery. They are the ones who have grown up, lived, and will die under conditions of poverty."[5] Many, probably most, of the aged poor were always in or on the margin of poverty.

Some individuals do experience impoverishment for the first time, however, as they grow old. Just as few people think about dying, few ever plan to grow old and retire. Only a small number of people make provisions for old age in spite of statistical evidence showing the diminished income during retirement. People's essential optimism is revealed in consumer surveys such as one disclosing that families who have not had as much as $500 in the bank during the last five years confidently anticipate a comfortable retirement. Confidence fades with age, however; among younger families, only 9 percent foresee hard times after retirement; among middle-aged families, 16 percent sense trouble ahead. But when they reach old age, at least 25 percent of these individuals end up in poverty.[6]

Aside from their own savings, aged persons may draw income either from private pension plans or Social Security. In fact, a 1981 poll sponsored by the President's Commission on Pension Policy disclosed that most workers expect Social Security and private pensions to provide most of their retirement income. These sources usually provide much less income than most persons anticipated. Pension plans are often great disillusionments. Many workers confidently subscribe to company pension plans only to find that they have no pension rights upon retirement. If a worker is laid off or disabled before working, say, nine years with the same firm, he or she may not be eligible for any pension payments.

Many workers fail to acquire pension rights because they work for companies without pension plans (most small firms), or because they don't work long enough for a company with pensions. At present, only 22 percent of all aged people receive private pensions. These pensions are generally reserved for the *non*poor aged, i.e., those with higher preretirement earnings and savings. Only 4 percent of all aged *poor* households receive a private pension and those pension benefits account for only 1 percent of their total income. Furthermore, even those receiving private pension benefits are often disappointed to learn that private pensions are typically not adjusted for inflation. As a result, the real value of private pensions diminishes with age.

---

[5]Harrington, *The Other America*, p. 105.

[6]The substantial discrepancy between actual saving rates and those required to support post-retirement living standards is illustrated in James A. Schulz and Guy Carrin, "The Role of Savings and Pension Systems in Maintaining Living Standards in Retirement," *Journal of Human Resources*, Summer 1972.

Social Security payments reach far more of the aged—90 percent presently—and constitute the single most important source of income for the elderly. Moreover, Social Security retirement benefits *are* adjusted for inflation, thereby retaining their real value. Nevertheless, Social Security benefits alone do not assure an adequate income. Because the amount of monthly benefits depends in large part on the amount of prior earnings, individuals who are poor while working are likely to be poor after retirement. The Social Security system is discussed in Chapter 12, along with other income transfer programs.

A final source of potential support for the aged may be found in their own families. The extended family unit has in the past represented the most dependable source of social and economic security for many people. However, continuing industrialization and urbanization have tended to disintegrate the extended family, leaving each core family unit to fend for itself. Despite the material and social benefits this development yields for others, it deprives the aged of a source of support, immediate companionship, and in many cases a roof over their heads. Today, less than a third of the aged live with relatives, and of those who do not, less than 3 percent receive any income support from their offspring. Accordingly, relatives rarely constitute a source of economic security for the aged and cannot be expected to provide an escape from poverty.

Even when the aged are supported by their families, such support may be regarded as a mixed blessing. Many aged people live with relatives simply because they cannot afford to live by themselves. Moreover, they may not be counted as "poor," because the income of the household in which they live exceeds poverty standards. Yet, these older people are truly dependent if their living arrangements are dictated solely by economic necessity. The basic issue is not whether the aged live with their relatives or not, but whether the aged command enough economic resources to make a free choice of their own.

The income sources of the aged are summarized in Table 6.1, which relates two distinct kinds of information. The middle column depicts the proportion of aged households receiving any income from the sources discussed above. Thus, an aged couple earning only $4.32 interest on their bank savings is included among those with asset income. If they receive Social Security payments, then they are also included in that category.

The right column of Table 6.1 depicts the relative importance of each income source; Social Security assets and earnings are clearly the most significant. It is interesting to note how the importance of asset income diminishes as we move from column two to column three: While 66 percent of the aged receive some asset income, that source accounts for only 22 percent of all income for the aged, implying that most asset holdings are quite small.[7] If a small minority of the aged have very large asset holdings (including savings, bonds, stocks, and

---

[7]Asset income is grossly underreported, however, particularly among higher-income households. See Daniel Radner, "Distribution of Family Income: Improved Estimates," *Social Security Bulletin*, July 1982.

TABLE 6.1   INCOME SOURCES OF THE AGED

SOURCE OF INCOME	PERCENT OF AGED HOUSEHOLDS RECEIVING SUCH INCOME	TOTAL SHARE OF INCOME PROVIDED BY SOURCE (%)
Earnings	23	19
Private pensions	22	7
Social Security	90	40
Other public pensions	12	7
Public assistance	10	1
Asset income	66	22
Other sources	32	4

Source: Melinda Upp, "Relative Importance of Various Income Sources of the Aged, 1980," *Social Security Bulletin,* January 1983.

property), then the rest of the aged own virtually nothing. This appears to be the case, since assets generate only 4 percent of the income of the aged poor, but over 30 percent of the income of high-income aged families.

Expenses of the Aged

The serious decline in the sources and amounts of income that the aged command creates enough momentum to impoverish a high proportion of these individuals. But dwindling incomes are not their only burden; the aged also confront very large, and often rising, expenses. The interaction of these two forces is a virtual guarantee that a still higher proportion of the aged will experience material want before they die.

Everyone realizes that the aged are likely to experience high rates of sickness and disability. Often forgotten, however, is the tremendous financial burden that such disabilities impose. In 1981, for example, the average health bill for a person 65 or older was $3,144, including the expenses of hospital care, physician's services, and all drugs. This is a bill the average aged person cannot afford to pay. These health costs are equal to one-third of an aged individual's annual income and over 50 percent of his yearly income if he or she is old and poor.

Even these average expenses understate the burden of illness for those most sick. Hospitalization expenditures, for example, are incurred by only a portion of the poor, and these individuals pay all the costs, not just the "average" cost (which amounted to $1,381 in 1981). Furthermore, those who have endured impoverishment and hard labor the longest are most likely to be sick and least able to afford the costs of sickness. Accordingly, many individuals who manage to fend off poverty during their working years succumb to financial impoverishment when illness strikes. For those who have always been poor, illness in old age represents one more burden and indignity.

Medicare and Medicaid have done a great deal to reduce the threat of impoverishment among the aged due to illness. By providing subsidized medical insurance (Medicare) and the purchasing power required to buy needed medical services (Medicaid), the government has greatly diminished a major financial burden of the aged. However, the financial protection provided by Medicare and Medicaid is not complete. Like most private health insurance plans, Medicare does not pay all medical costs and there are limits on the type and extent of coverage. Also, Medicare users must pay premiums and deductibles that many poor people cannot afford.

Medicaid pays a larger share of the medical expenses of aged recipients. However, an individual must be poor to receive Medicaid benefits.[8] Typically, this means that an aged individual must exhaust most personal income and assets before becoming eligible for Medicaid assistance. Moreover, neither Medicaid nor Medicare provides preventive health care. As a consequence, all too many older poor people are burdened with both discomfort and poverty, sometimes even relegated to unsympathetic and inadequate institutions to wait idly for death.

In many areas of the country, the aged are also burdened by taxes, particularly property taxes. For most of the aged, their homes represent the only significant asset they possess and embody a lifetime of savings. But because local property taxes continue to rise, many of the aged find themselves unable to maintain their investment. Property taxes alone may consume as much as 30 percent of the incomes of aged persons living just above the poverty line. As a result, the U.S. Senate Special Committee on Aging reports that hundreds of thousands of aged persons are driven from their homes by mounting property taxes. Still more are forced to liquidate other assets to pay their taxes. Thus, the only visible economic security of many of the aged may itself contribute to their impoverishment.

Home ownership often imposes another unforeseen cost. Many of the aged purchased their homes in central cities at a time when inner city locations seemed most attractive. As the years have passed, however, inner city neighborhoods have deteriorated. Younger families have sought the freshness and space of the suburbs, while racial segregation and hostility have contributed to a general depreciation of inner city property values. As a consequence, the aged often find themselves socially and racially isolated in neighborhoods they once thought attractive. They cannot afford to move because the value of their homes has fallen while suburban values have skyrocketed. Hence, they can only hold on until the burden of property taxes leads them to rented quarters or nursing homes.

---

[8]Income and asset limitations for Medicaid eligibility are determined by the states and are typically somewhat higher than federal poverty standards. For a summary of how health expenses of the aged are paid, see Robert M. Gibson and Charles R. Fisher, "Age Difference in Health Spending," *Social Security Bulletin*, January 1979.

Making Do

An aged person with diminishing income and mounting expenses has little hope for economic security. An aged person's chances have simply run out; past labors and thrift are able only to postpone impoverishment in most cases. The question arises, then, as to how the aged actually manage in the face of such imposing circumstances. The most succinct answer came forth in hearings before a committee of the U.S. Senate:

"How do you manage?" I asked. A lady replied, "It's hard, Pat, oh, it's hard." "Well, what do you do?" "We don't do," someone replied, "That's how we manage!"

"I don't" is a most accurate description of the older adult living in retirement. I don't entertain. I don't go out with friends. I don't eat in restaurants. I don't go to movies. I don't buy new clothes. I don't ride subways and buses. I don't buy cake. I don't eat a lot. I don't take care of my health like I should. I don't, I don't, I don't.[9]

For the aged, then, growing older means giving up one thing after another until there is nothing left. When that time comes, they can only wait for death; sometime before that, they are unquestionably poor.

Assessing Causation

Poverty among the aged is not a natural product of biological development. Rather, it emerges from a diminution of income sources, a lack of accumulated resources, and the imposition of frequently rising expenses. Maintaining income sources or providing financial relief from taxation and illness will effectively prevent many aged individuals from falling into poverty. For others, however, poverty does not emerge in old age but is, instead, a continuing condition. The causes of poverty for these people must be sought elsewhere and earlier. Identifying and eliminating the causes of poverty for the nonaged will help to prevent later poverty among the aged.

HEALTH

One way to assure individuals greater prosperity and security in old age is to maintain their good health in younger years. Better health contributes to economic security in two important ways: by permitting persons to earn more income; and by reducing financial expenditures arising from health needs. All

[9]Special Committee on Aging. *Economics of Aging: Toward a Full Share in Abundance*, U.S. Senate, 91st Cong., 2d sess., 1970 (Washington, DC: Government Printing Office, 1970), p. 34.

other things being equal, a person with good health is likely to accumulate greater financial reserves when he is young and to need them less when he is old.

It is not difficult to surmise the potential that poor health has for undermining a family's economic security. A sick or disabled father not only fails to earn a full income; he also increases household expenses. To appreciate how expensive illness can be, we may observe recent income losses and health expenditures. In 1981, for example, illness and disability imposed an income loss in excess of $70 billion on American workers, and more than $300 billion was spent for health maintenance and care. This works out to an average income loss of $1,190 per worker and average health expenses of $1,400 per person. Even if the poor experienced only an average amount of illness and disability, their incomes would be severely depleted by poor health.

The relationship between health and income status is not simple enough, however, to permit the use of averages in ascertaining the cost of illness to the poor. Just as illness may tend to deplete a family's resources and leave it poor, so may poverty itself increase the likelihood of getting sick. Poor families suffer notoriously from chronic malnutrition and unsanitary environments, both of which nurture ill health. As a consequence, they are apt to be ill or disabled more often than the nonpoor. Poor families have markedly higher disease and mortality rates and miss more than twice as many days of work due to illness than do the nonpoor.

Poverty and illness, then, interact in a reciprocal relationship. As shown in Figure 6.2, illness leads to poverty and poverty leads to poor health. However, the relationship is not equally strong in both directions. We may still ask how many families or persons actually fall into poverty as a result of illness or disability; that is, ask to what extent poverty is actually *caused* by ill health. Many persons were poor before they were sick, so we cannot claim that illness caused their poverty. At most, we may say that illness maintains their poverty or that it makes poverty more miserable.

The search for causal significance thus centers on the question of how many nonpoor persons sink into poverty as a result of illness. The answer, of course, depends on how far above the poverty line families begin and how much illness

Figure 6.2 Illness and Poverty

they contract. Also important is the extent to which families are protected by insurance from the impositions of work loss and medical expenses.

A family need not be far above the poverty line to have an adequate margin against the burdens of ill health. Our 1982 poverty line for a family of four is just under $10,000. Average yearly medical expenses for a family this size are around $1,600 per year. Hence, for the typical family, an income of over $12,000 would easily prevent slippage into poverty as a result of illness. Moreover, as we have already suggested, the incidence of illness falls as income rises, further immunizing the nonpoor against poverty. Families with higher incomes also have more private health insurance. As Table 6.2 reveals, nearly 80 percent of high-income families have private major medical insurance coverage, whereas only 8 percent of low-income families have such coverage. One out of six poor families has no health insurance of any kind, including Medicaid.[10] Higher-income families can better afford to safeguard their health and to protect their economic position when illness strikes. Consequently, for families with some margin of income above the poverty standard, only severe and protracted illnesses represent a real threat to economic security. Illness is still painful and may even lower standards of living for these families; it is unlikely, however, to lead to poverty.

Families on the margin of economic security are not so well fortified against the onslaught of illness. With an income of $9,000 to $10,000, a family has little financial reserve. Such families are likely to be ill more often and less likely to be protected by insurance (Table 6.2). Consequently, they are prone to fall into poverty when illness strikes. Near-poor families do, in fact, move back and forth across the poverty line with great frequency. In part, this movement is due to the sporadic occurrence of illness. Economic security for these families is vulnerable to any kind of setback, be it illness, increased unemployment, or other misfortune. We cannot say exactly how much poverty is caused by illness and disability, but it is safe to conclude that very few people fall into poverty from any significant height as a result of ill health.

TABLE 6.2 PRIVATE HEALTH INSURANCE, BY HOUSEHOLD INCOME

HOUSEHOLD INCOME	PERCENT OF PERSONS WITH PRIVATE MEDICAL COVERAGE
Under $5,000	8
$5,000–9,999	21
$10,000–19,999	51
$20,000 and over	79

Note: Data refer to health insurance provided in whole or part by employer or union.

Source: U.S. Bureau of the Census, *Characteristics of Households and Persons Receiving Selected Noncash Benefits: 1981* (Washington, DC: Government Printing Office, 1983).

[10] Robert J. Blendon, Drew Altman, and Saul Kilstein, "Health Insurance for the Unemployed and Uninsured," *National Journal*, May 28, 1983.

The intergenerational links between health and poverty are more discouraging. Until now, we have considered only the impact of health on an existing family's economic status. But the illness bred by poverty may leave scars that last for generations. A child born to a poverty-stricken mother is likely to be undernourished both before and after birth. Furthermore, the child is less likely to receive proper post-natal care, to be immunized against disease, or even to have his eyes and teeth examined. As a result, the child is likely to grow up prone to illness and poverty, and in the most insidious of cases, be impaired by organic brain damage. A 1976 study by the U.S. Department of Health, Education, and Welfare reported that poor children

- Suffer 23 percent more hearing impairment.
- Do not grow as tall as other children.
- Are more likely to have low hemoglobin values during their years of growth.
- Suffer a higher incidence of impetigo, gastrointestinal diseases, parasitic diseases, and urinary-tract infections.
- In urban areas, are more often the victims of lead-paint poisoning and insect and rodent bites.[11]

To what extent do these childhood health impairments affect later educations, job skills, or income? No one knows for sure. However, there is a strong suspicion that poverty in one generation may result in illnesses and disabilities that become a significant cause of poverty in the next generation.

Mental health, as well as physical health, is an important dimension of poverty. The issue here is the same as before: Does mental disability lead downward to the slums, or does slum life accentuate tendencies toward mental illness? The former question embodies a popular "drift" hypothesis. According to this thesis, failures from all walks of life drift into the slums, creating our present poor population. The available evidence, however, once again shatters the popular myth. One of the few detailed studies undertaken on this subject traced the socioeconomic histories of schizophrenic individuals. The results were unambiguous: 91 percent of such patients were in the same socioeconomic class as their parents.[12] There was no evidence of substantial drift. Instead, the results suggest that poverty is more likely to lead to ill health than to result from it.

SUMMARY

Age and illness are highly visible correlates of poverty and, because of this, are often assumed to bear a causal relationship to economic impoverishment. The

[11]U.S. Department of Health, Education and Welfare, Office of Child Health Affairs, *A Proposal for New Federal Leadership in Maternal and Child Health Care in the United States* (Washington, DC: Government Printing Office, 1976), pp. 9–10, 15.
[12]Rodger L. Hurley, *Poverty and Mental Retardation: A Causal Relationship* (Trenton, NJ: New Jersey Department of Institutions and Agencies, April 1968).

reasoning behind such an assumption is simple and appears eminently plausible. As logical as such a conclusion is, however, there are several reasons for attaching only limited causal importance to the impact of age and illness. Many of the aged poor, for example, were always poor, so that aging itself causes little change in their economic status. Similarly, poor persons are more prone to illness, and illness for them represents no sudden loss of well-being. Even for those who are driven to poverty for the first time by age or illness, the loss of economic status is occasioned by a variety of forces, none of which is inseparable from the natural processes of aging and illness.

It is not possible to attach exact quantitative significance to the amount of poverty caused by age and illness. Given the data reviewed in this chapter, however, we may tentatively estimate that no more than 10 to 15 percent of the poor are impoverished as a result of age or illness. This assumes that only one-half of the aged poor experience poverty for the first time in old age and that only 5 to 10 percent of the poor have been destituted by the effects of ill health.

FURTHER READING

Age

CLARK, ROBERT, JUANITA KREPS, AND JOSEPH SPENGLER. "Economics of Aging: A Survey," *Journal of Economic Literature*, September 1978.

PRESIDENT'S COMMISSION ON PENSION POLICY. *Coming of Age Toward a National Retirement Income Policy*. Washington, DC: Government Printing Office, 1981.

U.S. DEPARTMENT OF LABOR. *Employment and Training Report of the President, 1978*. Washington, DC: Government Printing Office, Ch. 4.

U.S. SENATE, SPECIAL COMMITTEE ON AGING. *Developments in Aging*. Washington, DC: Government Printing Office, annual.

Health

CONGRESSIONAL BUDGET OFFICE. *Catastrophic Health Insurance*. Washington, DC: Government Printing Office, 1977.

RODGERS, HARRELL R., JR. *Poverty Amid Plenty*. Reading, MA: Addison-Wesley Publishing Co., Inc., 1979, Ch. 6.

7
Family Size and Status

There are two persistent accusations leveled against the poor. One is that the poor do not limit their family size; the other is that they do not maintain stable families. The implication in both cases is that the poor exhibit too little self-control and are thus responsible for much of their own plight. These accusations are examined in this chapter. As in Chapter 6, the focus of the analysis is on probable causation, highlighting the temporal relationship between poverty and family size or status. Did either large family size or family instability precede economic impoverishment? If so, then there may be some validity to the claim that the poor caused their own poverty by creating conditions that make it difficult or impossible to hold a job that pays an adequate income. If not, then there exists a basic presumption that poverty was not caused by either phenomenon. Indeed, in such circumstances, we may be led to ask whether the sequence of causation is reversible, that is, whether poverty itself may lead to family instability or excessive procreation.

FAMILY SIZE

Children are a distinct threat to the financial security of a family. Not only do the physical needs of a family increase with the number of children, but the mother is also likely to be restricted to the home for more years than is the mother of a smaller family. If the mother chooses not to stay at home, she must pay someone else to tend the house while she works. Childbearing and rearing thus make it either physically impossible or economically unrewarding for many mothers to participate in the labor force. Confronted with more needs and fewer resources, many large families are unable to fend off poverty.

Figure 7.1 depicts the actual incidence of poverty for different family sizes. Obviously, the risk of poverty increases dramatically with the number of children. Whereas only 13.4 percent of one-child families are poor, a third of all families with four children are poor. Another way of summarizing this relationship is to note the percentage of all families with four or more children. Nearly one-fifth of poor families are so large, versus only one-twelfth of nonpoor families.

To grasp the implications of larger family sizes among the poor, we may ask how many larger poor families would move out of poverty if they had fewer family members. For example, we know from Table 1.5 that five-member families are considered poor if their 1982 incomes were under $11,684 but the same poverty standard for a family of four was $9,862. Hence, any family of five whose income was less than $11,684 but more than $9,862 would no longer be counted as poor if it could somehow eliminate one family member. Or, to put it slightly differently, we may say that such a family would not have fallen into poverty if it had bred one less child. By counting the total number of such families, we may estimate the potential of family planning as a means for reducing poverty.

The statistical exercise required to make such an estimate is summarized in Table 7.1. The exercise is carried out on two levels. The first calculation tells how many larger poor families (of five or more persons) would move out of poverty if they had one less member. Among poor five-person families, we look for all those whose current income could support four persons; among six-person families, incomes that will support five people, and so on. Based on these calculations, we

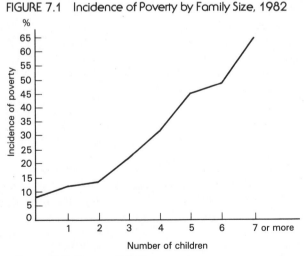

FIGURE 7.1   Incidence of Poverty by Family Size, 1982

Source: U.S. Bureau of the Census.

TABLE 7.1   THE POTENTIAL IMPACT OF FAMILY PLANNING (1981)

A. QUESTION: HOW MANY FAMILIES AND PERSONS WOULD NO LONGER BE COUNTED AS POOR IF EACH LARGER POOR FAMILY WERE REDUCED BY ONE PERSON?

ANSWER:	FROM 7-PERSON OR LARGER FAMILIES	FROM 6-PERSON FAMILIES	FROM 5-PERSON FAMILIES	TOTAL
Families	53,000	85,000	192,000	330,000
Persons	371,000	510,000	960,000	1,841,000

B. QUESTION: HOW MANY FAMILIES AND PERSONS WOULD NO LONGER BE COUNTED AS POOR IF EACH LARGER POOR FAMILY WERE REDUCED TO FOUR PERSONS?

ANSWER:	FROM 7-PERSON OR LARGER FAMILIES	FROM 6-PERSON FAMILIES	FROM 5-PERSON FAMILIES	TOTAL
Families	191,000	168,000	192,000	551,000
Persons	1,337,000	1,008,000	960,000	3,305,000

Source: U.S. Bureau of the Census.

observe that 330,000 poor families, a total of nearly 2 million individuals, would no longer be counted as poor if each family had one person less.

The second calculation summarized in Table 7.1 imposes an even stricter constraint on family size. Rather than trim all larger poor families by one person, it reduces all such families to the standard four persons. Hence, six-person families statistically lose two members, and their poverty line falls from $12,449 to $9,287. This kind of standardization creates an astounding reduction in the size of the poverty population. On these assumptions, over 500,000 families (3.3 million individuals)—nearly one-eighth of all the nonaged poor— would no longer be counted as poor.

Our statistical exercise leads us to the conclusion that mild restraints on family size (one person less) would reduce the nonaged poverty population by some 6 percent, while severe limits on family size (maximum of four) would effect a 12 percent reduction in the number of poor. Such results underscore the potential importance of the causal link between family size and poverty. Before turning to a discussion of causality, however, it is necessary to subject our statistical results to some critical scrutiny.

First, our statistical exercise tacitly assumes that there is no positive relationship between family size and family income. The statistical elimination of one family member is presumed to have no effect on family income. But this is not a realistic assumption. The amount of welfare, food stamps, or other assistance a family gets depends on its size. More children, then, implies more welfare. If we were to eliminate one family member, we would also have to reduce the family's income. As a result, far fewer families would escape poverty than Table 7.1 implies. Since over half of all poor families receive some form of welfare benefit, this is a serious qualification to our calculations.

Family income may also rise with family size for other reasons. The father of the family may be impelled to work overtime or at a second job as his family responsibilities expand; hence larger families may constitute a special kind of incentive to work. Larger families may also enable other family members to work; they may have a greater number of older children who can contribute directly to family income by working part-time or who enable the mother to work by assuming child-care responsibilities. Hence, the statistical reduction carried out above may, in fact, diminish sources of family income.

Further consideration must also be given to those families and persons whom we suppose statistically to escape poverty by our calculations. Some family members are constrained by our arithmetic to disappear, and we can ignore them for the moment. Surviving family members, however, improve their economic status only marginally, and we must recognize that their statistical "escape" is, therefore, not very impressive. Almost all such families remain within a few hundred dollars of our poverty standards, even after they manage to leave the poverty population.

These qualifications to our earlier calculations reduce the impact of family size as a cause of poverty; unfortunately, there is not enough information about the poor to make a meaningful estimate of its true impact. We can observe, however, that even if we envision only limited birth control (one less child in each larger family) and consider the foregoing qualifications important enough to reduce our estimates by at least half, then large family size still accounts for 3 to 4 percent of the nonaged poverty population. Under stricter family size controls, the reduction would amount to 6 percent.

The Causal Relation

Even when reduced by cautious skepticism, family size still appears to possess some potential for explaining the existence of poverty. Given the obvious association between these two phenomena, it would not seem necessary to pursue the subject of causation further. But the direction of causation is an important ingredient of policy decisions and must be examined. If the poor are mindlessly, even willfully, propagating beyond their financial means, policy intervention will be more difficult and less available; but if the poor are excluded from access to birth control, intervention is easier and more broadly acceptable. The former case comes closest to the position that excessive family size leads to poverty, while the latter case implies the reverse.

There is no evidence at all that presently large poor families ever enjoyed a more comfortable economic status. Larger families do have an effect on the dimensions of poverty to the extent that continued procreation may lengthen a family's stay in the poverty population rather than cause it to fall from nonpoverty to poverty. Large family size thus retards the flow of people moving out of poverty and contributes over time to an expansion of the poverty population. By itself, however, it creates very little new poverty.

Against this background, we must also ponder the accumulation of evidence suggesting that the poor continue to have little access to birth control information. Public schools, especially in low-income areas, are still reluctant to provide birth control information, while public welfare authorities are, in most cases, prohibited from providing it. Low-income families are also less able to afford abortions, even if they are desired. Even in quasi-public clinics, abortions cost several hundred dollars. Moreover, Congress has greatly limited the availability of Medicaid or other income transfers to pay for abortions.

Because of these constraints, poor families often end up with more children than other families, not because they want them, but because they are unable to prevent them. One study by the National Academy of Sciences indicated that over one-third of the least-educated families had unwanted children, and a survey of welfare mothers in New York yielded similar findings. Even more revealing are recent studies that indicate the extent to which unwanted births increase at lower income levels; 17 percent of all nonpoor families report unwanted births, compared to 26 percent for near-poor families, and a whopping 42 percent for poor families.[1]

Given the high incidence of unwanted births among the poor, it is evident that improved access to birth control information and contraceptive devices would lessen the amount of poverty, although not by a great amount. From this perspective, poverty is more a cause of excessive family size than the other way around, at least so long as access to birth control is conditioned on economic status. And there is evidence that this is the case. In addition to the statistics above we need only remind ourselves that the most reliable source of birth control information is the private family doctor, by and large an inaccessible luxury for the poor.

We must conclude that excessive family size is not an important cause of poverty on the basis of our earlier observation that poor families were, by and large, once smaller poor families rather than smaller nonpoor families. If causation were to be specified here, we would have to surmise that lack of access to birth control is one of the ways in which poverty itself creates more poverty. Eliminating family size as a significant independent cause of poverty should not, therefore, divert attention away from the potential of greater family planning efforts to alleviate the conditions of the poor. The fact remains that greater availability of birth control would help reduce the number that are poor.

[1]"Why the Poor Get Children: Findings of Two Major Studies," *Newsweek*, June 19, 1972. See also James Cramer, "Births, Expected Family Size, and Poverty," in James N. Morgan, ed., *Five Thousand Families: Patterns of Economic Progress* (Ann Arbor, MI: Institute for Social Research, 1974); and Sylvia B. Perlman, Lorraine Klerman, and E. Milling Kinard, "The Use of Socioeconomic Data To Predict Teenage Birth Rates," *Public Health Reports*, July-August 1981; and Joy G. Dryfoos, "Contraceptive Use, Pregnancy Intentions and Pregnancy Outcomes Among U.S. Women," *Family Planning Perspectives*, March/April 1982.

FAMILY STATUS

One-parent families, especially black ones, have long attracted the attention of social scientists, politicians, and the general public. They have been regarded with pity, with scorn, and even with a sense of fear. Single-parent, or broken, families do not fit easily into traditional American patterns and are often regarded as a threat to community morality, not to mention the whole institutional character of marriage. Recently, added concern over the existence of broken families has emerged from the observation that they tend to become financially dependent on the public purse. Within the confines of this chapter, there is hardly room for a thorough examination of the economics and sociology of one-parent families. Instead, the subject of family status, as of all other demographic characteristics, is treated with a focus on the existence of possible causal links to poverty.

In virtually all cases where only one parent resides in the family, that parent is the mother. Accordingly, the census classification "female-headed families with children" refers to nearly all those families whose social and economic life has been ruptured by the loss of a parent. Broken families actually arise from two different contingencies: Either a previously two-parent family is literally broken up by the death or separation (by divorce, legal separation, or desertion) of one parent; or the parents never formed a stable union, legal or otherwise. While the net effect in either case is to leave only one parent in the family, the economic and social ramifications of each situation may be quite distinct. A twenty-six-year-old widow, for example, may command more social support and economic resources than an unwed mother of the same age.

A one-parent family is severely handicapped in the effort to attain economic security. The loss of one potential breadwinner is a large and obvious constraint on economic stability. Potential family income is reduced by *more than half* with the departure of one parent. Where two parents exist in the family, one parent can devote full-time to labor market activity while the other is free to combine household and labor market activity. When only one parent resides in the family, such flexibility is diminished. The single parent is unable to devote all time to labor market activity, at least not without paying someone else to assume household responsibilities. Hence, the potential net income of a one-parent family is often closer to one-third rather than to one-half of a two-parent family's income. If women's employment opportunities in the labor market are further constricted by conventional sexual stereotypes, their potential income will be lower still. Accordingly, one-parent families bear an extraordinarily high risk of economic impoverishment.

The greater poverty of single-parent families is revealed in Table 7.2. Over a fourth of female-headed white families, and over half of female-headed black families are in poverty. Although single-parent families headed by men are also more likely to be poor than two-parent families, there are relatively few such families.

While the potential of family breakup (or nonformation) for impoverish-

TABLE 7.2 POVERTY AND FAMILY STATUS, 1982

FAMILY TYPE	NUMBER IN POVERTY (IN THOUSANDS)	POVERTY RATE (PERCENT)
White		
Two parent	3,104	6.9
Lone male parent	201	12.2
Lone female parent	1,813	27.9
Black		
Two parent	543	15.6
Lone male parent	79	25.6
Lone female parent	1,535	56.2

Source: U.S. Bureau of the Census.

ment is clear, the direction of causation is not necessarily so apparent. We need evidence that family breakup *leads* to poverty, and not the reverse, or at least that it effectively acts as an independent barrier to economic security.

Historically, there has seldom been any reluctance to "explain" the existence of one-parent families among blacks. As late as the 1920s, allegations of "animalism," "moral putridity," and "primitive sexualism" were often advanced as explanations for the great incidence of broken families among American blacks. The latent implication was always that blacks were responsible for their own destitution because they were morally, physically, or culturally unable to stabilize family relationships. Such explanations for black family instability and poverty have never fared well under scholarly examination. Among others, E. Franklin Frazier, an outstanding expert on the black family, has shown that family patterns are comprehensible only in the context of existing social and economic forces. Professors William Darity, Jr., and Samuel Myers, Jr., have offered an even simpler explanation for black family patterns. In 1981, there were only 86 black men for every 100 black women in the age group 25 to 44. Among whites the ratio was 100 to 100. Hence, a *shortage* of black men precludes many black women from forming two-parent families.[2]

Despite strong evidence against racial theories of causation between family status and poverty, the theories persist because people want to believe them. The whole subject experienced a certain rejuvenation in 1965 when President Johnson, speaking at Howard University, drew attention to the breakdown of black family structure as one of the most important causes of black poverty. While he did not seem to mean that black poverty could be explained on simple racial grounds, his words sparked instant misunderstanding and anger. James Farmer of CORE, for example, saw President Johnson's statement as a "massive academic cop-out for the white conscience" that would provide fuel for a new

[2]William Darity, Jr., and Samuel L. Myers, Jr., "Changes in Black Family Structure: Implications for Welfare Dependency," *American Economic Review*, May 1983. Sex ratios are reported in U.S. Department of Commerce, *Statistical Abstract* (annual).

racism. Martin Luther King, Jr., saw in the President's words a danger that the poverty of blacks would be attributed to innate black weaknesses, and therein he feared yet another basis for racial neglect and oppression.

Behind President Johnson's Howard University speech lay a theoretical paper written by Daniel P. Moynihan, then assistant secretary of labor. In what became known as the Moynihan Report, he had said:

At the heart of the deterioration of the fabric of Negro society is the deterioration of the Negro family.

It is the fundamental source of the weakness of the Negro community at the present time.

Once or twice removed, it will be found to be the principal source of most of the aberrant, inadequate, or antisocial behavior that did not establish, but now serves to perpetuate the cycle of poverty and deprivation.[3]

For most commentators, the Moynihan Report seemed to confirm black family structure as a cause of poverty. Moynihan himself, however, had in mind a more complex relationship. In the recesses of the report, Moynihan suggested, as had Frazier earlier, that family structure itself was shaped by prevailing social and economic forces. Hence, one could not argue that family breakup had caused poverty; at most, black family structures only reflected economic forces and made escape from poverty more difficult. Poverty and social injustice were more likely to cause family breakup, not the reverse.

One particularly interesting bit of evidence collected by Moynihan concerns the relationship between unemployment rates and family structure: Looking at the trend of unemployment rates and family structures, Moynihan found that the rates of separation and divorce followed economic events very closely. Thus, the rate of separations among black women shot up shortly after the economy faltered, while it sank when the economy prospered (see Figure 7.2). Family stability was apparently the result, not the cause, of economic events. As a family faced increased unemployment and deprivation, the father's position as breadwinner and family head became untenable; divorce, separation, or desertion often followed.

Further support for this position was found in illegitimacy statistics: In poor black neighborhoods rates of illegitimacy were more than triple those of black neighborhoods with middle-class incomes. Again it appeared that family formation itself was significantly affected by economic circumstances. Those parents with little prospect for economic security foresaw little hope for family stability; they decided not to marry.

---

[3]U.S. Department of Labor, *The Negro Family: The Case for National Action* (Washington, DC: Government Printing Office, 1965).

FIGURE 7.2   Black Unemployment and Separation Rates

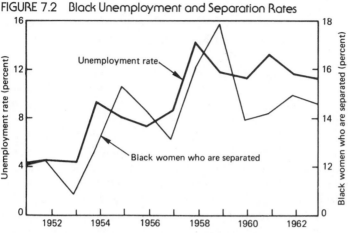

Source: U.S. Department of Labor, *The Negro Family: The Case for National Action,* March 1965, p. 22.

A. Philip Randolph, long a leader in labor and civil rights movements, found evidence similar to Moynihan's in World War II experience. During the exceptionally low unemployment years of the war, rates of divorce and illegitimacy among blacks took a sharp drop. Greater economic security thus manifested itself in greater family stability.

More recent information on families appears to further confirm Moynihan's observations and to extend his hypothesis to all families, black or white. Table 7.3 shows the pattern of marital status for men by income class. Among all married men aged 18 or older, 4.4 percent now have absent wives; they are separated or deserted. The incidence of absent wives varies enormously by income class, however. Over one-tenth of married men in the lowest income class no longer live with their wives, while only one out of forty men in the

TABLE 7.3   ABSENCE OF THE WIFE, BY INCOME CLASS, 1982

INCOME CLASS	PERCENTAGE OF MARRIED MEN* WITH WIFE NO LONGER PRESENT
Under $3,000	10.6
$3,000–5,999	8.9
$6,000–9,999	5.8
$10,000–14,999	4.5
$15,000–19,999	3.0
Over $20,000	2.6
All classes	4.4

*Aged 18 and older.
Source: U.S. Bureau of the Census.

highest income class are likely to be so positioned. This relationship conveys two important impressions. It appears to reconfirm the point that family stability is affected by economic conditions; and it suggests that economic impoverishment precedes family dissolution. Under these circumstances, restoration of the family would do little by itself to achieve economic security. A disproportionately high percentage of the departed fathers and husbands were, and are still, poor.

The impact of economic insecurity on marital instability was also noted in a seven-year study of 5,000 families. The families were first interviewed in 1967, then reinterviewed in each of the following years, until 1973. These observations, by the University of Michigan Survey Research Center, show how divorce and separation are often linked to economic status. In general, average family income turned out to be the best predictor of family stability, for both whites and blacks. In addition, families that owned their own homes in 1967 or had significant savings were much more likely to be still intact in 1973. By contrast, families in which the husband was encountering employment problems in 1967 were more likely to have broken up by 1973.[4]

The relationship between family status and poverty, then, is best described as dynamic. Continued economic deprivation is likely to undermine a family's stability. At some point, the family unit is ruptured, and the female-headed family is left to fend for itself. No loss of economic status is necessarily implied by the departure of the father, especially where he was unemployed and/or the female-headed unit turned to public assistance. In the University of Michigan study noted above, 20 percent of the families that broke up during the seven-year observation period did fall into poverty, and most of these turned to welfare. However, the average loss of income status amounted to only 6 percent of prior income status.[5]

While at any point in time a high proportion of poor families will be female-headed, family breakup cannot be identified as a major cause of poverty. Family disunity may help sustain poverty, but in most cases it appears that poverty preceded, and itself helped to cause, family dissolution.[6]

This conclusion does not necessitate a purely economic-deterministic view of family relations. Clearly, not all divorces and separations are occasioned by financial stress. Family dissolutions will continue to take place even after all

---

[4]Greg. J. Duncan and James N. Morgan, eds., *Five Thousand American Families: Patterns of Economic Progress*, Vol. IV (Ann Arbor, MI: Institute for Social Research, 1976). A parallel study of low-income and welfare families in Camden, New Jersey, found that the husband's economic performance was important for family attitudes and stability (see Samuel Klausner, "Six Years in the Lives of the Impoverished: An Examination of the WIN Thesis" (Philadelphia: Center for Research on the Acts of Man, 1978).

[5]Larger income losses are reported for nonpoor families; see Duncan and Morgan, *op. cit.*, Vol. IX.

[6]Evidence that economic stress contributes to mental illness and changes people's perception of self, family, and society is contained in D.D. and B.M. Braginsky, "Surplus People: Their Lost Faith in Self and System;" and Berkeley Rice, "The Worry Epidemic," *Psychology Today*, August 1975.

families are assured economic security. The point is that a disproportionately high percentage of family breakups occurs among the poor due to economic stress and that relatively few broken poor families were decidedly nonpoor before family dissolution occurred.

SUMMARY

Large families and broken families are among the most salient characteristics of the poor. Nearly 30 percent of all the poor are in families with at least five members, while one-fourth of the poor are in broken families; many of the latter are also from large families. Accordingly, there exists a strong presumption that family size and status are important causes of poverty. However, the presumed causal significance of family size and status does not fare well upon closer examination. For most of the families in question poverty prevailed before the family either grew larger or broke up. Moreover, economic insecurity itself may have contributed to the dissolution of the family or to excessive reproduction. Hence, stronger causality appears to flow from poverty to family size and status than in the opposite direction.

Some families do fall into poverty as a result of the burdens of additional children or an absent parent, but the number appears to be small. Family breakup and growth are more likely to extend and deepen a family's poverty than bring it about. Efforts to increase the economic opportunities of the poor should promote greater family stability and smaller family size. At the same time, direct efforts to make birth control available to the poor will do much to alleviate present poverty and retard its intergenerational transmission.

FURTHER READING

On Family Size

Bogue, Donald J.   "A Long-Term Solution to the AFDC Problem: Prevention of Unwanted Pregnancy," *Social Science Review*, December 1975.

Podell, Lawrence.   *Families on Welfare in New York City*. New York: City University of New York Press, 1968.

Sheppard, Harold L.   *Effects of Family Planning on Poverty in the United States*. Kalamazoo, MI: Upjohn Institute, 1967.

Shostak, Arthur.   "Birth Control and Poverty," in *New Perspectives on Poverty*, Arthur Shostak and William Gomberg, eds. Englewood Cliffs, NJ: Prentice-Hall, Inc., 1965.

On Family Status

LIEBOW, ELLIOT. *Tally's Corner: A Study of Negro Streetcorner Men.* Boston: Little, Brown and Company, 1967.

PEARCE, DIANA, and HARRIETTE MCADOO. *Women and Children: Alone and In Poverty.* Washington, DC: National Advisory Council on Economic Opportunity, September 1981.

RAINWATER, LEE, and WILLIAM L. YANCEY. *The Moynihan Report and the Politics of Controversy.* Cambridge, MA: The MIT Press, 1967.

ROSS, HEATHER, and ISABEL SAWHILL. *Time of Transition: The Growth of Families Headed by Women.* Washington, DC: Urban Institute, 1975.

TIENDA, MARTA, and RONALD ANGEL. "Headship and Household Composition among Blacks, Hispanics, and Other Whites," *Social Forces,* December 1982.

Culture and Race

Accusations that the poor bring about their own deprivation through excessive procreation or family instability are generally elements of a broader perspective. When people suggest, for example, that "welfare mothers would rather have another kid than a job," they are ascribing a whole complex of attitudes, norms, and values to the welfare poor. The demographic forces we have reviewed tend to be mere details of the Flawed Character perspective. What makes theories of cultural and racial inferiority so interesting is that they are so much more explicit about Flawed Characters. Simply put, the cultural theory of poverty argues that the poor lack the aspirations, values, and motivation required to "get ahead." The poor just don't give a damn about improving their economic status. In this sense, poverty is self-imposed.

Racial theories of poverty build on the notion of cultural differences, but add another dimension as well. Racial theories assert that blacks (or Hispanics, Indians, etc.) not only have lower motivation, but that genetic deficiencies inherently constrain their economic status. In terms of either the cultural or racial manifestations of the Flawed Character perspective, then, the poor bring little human capital to the labor market and are rewarded accordingly.

Although theories of racial inferiority have fallen into distinct disfavor in recent years, they are far from dead. On the contrary, they have enjoyed a certain renaissance in recent debates on IQ, and have persuaded at least one leading writer on the subjects of labor and poverty to conclude that the higher poverty rate among blacks is "the result of racial differences in endowment with genetic human capital."[1] But before examining the basis for such views we will consider

[1]Lowell E. Gallaway, *Poverty in America* (Columbus, OH: Grid Publishing, Inc., 1973), p. 149.

the content of theories of cultural inferiority, theories that need not be restricted to one racial group among the poor.

THE "CULTURE OF POVERTY"

In colonial America poverty was regarded as the manifestation of vice and sin. Because everyone except Negro slaves was thought to enjoy the opportunity to acquire economic security by his own labor, those who did not attain such security were deemed to be morally flawed. Poverty thus became proof of moral bankruptcy, and the poor were treated accordingly. In Pennsylvania, paupers had the shoulders of their right sleeves adorned with the letter *P* to warn unsuspecting strangers. In other jurisdictions the poor were sent packing, sometimes after a public whipping. As the puritanical Humane Society summarized the situation in 1809, ". . . by a just and inflexible law of Providence, misery is ordained to be the companion and punishment of vice."[2]

In more modern times the theoretical link of poverty to sin has not fared well. There now exists a general reluctance to ascribe the misery of the poor to the laws of Providence. Nevertheless, belief in the universality of economic opportunity remains firmly embedded in the American consciousness. Accordingly, we need a substitute explanation for the persistence of poverty in a land of abundance and opportunity. This, in part, explains the ascendency of cultural theories of poverty. To formulate a cultural theory of poverty is to assert that the poor lack sufficient desire and motivation to escape poverty. It is to allege that the goal of economic security is of lesser importance in the value matrix of the poor. By this hypothesis the poor are impoverished because their "culture" prevents them from taking advantage of opportunities to escape poverty.

If the poor are culturally bound to poverty, then the task of eliminating poverty becomes infinitely more difficult and time-consuming. Public efforts must be directed toward changing attitudes and environments, rather than simply toward changing opportunities. Communication between poor and nonpoor groups will also be more difficult, with interclass tension and anxiety the likely results. The culture of poverty thesis cannot be dismissed lightly.

Norms vs. Traits

A completely satisfactory definition of *culture* is not easy. Nevertheless, for the purposes of this inquiry, we may understand culture to refer to the norms, values, and aspirations of an individual or group. These components of culture are not observable. We must *infer* underlying aspirations and values from

---

[2]Cited by Paul Jacobs in Jeremy Larner and Irving Howe, eds., *Poverty: Views from the Left* (New York: William Morrow & Company, Inc., 1968), p. 40.

observations of behavior. This means that the assertion of distinct cultural attributes among the poor is largely founded on observations of distinct behavioral patterns. The assertion, however, is vulnerable to criticism, as not all behavioral differences reflect cultural differences. Even persons with identical norms and aspirations may behave differently in various situations. Our task is to determine whether the inferential reasoning that underlies the cultural hypothesis is valid.

Consider the case of a welfare recipient who declines what appears to be a reasonable job offer. For many middle-class observers, such a rejection constitutes incontrovertible proof that the recipient lacks normal initiative, aspirations, and goals—clear evidence of a culture of poverty. Middle-class individuals, it is argued, would never reject an offer to improve their economic status, especially in the dire financial straits of the welfare recipient. The accusation can be challenged, however. The rejection of employment opportunities may reflect other circumstances not readily apparent to the nonpoor observer. The job offer itself may, of course, be inherently unattractive and provide no economic advancement. But the rejection may also be based on public welfare policy. If it is difficult and time-consuming to obtain public welfare assistance, then the individual who leaves the welfare roles for employment incurs a distinct risk. If the job proves to be unsatisfactory or temporary, then he and his family are left without any financial support while he awaits a new job or more welfare. For families at the margin of impoverishment and confronting largely transitory kinds of jobs, such a risk may be unwarranted. Thus, the job rejection may proceed not from different values and aspirations but from tangible behavioral constraints.[3] Middle-class job-seekers, with savings accounts and better job prospects, are not subject to these same constraints.

The culture of poverty hypothesis requires rather stringent evidence. It must be shown that the norms and aspirations—not just the behavior—of the poor are different and that these differences impede escape from poverty. It should also be shown whether and to what degree such differences would disappear under changing socioeconomic circumstances.

Oscar Lewis is the most familiar and forceful proponent of the culture of poverty thesis. His observations of life-styles among the poor convinced him that the behavior patterns of the poor are different and that these differences reflect distinct values. Although his empirical research was confined largely to Mexico and Puerto Rico, he believed that these differences transcend national boundaries. He offered the following explanation for the perpetuation of poverty:

Once [the culture of poverty] comes into existence it tends to perpetuate itself from generation to generation because of its

---

[3]Additional disincentives to work confronting a welfare recipient—some of which are clearly part of the Big Brother argument—are discussed in Chapter 12.

effect on the children. By the time slum children are age six or seven they have usually absorbed the basic values and attitudes of their subculture and are not psychologically geared to take full advantage of changing conditions or increased opportunities which may occur in their lifetime.[4]

From Lewis's perspective, the poor are clearly prolonging their own impoverishment. As evidence, he identified no less than seventy behavioral traits that distinguish the poor, including little use of banks or museums and nonparticipation in labor unions. Although he acknowledges that the poor may be aware of, and even profess, middle-class values, he regards their aberrant behavior as proof that they do not share those values.

Other sociologists and anthropologists have been quick to follow Lewis's lead. Another popular diagnosis of the poor, for example, focuses on their alleged self-indulgence. Out of Lewis's more general depiction of lower-class culture, other observers claim to perceive a pattern of nondeferred gratification: Whereas the middle-class person supposedly feels the need and desire to save, postpone, and renounce certain immediate pleasures, the poor person is alleged to experience no such motivations. This alleged impulse following is presumed to be embedded in the personality dynamics of the poor individual, thus obstructing his self-improvement.

This pattern of self-indulgence is additionally presumed to have strong intergenerational effects. Self-indulgent parents have little interest in their children's futures, thus contributing to further poverty. As one observer has asserted:

Where middle and upper class parents think in terms of a college education for their offspring, lower class parents' aspirations usually stop at a high school diploma, at the very best. Poor parents, with little education, are more likely to believe in luck than in education and to be contemptuous of "book learning". . . . Indeed, among low-income families, both the low educational attainments of the head of the household and the quality of family life create a social environment that leads the poor to believe that "education is not for them."[5]

A Question of Opportunities

Not all sociologists, of course, share these views of lower-class culture. On the contrary, much recent sociological discussion has focused on some of the

[4]Oscar Lewis, *La Vida* (New York: Random House, Inc., 1966), p. xiv.
[5]Oscar Ornati, *Poverty Amid Affluence* (New York: The Twentieth Century Fund, 1966), p. 66.

basic weaknesses in the culture of poverty thesis. It has been pointed out, for example, that the attribution of cultural differences based on the observation of behavioral differences incorporates many assumptions of questionable validity. Within the subject area of deferred gratification, the following conditions must be fulfilled before a valid inference about differential values can be made:

1. The satisfaction being deferred must be equally important to the poor and nonpoor.
2. There must exist equal opportunity to defer the satisfaction.
3. The poor and nonpoor must equally suffer from deferment.
4. The probability of obtaining gratification at the end of the deferment period must be equal for both groups.

If any or all of these conditions are violated, then behavioral differences may be explained by situational differences, by differences in opportunity; no reference to alleged cultural phenomena is necessary.

The case of educational attainment illustrates some of the foregoing conditions. The children of the poor undeniably drop out of school earlier than other children. But does this behavioral difference reflect cultural orientations? Schools in lower-income areas are notoriously ill-equipped to transmit interest, enjoyment, or ability. The third and fourth conditions in our list are violated: Middle-class school experience is both more pleasant and more profitable. Furthermore, the low-income family cannot afford to support a child's education for as long as a middle-class family; thus, the second condition is also violated. Given these inequalities in opportunity, it might be equally valid to conclude that the poor value education *more* highly than the nonpoor because of the greater sacrifices they make to get as far as they do.

A similar array of qualifications to the "impulse following" hypothesis is encountered when saving behavior is considered. The poor save less money less often than the nonpoor. Does this reflect a present-time orientation (as contrasted with a future-time orientation)? Perhaps not. The poor have very little to save in the first place. Whatever they do manage to put aside represents a real sacrifice in terms of present consumption. Hence, there is no foundation for inferring cultural inadequacies on the basis of observed differences in saving.

The central weakness of the culture of poverty proposition is the assumption that behavioral differences between the poor and nonpoor reflect differences in goals and aspirations. In reality, the poor do not have an equal opportunity to fulfill, or even to pursue, their goals. Hence, there is a sharp divergence between the aspirations and the behavior of the poor that does not exist among middle-class groups. With more equal opportunities for achievement, there is a strong presumption that the entire foundation of the culture of poverty theses would disintegrate. At the very least, we may say that the cultural thesis rests on a very uncertain foundation until equality of opportunity is fully achieved.

If testimony of the poor themselves is valid, there is little reason to believe that their behavior patterns will remain the same under improved socioeconomic conditions. Welfare mothers, for example, express a strong desire to see their children attain better social and economic positions. Moreover, they perceive clearly—more so than many academic observers—the great divergence between their aspirations and their actual opportunities. One survey, for example, questioned welfare mothers about their desires and expectations for their children's employment. The responses, portrayed in Table 8.1, are illuminating. Seventy percent of the mothers have white-collar aspirations for their eldest child, yet only 46 percent have any expectation that their children will attain this status. (Even fewer actually do.) The lower occupational status of poor children apparently does not reflect their parents' aspirations so much as it reflects the opportunities of the poor.

Other studies have come to similar conclusions regarding work orientations and other dimensions of "culture." When poor families are compared to nonpoor families of the same ethnic background (e.g., white, black, Hispanic), no significant cultural differences appear.[6] This conclusion also applies to welfare recipients. After reviewing available studies of work attitudes and behavior of welfare mothers, Leonard Goodwin concluded that "welfare recipients do not differ markedly from other Americans with respect to general personality characteristics or with respect to the work ethic and basic life goals."[7]

TABLE 8.1   WELFARE MOTHERS' DESIRES AND EXPECTATIONS FOR ELDEST CHILD'S OCCUPATIONAL STATUS (PERCENT)

OCCUPATION	DESIRE	EXPECTATION
Professional and managerial	48	27
Clerical	22	19
Craft	8	8
Police, army	2	6
Other paid work	6	14
Housewife	1	4
Don't know	13	23

Source of data: Lawrence Podell, *Families on Welfare in New York City* (New York: City University of New York Press, 1968), Tables 7-C and 7-D.

[6]See, for example, Barbara Coward, Joe Feagim, and J. Allen Williams, Jr., "The Culture of Poverty Debate: Some Additional Data," *Social Problems,* June 1974; Chandler Davidson and Charles Gaitz, "Are the Poor Different?: A Comparison of Work Behavior and Attitudes Among the Urban Poor and Nonpoor," *Social Problems,* December 1974; also Roberta H. Jackson, "Some Aspirations of Lower Class Black Mothers," *Journal of Comparative Family Studies,* Autumn 1975.

[7]Leonard Goodwin, "What Has Been Learned from the Work Incentive Program and Related Experiences: A Review of Research with Policy Implications" (Worchester, MA: Worcester Polytechnic Institute, 1977), p. 31.

If their aspirations and values were really as different as some observers claim, then the poor would be satisfied with their standard of living and resistant to new opportunity. Many modern cultural theorists argue, in fact, that the poor are content and unable to progress. (Similar arguments were once employed in defense of slavery.) Such views are not consistent with reality. Not only have organized groups of the poor repeatedly expressed their discontent, but the poor have demonstrated a marked ability to move out of poverty when economic opportunities improved (see Chapter 2).

Even the most adamant exponents of the culture of poverty do not argue that all persons in poverty are psychodynamically attached to impoverishment. Oscar Lewis himself estimated that only 20 percent of the poor in America are culturally bound to poverty. Walter Miller, another advocate of the culture of poverty theory, does not specify what proportion of the poor are so afflicted but warns that the proportion is rising. Nevertheless, the basis for these propositions is no stronger than that for the rest of the theory.

Among the 34 million people who were officially poor in 1982, there were, no doubt, some individuals with extraordinarily low aspirations. Many (e.g., discouraged workers) may even have succumbed to a fatalistic attitude regarding their condition and future prospects, thus diminishing their ability to exploit new opportunities. We cannot assume, however, that this fatalism emerged from a cultural orientation or that it is totally impervious to changing circumstances. Yet the culture of poverty theory rests on these assumptions. To the extent that some of the poor do believe their chances for advancement are negligible, new opportunities will be grasped hesitantly. The more the poor experience repeated failure and disappointment, the more skeptically they will respond to new policy initiatives. This does not necessarily imply cultural dissonance; their skepticism may very well be a rational response based on prior experience.

THE RACIAL INFERIORITY THEORY

Poor blacks are apt to appear particularly constrained by "cultural" patterns. They have been extended more new promises more often than any other group among the poor. Some promises of improved opportunity were well-intentioned, others were not; many remain unfulfilled. Many poor blacks respond accordingly—with cynicism and hesitancy—when still further promises and programs are offered. Unfortunately, whites tend to regard this absence of unbridled enthusiasm as additional evidence that blacks lack aspiration.

Those viewing previous policy initiatives and present opportunities as generous offer other explanations for the poverty of blacks and other minorities. In addition to the culture allegation, many whites continue to regard the inferior socioeconomic position of blacks as a natural consequence of racial disabilities.

In this section, the nature and basis of such racially based perspectives are examined.

In 1982 mean family income among black Americans was $17,259, while among white Americans it was $28,603. As we have already seen, one out of every three blacks was poor, compared with only one out of nine whites. There is no question about whether a link exists between race and poverty; instead, we are concerned with the causal nature of the established link. Furthermore, in discussing the causal association between race and poverty, we need not worry about the circular relationships that attracted our attention earlier. Poverty may lead to ill health, broken families, or more children, but there is no prospect of poverty changing people's skin color. Accordingly, both the existence of a link and the direction of causality are known: Being black does lead to poverty.

The causal path leading from race to poverty may be explained in two ways. Inherent racial disabilities may limit income-earning abilities. This, of course, is the racial argument that has arisen before. Another possible explanation for the established path emanates from the alleged existence of discrimination. By this argument, blacks are more apt to be poor, not because of different physical, mental, or cultural capacities, but because they are treated differently by society. Whites have no difficulty in choosing between the alternative explanations of black status: The President's National Advisory Commission on Civil Disorders discovered that white Americans favor the racial explanation three to one. As recently as 1978, one out of two white Americans asserted that blacks have less ambition than whites. Fewer than one out of six whites saw racial discrimination as a serious problem.[8] Accordingly, we postpone a discussion of the discrimination argument until Chapters 10 and 11.

The thesis of racial inferiority is not new. Aristotle, for example, used it to explain Greek superiority over the European barbarians. Still later, the barbarians, who by then had produced Shakespeare, Kant, and Newton, used this argument to explain their superiority over the Greeks. Later still, English intellectuals were predicting that America would never achieve greatness because its colonies were heavily populated by the rejected and inferior classes of Europe.

Despite the somewhat dismal record of racial theories, they remain popular. Among the most quoted proponents of a racial explanation of black socioeconimic status in America is Dr. William Shockley. Shockley is an inventor of the transistor and a recipient of the Nobel Prize in Physics. As he explained to the National Academy of Sciences in 1969: "The major deficit in Negro intellectual performance must be primarily of heriditary origin and thus relatively irremediable by practical improvements in the environment." In other words, blacks are poor because they are not smart, and they are not smart because they are black.

[8]Louis Harris and Associates, *A Study of Attitudes Toward Racial and Religious Minorities and Toward Women* (New York: National Conference of Christians and Jews, 1978).

Shockley's position is rather extreme, but he is not alone in his beliefs about innate racial differences. Such beliefs are a common component of racial prejudice and linger on in the minds of many. They even acquire a certain plausibility for most people because of the demonstrated link between genetic characteristics and achievement: Nearly everyone accepts the notion that smarter people do better and get further. Such a notion leads easily to the position that blacks fare poorly because they are not as smart as whites. The argument is readily extended to Puerto Ricans, Mexican Americans, American Indians, and other poor minorities.

Intelligence and Status

What keeps the racial inferiority debate going (aside from ingrained prejudices) is the fact that intelligence is an unobservable dimension of an individual's genetic endowment. Although we all give nodding agreement to the notion that mental capacities, like physical capacities, are inherited, we have no direct way of weighing or measuring that inheritance. Accordingly, we depend largely on inferential reasoning to provide clues about the relationship of intelligence to economic status. Unfortunately, such reasoning often turns out to be circular. We have all heard statements like "Wow! John made a fortune in the dry cleaning business; I never realized he was so smart." From this perspective, the true test of intelligence is a person's tax return. According to this test, poverty *must* be explained by a lack of intelligence. If blacks tend to be poorer than whites, their plight must be explained in the same way.

Fortunately, our knowledge of the relationship between intelligence and economic status does not depend exclusively on such superficial reasoning. We know, for example, that identical twins inherit identical genes, and thus identical intelligence (even if we cannot measure that intelligence). Accordingly, if genetic endowments are important for economic status, identical twins should end up with the same status. And they tend to. A study by English sociologists determined that even when they are separated and reared in different environments, identical twins attain very similar socioeconomic statuses. Such observations confirm the significance of inherited abilities, at least for differences among *individuals*.

Demonstrating that genetic abilities are important for economic status does not deny the existence of environmental influences, however. In the studies of English twins, varying environments were shown to have *some* effect on achievement. Those effects would be still stronger where environmental differences were greater. The Osage Indians in America provide a dramatic illustration: Not only achievements, but even measured IQ increased substantially after the tribe discovered oil!

A broader understanding of human achievement recognizes that both genetic and environmental factors influence the attainments of individuals and puts the issue of racial differences in an entirely different setting. Because black and white Americans live in distinct areas and under different conditions, racial abilities alone cannot explain disparities in economic status. To the extent that differences in racial abilities exist at all, we are led to inquire what *proportion* of observed status disparities can be attributed to them. In logical order, then, we must focus on three separate questions:

1. Do genetic differences exist between whites and blacks?
2. If so, how large are any such differences?
3. What is the relative significance of any such differences for observed socioeconomic status?

Very little interest attaches to the question of physical differences between whites and blacks, at least as far as socioeconomic status is involved. Instead, the issue of genetic differences focuses on the relative mental abilities of the two races. The first question, then, really asks whether whites are innately more intelligent than blacks.

IQ Scores

Because we have no way of directly measuring intelligence we cannot answer the foregoing questions directly. Instead, we must first find some independent indicator of intelligence, then test for differences among people on this basis. This is where IQ tests come in: An IQ score indicates how well an individual has performed on a standardized test relative to others of the same age. An IQ score of 100 indicates that one has performed up to average, while higher or lower scores indicate above- or below-average performance. There are a variety of such tests available, but all incorporate exercises of perceptual, verbal, arithmetical, and reasoning abilities.

Since the nineteenth century there have been literally hundreds of research studies directed toward measuring the relative IQs of blacks and whites. All of them have demonstrated that blacks, on average, score lower on intelligence tests than whites. The average difference between whites and blacks amounts to 15 to 20 IQ points, indicating that the typical black has an IQ of 80 to 85. These figures are now widely accepted; what is still debated is how they should be interpreted.

Basically, an IQ test measures various kinds of performance abilities, such as perception, memory, and verbal knowledge. Accordingly, it is subject to the influences of both genetic intelligence and environmental experience. A child who has never seen a giraffe or a waterfall, for example, has difficulty identifying them in an IQ examination, whatever his native intelligence may be. Because IQ scores incorporate both environmental and genetic experiences, there is no easy method for isolating genetic factors. All we can say with assurance is that IQ differences reflect genetic differences when administered to children who have shared very similar environmental experiences. Clearly, black and white children do not satisfy this condition.

The nature of IQ-score determinants suggests that black and white IQ scores could be brought into harmony by appropriate environmental changes. In fact, studies that have attempted to control for such differences by testing black and white children from similar backgrounds have narrowed the average IQ score difference to as little as five points. Black children adopted by white parents have also scored higher on IQ tests. Other research has demonstrated that the IQ test performances of blacks and whites move further apart the longer they are maintained in unequal situations—ghetto schools, for example. Accordingly, it appears that there is nothing natural or unchangeable in any observed racial pattern of IQ scores.

Further evidence of environmental impact on IQ scores is provided by the variation in these scores for individuals and groups. We have already noted the effect of oil discoveries for the Osage Indians. For the country as a whole, IQ scores have been rising consistently over the last fifty years. This suggests either that we are breeding selectively or that IQ scores are subject to environmental improvement (and perhaps even familiarity with testing procedures). More to our point, it has also been observed that black children moving from rural to urban areas raise their IQ scores significantly, reflecting an improved environment. Still other studies have shown that intensive teaching and supportive environments can materially improve the IQ scores of any group, even mentally retarded children! And finally, it has been demonstrated that improving the diets of poor expectant mothers results in higher IQ scores for their children.

Resolving the Issues

The relationship between intelligence, IQ scores, and economic status is summarized in Figure 8.1. Notice that IQ scores and economic status are directly affected by intelligence. But notice also that both IQ scores and economic status are influenced by environmental factors as well. Accordingly, any demonstrated link between IQ and status may be explained by environmental forces alone. At least we may be certain that differences in IQ scores and status are less likely to reflect intelligence differences the greater are the environmental differences between the two individuals or groups in question. And this turns out to be an important qualification when comparing blacks and whites in America.

Guided by Figure 8.1 and our previous discussion, we can answer the three questions posed before. First, we must note that there is no basis for concluding that genetic differences in intelligence exist between blacks and whites. This conclusion emerges from the fact that we do not really know what intelligence is and from the observation that the test scores we use to measure intelligence are themselves subject to environmental influence. We could just as easily assert that

FIGURE 8.1   Intelligence, IQ, and Economic Status

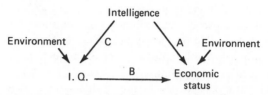

blacks are *more* intelligent than whites as the reverse. Indeed, many people argue that the entire search for an *explanation* of IQ differences is misplaced and racist. If IQ scores don't measure intelligence, then there is no white–black gap to explain.[9] In the absence of any evidence to the contrary, it seems most reasonable to conclude that there are no such genetic differences between the two racial groups.

Even if one were to adhere adamantly to the position that IQ scores accurately reflect intelligence, there would still be little basis for attributing the inferior economic status of blacks to genetic deficiencies. At most, such an argument would have to rely on the average IQ score difference of five to ten points obtained in controlled tests. Suggesting that this difference could account for an existing income disparity of over $10,000 a year would be extremely tenuous, if not comical. One would then be arguing that a 5 or 10 percent difference in intelligence could account for a 40 percent disparity in income, and that status differences were not at all affected by differences in opportunities. Even the unfounded assertion that genetic differences do exist between blacks and whites leads to the conclusion that such differences are of relatively minor significance for observed socioeconomic status.

Other Weaknesses of the Racial Doctrine

The foregoing observations demonstrate the essential weaknesses in the racial inferiority doctrine. The evidence presented has been rather technical, but there are even simpler inconsistencies that discredit racial theories of black poverty. To begin with, blacks do not fare equally well or poorly in all regions of the country. For the nation as a whole, black incomes in 1981 were 62 percent as large as white incomes. In the South, however, they were only 60 percent as large, while in the West, 70 percent. Hence, to argue that genetic disabilities account for status disparities would require one to argue that western blacks are genetically better equipped than southern blacks.

A similar problem arises with the rise in black status over time. In the last

[9]See James Cronin, et al., "Race, Class, and Intelligence: A Critical Look at the IQ Controversy," *International Journal of Mental Health*, Winter 1975; also Cedric X. (Clark), "The Shockley-Jensen Thesis: A Contextual Appraisal," *The Black Scholar*, July 1975.

ten years, black incomes have risen considerably relative to white incomes. A theory of racial determination would be compelled to explain this development on the basis of improving genetic abilities among blacks or declining genetic potential among whites.

Finally, and most damaging to the doctrine of racial superiority, is the concept of *race* itself. There is not, and never has been, a clear understanding of what the term race means, or for that matter, of how many races exist. As an English zoologist has noted, "geneticists believe anthropologists know what a race is, ethnologists assume their racial classifications are backed up by genetics, and politicians believe that their prejudices have the sanction of both genetics and anthropology."[10] In the resultant confusion, anywhere from three to thirty separate races have been identified at various times. In the American context, the term is used interchangeably to refer to religious, national, or ethnic groups. In the context of the immediate discussion, the term refers basically to skin color. Given the history of miscegenation in America, no one could conceivably argue that distinctive pure white and black genetic characteristics exist: It is estimated that over 90 percent of American blacks have some white ancestry. Hence, American blacks hardly comprise a suitable test for racial theories of inherent differences.

Interestingly enough, adherents to the racial doctrine have attempted to employ this phenomenon of miscegenation to their advantage. They argue that the success of mulattos is due to the presence of "white" genes, which improve their intellectual endowments, proving the thesis of racial superiority. The argument is also used to explain rising black status over time. The evidence presented, however, is exceedingly weak. Mulattos apparently did fare relatively better than "pure" blacks during and shortly after the slave era, but children of mixed parentage were often favored by their white father-masters. Thus, they received greater opportunity and support. Other research has shown that more successful blacks today do not differ in patterns of white ancestry. Moreover, the highest black IQ score yet reported—200—was attained by a child who had no traceable white heritage whatsoever. Hence, whatever the other virtues and liabilities of miscegenation may be, its effects on genetic abilities appear to be negligible.

SUMMARY

Theories of poverty causation based on cultural or racial phenomena have long commanded a certain acceptability. In part, they are based on prejudices of the nonpoor against the poor and, in part, on the confidence with which the nonpoor perceive economic opportunity to exist for all. Since the earliest days of

[10]Anthony Smith, *The Body* (New York: Walker and Company, 1968), p. 14.

colonization it has been asserted that anyone with enough stamina and initiative could succeed in America. Accordingly, those who did not succeed have been regarded variously as immoral, culturally apart, or racially inferior. This chapter has considered the latter two allegations and examined the direct evidence on which they are based.

The argument that the poor do not possess enough aspiration and initiative to raise themselves out of poverty rests on misconceptions rather than factual evidence. Divergent behavioral patterns do not prove the existence of divergent aspirations and goals; instead, they may well represent rational responses to continuing inopportune circumstances. The sometimes different behavior of the poor, in the areas of saving, education, and job acquisition, for example, may reflect great aspirations equally as well as small ones. Direct research on the goals and ambitions of the poor suggest that they share middle-class goals and await improved opportunities to pursue them.

Allegations about racial disabilities suffer equally from misconception and prejudice. There is no basis for concluding that differences in intelligence exist between whites and blacks. Not only do we not yet know what intelligence is, but the instruments we assume to measure it yield ambiguous results. Moreover, even the most extreme assumptions about the meaning and reliability of observed IQ scores would still lead to the conclusion that genetic factors are of negligible significance in explaining the existing economic disparities between whites and blacks.

FURTHER READING

On Culture

GOODWIN, LEONARD. *Do the Poor Want to Work?* Washington, DC: The Brookings Institution, 1972.

LEWIS, OSCAR. *La Vida.* New York: Random House, Inc., 1966.

LIEBOW, ELLIOT. *Tally's Corner: A Study of Negro Streetcorner Men.* Boston: Little, Brown and Company, 1967.

MERCY, JAMES A., and LALA CARR STEELMAN. "Familial Influence on the Intellectual Attainment of Children," *American Sociological Review*, August 1982.

PADILLA, AMADO, ed. *Acculturation: Theory Models and Some New Findings.* Boulder, CO: Westview, 1980.

VALENTINE, CHARLES A. *Culture and Poverty.* Chicago: University of Chicago Press, 1968.

WINTER, J. ALAN, ed.   *The Poor: A Culture of Poverty or a Poverty of Culture.* Grand Rapids, MI: Wm. B. Eerdmans Publishing Co., 1971.

On Race

CARTWRIGHT, WALTER J., and THOMAS R. BURTIS.   "Race and Intelligence: Changing Opinions in Social Science," *Social Science Quarterly,* December 1968, pp. 603–18.

CLARK, CEDRIC X.   "The Shockley-Jensen Thesis: A Contextual Appraisal," *The Black Scholar,* July 1975.

GREEN, ROBERT, and ROBERT GRIFFORE.   "Standardized Testing and Minority Students," *Educational Digest,* February 1981.

HARVARD EDUCATIONAL REVIEW, Winter, Spring, and Summer issues, 1969.

HERRNSTEIN, RICHARD.   "I.Q.," *The Atlantic Monthly,* September 1971, pp. 43–64.

MYRDAL, GUNNAR.   *An American Dilemma.* New York: Harper & Row, Publishers, 1962, Chs. 4–6.

SOWELL, THOMAS.   *Race and Economics.* New York: David McKay Co., Inc., 1975.

WOLFE, JOHN R.   "The Impact of Family Resources on Childhood IQ," *Journal of Human Resources,* Spring, 1982.

Education
and
Ability

The empirical relationship between education and ability on the one hand and economic status on the other are essential components of American folklore. In fact, the observations that "to get ahead, get an education" and "you can't keep a good man down" have acquired the aura of ideological convictions. Everyone has heard of Horatio Alger, and no one doubts that doctors get rich. Conditioned by these examples and mindful of their own security, Americans react accordingly. Middle-class parents begin preparing their children for college soon after birth, and the children themselves learn to regard success as the reward to virtue, ability, and good grades in school. By the same token, those who do not succeed are regarded as less virtuous, less able, or less diligent in the pursuit of education. From this perspective, lack of ability or education emerges as an important cause of poverty. The distribution of poverty even acquires a democratic flavor, as it is also presumed that the development of abilities and education is largely a matter of individual choice.

The conviction that education and ability lead to material success is not easily challenged. Few persons even pause to reflect on the nature and reliability of the underlying associations. With educated people moving ahead all around them, how many individuals can take the time and effort to question the pace of events? Nevertheless, the implied importance of education for the existence of poverty demands that such an inquiry be made. Our discussion focuses on two issues: (1) whether educational achievement determines who is poor; and (2) whether the level of educational achievement determines *how many* people are poor. The same questions are asked of the relationship between ability and poverty.

EDUCATION AND INCOME

The conviction that more education leads to higher income finds extensive support in statistical data. The simple correlation between educational attainment and income is very strong and consistent: More years of education *do* lead to higher income. In 1982, for example, men with no more than eight years of schooling had a median income of only $8,072; high school dropouts commanded median incomes of $12,079; high school graduates had incomes of $17,055; and college graduates had median incomes above $26,000. Hence, there is an impressive foundation to the belief that education pays.

The relationship between education and income is equally effective in separating the poor from the nonpoor. The typical nonpoor family head has a high school diploma, while the average poor family head has completed fewer than nine years of school. This disparity in educational attainment is reflected in the incidence of poverty. As Table 9.1 confirms, the likelihood of impoverishment declines rapidly as a person scales the educational ladder. Only one out of twenty people who had attended college ended up in poverty in 1982, while more than one out of five high school dropouts were so misfortunate.

Higher educational attainment contributes to income in several ways. It increases a person's productivity (his human capital) by expanding his knowledge and skills. Prospective employers also tend to regard educational degrees as proof of commendable diligence. Diplomas, regardless of their content, are likely to provide access to more jobs. Educational institutions may also serve as job placement services, providing employers and students with ready access to each other. The combination of these factors suggests that the person who stays in school longer will be treated and will perform differently in the labor market. Educational attainment affects every facet of labor market success. A person's participation in the labor force, his or her occupation, the frequency of his and her employment, the number of hours worked, and the wage rate received are all affected by the schooling the person has achieved. In conjunction, these factors determine an individual's income.

People with little education are least likely to get and hold a job. If they do obtain jobs, they are first to be laid off by employers when production schedules change. With fewer skills and credentials, their ability to acquire other jobs will

TABLE 9.1   INCIDENCE OF POVERTY, BY EDUCATION OF HEAD OF FAMILY, 1982

EDUCATION	NUMBER IN POVERTY	INCIDENCE OF POVERTY (%)
Elementary school	1,901,000	22.0
High school dropout	1,533,000	20.0
High school graduate	2,071,000	10.2
College (1 year or more)	1,001,000	4.8

Source: U.S. Bureau of the Census.

be restricted. Consequently, they are apt to be unemployed far more often and for longer periods than those with greater educational attainments. In early 1983, high school dropouts experienced a 20.6 unemployment rate, while high school and college graduates confronted unemployment rates of 11.7 and 3.8, respectively (Table 9.2).

As was noted in Chapter 4, long and repeated spells of unemployment may induce people to leave the labor force altogether. Frustrated by lack of employment opportunities, they may give up the job search, relying instead on public or private financial assistance. Few men can, however, resign themselves to nonparticipation, in part because available social and financial supports are extremely limited. Nevertheless, the impact of educational attainment is discernible in the relevant statistics. Whereas over 90 percent of all male high school and college graduates participate in the labor force, only 83 percent of high school dropouts do so.

Getting and holding a job does not guarantee financial success, of course. The nature of the job one obtains, how many hours one works, and what wage one is paid are equally as important. On all these fronts, the less educated individual fares poorly. High school dropouts are disproportionately concentrated in the blue-collar occupations as unskilled laborers, operatives, service workers, and craftsmen. By contrast, high school graduates are most heavily concentrated in the lower white-collar occupations, at the clerical and sales levels, and in the higher blue-collar positions. College graduates crowd the professional and managerial classes and are virtually nonexistent in the lowest job categories.

The cumulative impact of these labor market phenomena sharply differentiates the incomes of the lesser- and greater-educated. As we have already noted, the income differences amount to thousands of dollars a year. Over a lifetime, this disparity becomes tremendous. During their careers, high school graduates can anticipate earning $300,000 more than high school dropouts, while college graduates will earn $300,000 more than high school graduates before retiring.[1]

TABLE 9.2   EDUCATION AND THE LABOR MARKET

	HIGH SCHOOL DROPOUTS	HIGH SCHOOL GRADUATES	COLLEGE GRADUATES
Unemployment rates (%)	20.6	11.7	3.8
*Labor force participation (%)	83.4	90.7	95.4
*Full-time workers (%)	74.9	89.7	90.6
Occupation status	Blue collar	Clerical	Professional
Average earnings	$9,291	$12,092	$20,223

*For male workers aged 25 to 64.

Source: U.S. Department of Labor (1981–1983 data).

[1]Because these estimates do not account for productivity or price increases, they understate income differences; see U.S. Bureau of the Census, *Lifetime Earnings Estimates for Men and Women in the United States: 1979* (Washington, DC: Government Printing Office, 1983).

Education and the Distribution
of Income

The weight of accumulated evidence on the association between income and education reinforces the belief that inadequate education is a major cause of poverty. That the least-educated will bring the least amount of human capital to the labor market and therefore receive the least income appears obvious. From this perspective poverty can be explained by a failure to stay in school, by underinvestment in one's own human capital.[2] Before fully accepting this interpretation, however, several additional issues must be considered.

Even if, on average, better-educated individuals can earn more money, all persons with more schooling will not necessarily have higher incomes. No one has seriously suggested that education is the *only* determinant of income. Inherent ability, inherited wealth, geographical location, discrimination, economic conditions, and simple luck will all influence a person's income opportunities. We want to determine how consistent the relationship is between education and income, and how much poverty can be explained by education alone.

The relationship between education and income is far from perfect. Indeed, the labor market rewards the educational attainments of some people much more handsomely than that of others. Consider Figure 9.1, for example: Each step up the educational ladder clearly improves the incomes of both blacks and whites. Even more striking, however, is the gross disparity shown on the graphs that exists between white and black males. The average black college graduate, for example, earns less ($17,622) than a white high school graduate ($18,677); while a white high school dropout earns more ($14,270) than a black high school graduate ($13,178). Whatever benefits education provides, they are clearly not equally accessible to all. Hence, if lack of education is regarded as an explanation for poverty, it must be recognized at the outset that the explanation is not complete.

The same disparity can be observed between men and women (see Figure 9.2). Women college graduates earn less on average ($11,360) than men who complete just eight years of school ($11,516). Moreover, the average male high school graduate commands an income ($18,139) that is higher than all groups of women, including those who have attended graduate school. Again, the rewards for educational achievement, while perhaps large, are not evenly distributed.

Explanations for the income disparities that exist between races and sexes are not difficult to find. Some of these are discussed more thoroughly in Chapters 10 and 11. For present purposes, we may confine ourselves to the observation that more education does not guarantee escaping poverty. Keeping some poor persons in school longer may not effectively raise their incomes. Even in situations where racial or sexual discrimination is not present, the link between education and income is not perfect. There are over a million white high school dropouts, for example, who earn more money than one out of three

---

[2] The link of this perspective with cultural theories of poverty (Chapter 8) should be apparent.

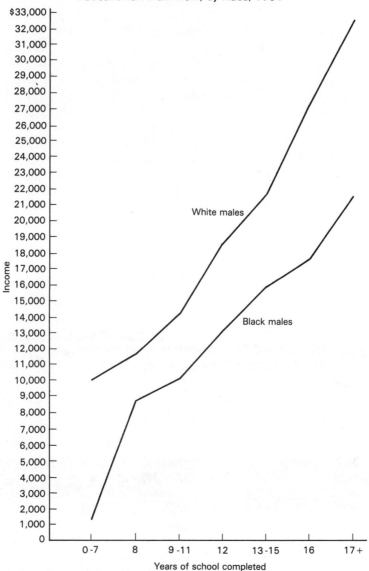

FIGURE 9.1 Mean Incomes of Males 25 years of Age and Over, by Educational Attainment, by Race, 1981

Source: U.S. Bureau of the Census.

FIGURE 9.2   Mean Incomes, by Educational Attainment, by Sex, 1981

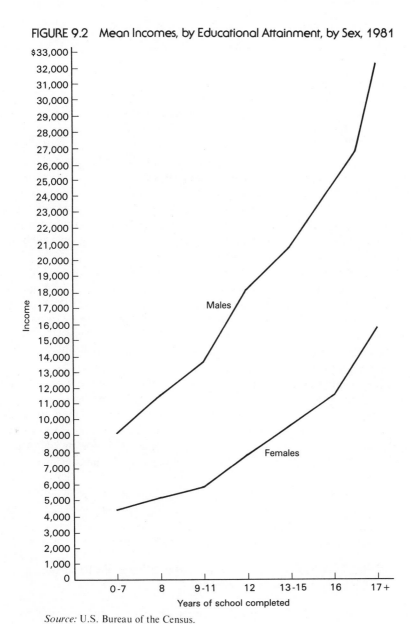

Source: U.S. Bureau of the Census.

college graduates. There are also more families in poverty headed by white male high school graduates than by white high school dropouts.

Education as a Sorting Device

The full significance of education for the distribution and extent of poverty can be understood only in the framework of the entire labor market. As we have seen, observing the relationship of average incomes to average educational attainments can lead to erroneous impressions about the importance of education. A certain quantity of job vacancies and prospective employees exists in any labor market. When the number of vacancies falls far short of the number of job-seekers, the economy is in a depressed state, and unemployment rates are high. This implies that employers will be able to choose among many applicants in filling any job vacancy. How will the employer proceed? That is, on what basis should he or will he make his selection?

In Chapter 4, we suggested that employers will tend to select new employees on the basis of their human capital, their potential contribution to output. In some cases, the process of selection is comparatively simple. If the job is highly technical, identifying the most competent applicants on the basis of tests or prior accomplishments may be easy.

But differences in human capital are not always large or easily observed, compelling employers to depend on some guesswork. In these cases—probably the majority—employers come to rely on only a few selection criteria, educational attainment being one of the most important.[3] The employer has several reasons for separating the more-educated from the less-educated in the application process. First, it is assumed that more schooling results in greater ability. The employer may also feel that perseverance in school merits greater opportunity. And finally, educational minimums constitute a cheap and easy means for holding down the time and cost of interviewing.

These considerations transform educational credentials (e.g., a high school diploma) into admission tickets for job interviews, especially in times of high unemployment. The recession of 1971 amply illustrated how selective employers can become; consider this help-wanted ad from the Austin, Texas, *American:*

TOPLESS DANCERS. Must have two years college. Prefer English major, languages or humanities.[4]

From the standpoint of this employer, all prospective go-go girls are in competition for available jobs, and educational attainments separate the finalists from the rejects. Other employers are likely to react similarly when jobs are scarce.

[3]Other important criteria are race and sex, implying that otherwise qualified blacks and women will gain access to jobs only after available white males have been hired (see Chapter 11).
[4]Cited in *Playboy*, December 1971, p. 26.

For example, even though a high school dropout could easily perform the responsibilities of a salesclerk, he is not given the opportunity if high school graduates are also available. As a consequence, he remains unemployed and poor.

The implications of this selection process for the relationship of education to poverty are profound. The distribution of edcuation will have a significant impact on the distribution of poverty. As a rule, those with the least education will end up in poverty. This will be especially true among otherwise similar labor market, racial, and sexual groups. But what about the extent of poverty? Will education have a similar influence in determining how many persons are poor?

Consider again the case of the high school dropout seeking the job of salesclerk. A high school diploma would undoubtedly make his competitive position stronger. But would his graduation, by itself, increase the number of available jobs? Clearly not. His graduation may enable him to compete successfully for the available job, but his success will leave someone else unemployed. If there is only one job and four applicants, no amount of educational improvement or redistribution will succeed in leaving fewer than three persons unemployed. Education may influence who gets the available jobs, but the demand for labor will determine how many jobs there are (recall Figure 4.1, illustrating the interaction of market demand and supply).

Confusion about the causal significance of education comes from the failure to distinguish between individual and group needs, or, as an economist would say, between micro- and macro-phenomena. Observing that individual incomes are related to educational attainments easily leads to the supposition that raising the educational attainments of all the poor will eliminate poverty. Yet, bestowing a high school diploma, or even a Ph.D., on all the poor will do little to alter the number or kinds of jobs available. A few more vacancies might be filled, but the greatest impact would be to alter the composition of the poor and to raise their educational attainments. By itself, such an effort would do little to reduce the extent of poverty.

The Content of Education

The foregoing discussion said nothing about the content of education. Instead, the term has been used to refer to schooling in general. Accordingly, some of the most vital and controversial issues relevant to the education-income nexus have been neglected. Among the more salient of those issues are the questions of how much vocational content should be offered in school curricula and who should provide it. Training in specific skills might be especially valuable to those who are not going to pursue higher education. One recent study suggests that the incomes of black workers are particularly sensitive to the

degree of vocational instruction in their high school curriculum.[5] Greater earning potential could be generated by simply restructuring educational curricula
rather than by extending them.

Of even greater importance for policy consideration is the question of
access to education. Because educational attainments significantly determine
who will be poor in any given economic situation, we must also determine who
receives the necessary credentials and why. Some consideration of these issues is
taken up in Chapters 10 and 11. For the present, we may note that neither the
issue of educational content nor of access materially alters the conclusions cited
above. Regardless of what is taught or who it is taught to, education by itself, can
do very little to alter the number of jobs available at any given moment.[6]

ABILITY AND INCOME

Ability, like education, is presumed to be an important determinant of income.
In fact, it is generally deemed desirable for the distribution of incomes to reflect
the distribution of productive abilities. We are accustomed to thinking that
greater ability merits richer rewards and, indeed, that material success manifests
ability. The idea that income *should* reflect ability can be questioned, however.
Why, for example, should a man who inherits the capacity to learn to steer
rockets through space command a higher income than the man who is born with
the capacity to learn to drive buses? Are justice and equity any better served
when rewards are distributed according to inherited genes rather than according
to inherited dollars?

In Chapter 8, we encountered some of the difficulties that engulf discussions of individual ability. The term *ability*, as it is commonly employed,
incorporates elements of both innate capacity and developed performance.
Accordingly, there is a certain vagueness in the question whether the income
distribution reflects the ability distribution. If we refer to innate abilities, then we
really have no means for answering the question because we do not know
precisely what innate abilities are or how to measure them. However, if we look
only at developed performance, we must recognize that we are departing from
the pattern of innate abilities, because all individuals do not share equal opportunity to develop their capacities. An income distribution based on performance
abilities may not meet our standards of equity.

Another problem with the measurement of performance ability is the fact
that no single, all-inclusive performance criterion exists. The ability to sing or to
run is distributed differently from the ability to solve complex mathematical

[5]Alan C. Kerckhoff and Robert A. Jackson, "Types of Education and the Occupational
Attainments of Young Men," *Social Forces*, September 1982.

[6]Over a longer period of time rising educational attainments may increase national productivity and employment, even if there is little immediate impact on the level of poverty.

problems. There are literally hundreds, if not thousands, of varied abilities, all uniquely distributed among the population. Determining whether incomes accurately reflect performance ability is impossible. At most, one could assert that the distribution of incomes reflects the distribution of abilities valued highly in the market place. But even that cautious assertion masks a tautology. One could assert that *any* income distribution reflects the same thing. There is no means for determining whether a given income distribution departs from the distribution of abilities. In the face of this impasse, we usually proceed in reverse. That is, we infer the distribution of abilities from the distribution of incomes: People with more money are *assumed* to be more able. In this way the income distribution justifies itself.

In view of these considerations, we apparently have little basis for objectively assessing the fairness or appropriateness of any existing income distribution. At most, we may simply observe how well the distribution reflects certain specific kinds of attainments or characteristics. We must then resort to our own values to determine how appropriate these criteria are and how equitable they are reflected in incomes. The inherent subjectivity of this approach does not render it impracticable, but it does make consensus difficult.

Two kinds of abilities continue to attract the most attention in discussions of income distribution—measured IQ and educational attainment. IQ is of interest both because it gauges highly valued performance abilities, such as perception and problem solving, and because, despite admonitions to the contrary, it is assumed to reflect innate capacities. Educational attainment is of interest for much the same reasons. Accordingly, we may ask how well the existing income distribution reflects these criteria. Figure 9.3 provides the answer to this question.

The educational, IQ, and income distributions are all depicted in Figure 9.3. One can see, for example, that slightly less than 30 percent of the male population had completed just twelve years of school in 1965; that somewhat under 10 percent had an income of about $2,000; and that approximately 15 percent had exactly average IQs. One striking impression obtained from the graphs in Figure 9.3 is that the shape of the income distribution is very different from those of the education and IQ distributions. There is a relatively high concentration of persons in the lower end of the income scale, say under $5,000, while relatively few people are in the lower educational or IQ categories. One way of expressing this disparity is to say that incomes are distributed much less equally than are IQs or educational attainments. Or, one could say that the distribution of poverty is not well explained by the distributions of either IQ or educational achievement.

Some interesting implications follow from Figure 9.3 and our previous discussions of ability and education. We have already suggested that high IQ scores are not equally accessible to all individuals of similar genetic capacity (see Chapter 8). Black children, for example, have less of an opportunity to develop

FIGURE 9.3   Distribution of Income, Education, and IQ for Males, 25 Years of Age and Over, 1965

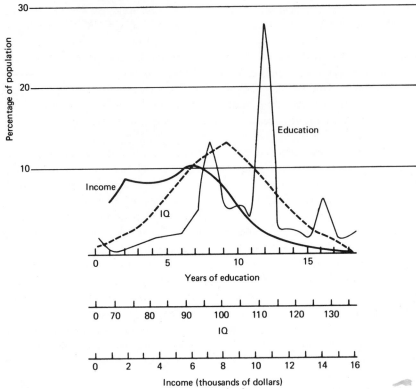

Source of data: Lester C. Thurow, *Poverty and Discrimination* (Washington, DC: The Brookings Institution, 1969), p. 68.

their capacities into performing abilities. This implies that the income distribution is even less representative of innate capacities than is suggested by its observed relationship to IQ. Similarly, we should note that educational attainments depart considerably from the IQ distribution, suggesting that access to, and the quality of, education are not uniform. These observations are considered further in Chapter 10.

SUMMARY

Individuals with greater educational attainments unquestionably earn more money, on average, than persons with less education. Persons with highly-valued abilities also tend to earn larger incomes. Accordingly, it is hardly surprising to discover that the poor tend to have less education and fewer marketable skills than the nonpoor. While the evidence reviewed in this chapter demonstrates that these relationships are not perfect, they do have a general validity. More important than the question of association, however, is that of causality. What we really seek to discover is not whether the poor are undereducated or underskilled, but whether a lack of education or skills is responsible for their poverty.

Education does operate as a powerful mechanism in determining the distribution of poverty. Where only a limited number of income opportunities are available, they will be reserved on a "least-educated last" basis. That is, the person with educational credentials will have a competitive edge in the labor market, at least within racial or sexual population groups. There is, therefore, some basis for attributing the poverty of individuals to educational deficiency.

The relationship between education and poverty is not so simple on an aggregate basis, however. The competitive position of all workers cannot be raised simultaneously; if one individual's relative educational position rises, someone else's falls. Education cannot be a cause of aggregate poverty unless direct links from educational attainments to social productivity to wages can be demonstrated. Such links are plausible, especially in the long run. In the short run, however, the link between education and the extent of total poverty is not so apparent.

The relationship of ability to poverty is also more complex than commonly assumed. Because we lack standard definitions and measurements of ability, there is no firm basis for declaring that the poor are less able. At most, such an observation means only that the poor make less money. Even when confined to measures of performance, such as IQ, we find that the relationship of ability to income is oblique. The distribution of incomes diverges considerably from educational or IQ distributions and even further from the distribution of innate talents.

FURTHER READING

BERG, IVAR. *Education and Jobs: The Great Training Robbery.* New York: Frederick A. Praeger, Inc., 1970.

BRITTAIN, JOHN A. *The Inheritance of Economic Status.* Washington, DC: The Brookings Institution, 1977.

DACHTER, LINDA P. "Race/Sex Differences in the Effects of Background on Achievement," in *Five Thousand Families,* Vol. IX, Martha S. Hill, et al., eds. Ann Arbor, MI: Institute for Social Research, 1981.

HAUSER, ROBERT M., and THOMAS N. DAYMONT. "Schooling, Ability, and Earnings: Cross-sectional Findings 8 to 14 Years After High School Graduation," *Sociology of Education,* July 1977.

JENCKS, CHRISTOPHER, et al. *Inequality*. New York: Basic Books, Inc., 1972.
_____ .*Who Gets Ahead? The Economic Determinants of Success in America*. New York: Basic Books, 1979.

SCHILLER, BRADLEY R. "Equality, Opportunity, and the 'Good Job,'" *The Public Interest*, Spring 1976.

THUROW, LESTER, and ROBERT LUCAS. "The American Distribution of Income: A Structural Problem," a study prepared for the Joint Economic Committee, U.S. Congress. Washington, DC: Government Printing Office, 1972.

Discrimination in Education

Education appears to have a major impact on the distribution, if not necessarily the extent, of poverty. Anyone denied equal opportunity to education has an increased probability of being poor. In other words, discrimination in education helps determine who will be poor.

Discrimination in labor markets has similar effects. To achieve nonpoverty status, an individual must be able to employ his abilities in the labor market. Acquisition of acceptable characteristics alone is no guarantee of escape from poverty. If there exist forces that prevent or limit access to the labor market, the rewards to demographic achievements are never realized.

Barriers to either the acquisition or utilization of one's demographic characteristics, or, in economic terms, one's human capital, are the subject of this and the following chapter. The discussion in this chapter begins with a consideration of the meaning and nature of "discrimination" and ends with an examination of discriminatory barriers in the educational system. Chapter 11 focuses on discrimination in the labor market.

DISCRIMINATION

The terms *discrimination, prejudice,* and *racism* are widely used. Seldom do they fail to evoke emotional, often heated responses. While most people do not always understand what is meant by these concepts, they stand forever ready to deny or proclaim the significance of each. The report of the National Advisory Commission on Civil Disorders (the "Riot Commission") in early 1968 provides a striking example of this volatility. In searching for an explanation of the urban strife that was becoming characteristic of American cities, the commission concluded that white racism was a principal source of injustice and unrest. Very few white Americans, President Johnson included, were ready to accept the commission's sweeping indictment. White Americans generally felt neither significantly prejudiced nor sufficiently involved in the ghetto to be responsible for the conditions therein.

Much of the misunderstanding revolving around the commission's report can be traced to the vague meaning of the term *racism*. For many people, racism means burning school buses, racial taunts, or protesting equal opportunity. Relatively few Americans identify easily with such characterizations. Racism, however, has other meanings. In fact, as used by the commission, the concept transcends the attitudes and behavior of individuals. The commission's indictment refers to entire patterns of racial interaction and the institutional character of much discrimination.

To understand the nature of racism, we must begin by distinguishing between attitudes and actions. People often think differently than they act. As a result, they may adopt patterns of behavior that are injurious to others without consciously wishing to inflict injury. Conversely, they may harbor hostile feelings toward particular individuals or groups but refrain from acting them out due to personal, moral, or legal inhibitions. The term *prejudice* refers to the unfavorable feelings and attitudes that people harbor against others, especially other population groups. These are to be distinguished from unfavorable actions or behavior, which fall under the heading of discrimination. Therefore, prejudiced individuals may or may not discriminate, and discrimination does not necessarily imply the existence of prejudice.

While people's prejudices are often the origin of discriminatory behavior and may be appropriate targets for public policy, they are relevant to our discussion only insofar as they find expression in behavior. Accordingly, we focus on the nature of discrimination. We may note here, however, that the broader term, racism, encompasses the concepts of both prejudice and discrimination.

The concept of discrimination need not convey notions of injustice or injury. In general, it refers only to the differential treatment of persons. Thus, we discriminate when we assign the tallest boys to the basketball team or when we cheer for the local football team. Yet we hardly think of these phenomena as being related in any meaningful way to, say, the exclusion of blacks from higher status jobs or classrooms. Clearly, a general concept of discrimination encompassing both situations is too anemic for practical use. But how, then, are we to identify the kind of discriminatory treatment that we regard as the proper concern of public policy?

We can move closer to a relevant concept of discrimination by recognizing the criteria on which differential treatment is based. Assigning taller boys to a basketball team, for example, serves a very specific and productive function. In this case, the criterion of selection is directly relevant to the task at hand. The same cannot be said for the selection of a less qualified white competing with a more qualified black. Here the basis of selection, color, is irrelevant to the task at hand, and the resultant choice is actually counterproductive. Hence, we could refine our concept of discrimination by incorporating the relevancy of selection criteria. The kind of discrimination that is based on irrelevant or nonproductive criteria must be considered as injurious to the public welfare.

The U.S. Supreme Court employed this "relevancy" concept of discrimination when it restricted the use of aptitude tests for job-seekers. The Court observed that intelligence tests and other hiring criteria used by the Duke Power Company were not related to job performance. That is, the tests performed no useful economic function. Yet they were effective in screening out black job-seekers. In *Griggs* v. *Duke Power Company* (1971), the Court ruled that such practices were unfairly discriminatory.

Unfortunately, even this refinement of the concept of discrimination does not provide a completely workable definition. There remain many choices we would consider socially injurious that are still not identifiable by the criterion of relevancy. The choice of one's neighbors is an example: The only obviously relevant criterion in choosing neighbors is one's own desires and satisfaction. Thus, the choice of a white neighbor over a black one conforms to a certain standard of relevancy. Nevertheless, we have come to regard racial discrimination in housing as a socially pernicious practice. On what grounds do we distinguish this kind of individual choice from others? Are there fundamental differences between the situation where a homeowner chooses a white neighbor and, say, the situation where you choose to listen to a rock singer rather than an opera singer? Both situations reflect the free expression of individual choice.

There are few objective grounds for distinguishing between the choice of neighbors and the choice of singers. In both situations, someone is harmed by the selection decision: The opera singer loses potential income and the black home-seeker loses a potential residence. Our distinction between the two situations rests instead on more subjective grounds. Racial discrimination in housing is singled out for special attention because it violates our subjective notions of social justice. Against a combined background of religious, moral, legal, and historical considerations, we have collectively determined that racial discrimination is a particularly deleterious form of individual choice. It is on the basis of this subjective determination that racial discrimination has become a pressing public concern.

An important factor in our subjective judgment about the nature of racial discrimination is our perception of its effects. Where all whites discriminate against all blacks, the expression of free choice becomes especially pernicious. The black home-seeker is denied not one potential home, but all potential homes in white areas. Free choice for whites thus implies restricted choice for blacks and, hence, violates a basic dimension of freedom. Other choices that are less uniform or pervasive are not equally worthy of public concern. Racial discrimination itself would cease to be a public concern were it the practice of only a relatively few, scattered whites.

Costs and Benefits of Discrimination

While it is obvious that blacks, Hispanics, and other targets of discrimination suffer real and intangible losses from the practice of racial discrimination, it is not so apparent whether or how the white community gains. Psychologically, of course, many whites will feel better off for having subordinated someone else. And if majority white individuals actually feel uncomfortable around minorities, on the job, in school, or at home, we may conclude that they are even happier as a result of discrimination.[1] But the economic costs and benefits that may accrue to the white community is our immediate concern.

Many whites do reap tangible benefits from the practice of discrimination. When blacks and Hispanics are discriminated against in the labor market, for example, they will receive lower wages than white workers who possess equal qualifications. As a result, two groups gain: White workers who are immunized against competition from minority workers obtain higher wages than otherwise; and those employers (laundries and hotels, for example) who actually hire minority workers benefit by getting higher quality labor than they are, in fact, paying for. In the educational field, white children gain from discrimination by monopolizing better facilities and teachers. As long as racial discrimination is practiced, white children of lesser ability are also released from the necessity of competing with more able minority children in the quest for admissions.

Not all whites gain directly, however, from racial discrimination; some, in fact, actually lose. White workers who cannot escape menial occupations suffer from increased competition from minority workers. The wages of white laundry and hotel workers, for example, will be held down by the large number of blacks, Hispanics, and Asians excluded from other occupations. This relationship is illustrated in Figure 10.1. Some employers, too, will suffer losses. In a segregated community employers will often incur higher labor costs through the use of lesser-qualified whites. In the field of education, many whites will suffer from racial discrimination. Not all whites can flee the inner city. Those left behind, primarily the poorest, will be trapped in increasingly inferior educational systems, unable to enjoy the fruits of suburban white monopolies. They, like their black and Hispanic neighbors, will find their human capital potential underdeveloped.[2]

[1]The perception of psychological benefits may, of course, rest on prejudices, in which case the nature of benefits could be altered by illuminating and reducing racial stereotypes.

[2]As we shall note later, some whites may also suffer from policies designed to eliminate vestiges of discrimination against blacks; where blacks are given *preferential* (not just equal) access to schools or jobs some whites suffer reverse discrimination.

FIGURE 10.1

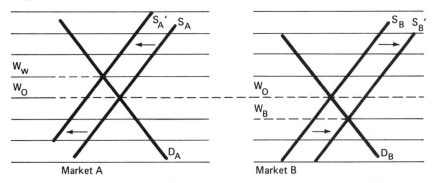

Market A   Market B

Suppose there are only two kinds of jobs, those in Market A and those in Market B. If everyone is allowed to move freely from one market to another, the equilibrium wage will end up at W_O in both markets. Why? Because if wages were higher in A than B, people would move out of B and into A, thus lowering the marginal revenue productivity in A while raising it in B. Hence, freedom of movement between Markets A and B assures an equality of average wage rates.

But now suppose black workers in A are kicked out and sent to Market B, making A a "whites only" preserve. This has the effect of shifting the labor supply curve in A to the left (to S_A') and the labor supply curve in B to the right (to S_B'). The net result indicated by the new supply and demand intersections is to raise wages in A (to W_W) and to lower wages in B (to W_B). Thus, black workers and any white workers trapped in Market B suffer lower wages, while the white workers in Market A end up with higher wages.

On an individual basis, then, some whites gain and some lose as a direct result of discrimination, making it difficult to calculate the net microeconomic gain or loss to the white community. No such ambiguity attaches to the indirect losses that are incurred on an aggregate, or macroeconomic, level, however. Where discrimination against minorities is pervasive, society as a whole loses potential human capital. The abilities and creativity of the minority communities remain underdeveloped and underemployed. Hence, total output of goods and services is less than it would be in the absence of discrimination. Estimates of the size of this loss run into tens of billions of dollars a year. In addition, much of the output we do produce is directed to relatively unattractive uses such as the surveillance of homes, streets, jails, and welfare case loads. Thus, whatever direct gains or losses individual whites incur are overwhelmed by the very large indirect losses to the economy as a whole.[3]

Proving Discrimination

Given the potential socioeconomic cost of discrimination, it is clearly in society's interest to recognize its existence and eliminate it. The identification of discrimination is not always easy, however. Consider a situation where a white worker and a Hispanic worker both apply for the same job. The white applicant is accepted, and the Hispanic applicant claims that he was unfairly discriminated against. What grounds do we have for accepting the charge of discrimination, as opposed to, say, the charge that the Hispanic applicant is simply a poor loser?

The easiest cases of discrimination to prove are those that involve blatant discrepancies in treatment. In our example, if the Hispanic applicant was required to take special tests or possessed identifiably superior qualifications, the issue is readily resolved. The same simplicity exists where black children are confined to dilapidated schools or a prospective black home buyer is turned down after offering to pay the full retail value of a house.

But the practice of discrimination is not always so apparent. Indeed, with the public eye focused on discrimination, those who engage in discriminatory practices are likely to develop great subtlety. Accordingly, evidence of discriminatory treatment may have to rest on the observation of end results. If a metropolitan area company has four thousand employees, none of whom is black, there exists a strong presumption that its hiring procedures are not impartial. So it is with the schools: If blacks and whites go into the educational system comparatively equal but come out with gross disparities in ability, we may conclude that they were treated differently somewhere along the line. Evidence of discriminatory treatment may be gathered by direct observation of treatment or by inference from results. Both types of evidence will be considered in our discussion of the educational and labor market systems.

RACIAL DISCRIMINATION IN EDUCATION

Discrimination in the American educational system was once both blatant and pervasive. In the eighteenth and early nineteenth centuries, the teaching of slaves was barred in most southern states. In 1885, California adopted a school segregation law allowing the exclusion of Chinese and Mongolian children from white public schools. A county school superintendent in Texas proclaimed that

[3]White workers as a class may also lose if racial discrimination weakens worker solidarity, reducing labor's share of total income. See Michael Reich, "Who Benefits From Racism? The Distribution Among Whites of Gains and Losses From Racial Inequality," *Journal of Human Resources*, Fall 1978; and his "Changes in the Distribution of Benefits from Racism in the 1960s," *Journal of Human Resources*, Spring 1981.

"our Mexicans" were better off transplanting onions than going to school. In 1876, a black student admitted to the University of Pennsylvania Medical School was asked to sit behind a screen in the classroom, so as not to offend the white students. White students at Harvard University simply ejected the black entrants.[4]

The U.S. Supreme Court effectively condoned all this behavior by declaring in 1896 that "separate, but equal" education was constitutional (*Plessy* v. *Ferguson*). Even separate but *un*equal was tolerable, as long as the inequalities were not motivated by racial hostility (*Cumming* v. *Richmond County Board of Education,* 1899).

Discrimination still exists in American schools, even though it is much less pervasive or blatant than in the past. While this assertion will surprise very few readers, it is worthwhile to review the evidence on which it is based. Blacks and whites go into the educational system comparatively equal but come out of the system very different. By the time they are nine years old, black and Hispanic students are about 25 percent behind majority white students in reading, science, and math. These disparities continue to grow, so that by age 17 black students are over 30 percent behind white students in measured performance.[5]

Strong as these grounds are for believing that the education provided whites and blacks is not equal, they tend to *understate* disparities in black and white educations. The ability comparisons of black and white high school seniors, for example, necessarily exclude those students who dropped out of school before reaching the twelfth grade. Yet, the decision to quit school may itself reflect inferior educational opportunities and recognition of widening achievement disparities. Seen in this light, black dropout rates are especially disturbing. While 85 percent of white students now graduate from high school, less than 80 percent of black students graduate.

Perhaps the most complete statement of black educational deficiencies is the rate of functional illiteracy among black youth. In 1975, the U.S. Office of Education sponsored a survey of the nation's seventeen-year-olds still in school. Students were asked to respond to eighty-six questions on reading items encountered in everyday life (e.g., street signs, telephone directories, store coupons). Ninety-two percent of all white seventeen-year-olds were rated as functionally literate, having answered correctly at least three-fourths of all the questions. By contrast, only fifty-eight percent of the black seventeen-year-olds were considered functionally literate.[6]

[4]These and other historical examples are cited in U.S. Commission on Civil Rights, *Toward Equal Educational Opportunity: Affirmative Admissions Programs at Law and Medical Schools* (Washington, DC: Government Printing Office, 1978).

[5]National Center For Education Statistics, *Digest of Education Statistics, 1982* (Washington, DC: Government Printing Office, 1982).

[6]Congressional Budget Office, *Inequalities in the Educational Experiences of Black and White Americans* (Washington, DC: Government Printing Office, 1977), pp. 8–9. Recent studies suggest that these disparities are shrinking; see Lyle Jones, "White–Black Achievement Differences: The Narrowing Gap," University of North Carolina, 1983, unpublished paper.

Table 10.1 offers one final perspective on the outcomes of the educational process. This table shows the percentage of different groups that complete at least four years of college. One-fourth of all white males graduate from college. Only eleven percent of black or Hispanic males attain that much education. Among females, the same kind of differences are apparent. If minorities and whites really do enter the educational system with equal potential, these differences in educational outcomes require further explanation.

Segregation in the Schools

The indirect evidence indicating discriminatory treatment in the educational system is highly suggestive. In fact, the observed disparities in achievement between white and black students are so great that direct evidence of discrepancies in educational opportunity should be easy to find. Segregation of facilities provides one such example: Where separate schools are maintained for whites and blacks, the documentation of inequalities is simple.

Before looking at the extent of continuing racial segregation in American schools, we need to establish some perspective on the meaning of segregation. When most people refer to *integrated schools*, they are encompassing all schools serving both whites and blacks. Such a definition is deceptive, however. Consider the case of a city with only two high schools: School A has 2,000 students, only one of whom is black; School B's 1,000 students, on the other hand, are all black. By the usual criterion of biracial enrollment, School A would be regarded as integrated, yet the racial isolation common in both schools is surely of greater significance than School A's dubious claim to biracial enrollment.

A more meaningful concept of integration must refer to the proportion of students attending school with children of another race. From this perspective, we are able to identify the completeness of integration. Complete integration, of course, would be a situation where all black students attended school with white

TABLE 10.1   COLLEGE COMPLETION RATES, BY ETHNIC BACKGROUND, 1982

RACIAL/ETHNIC GROUP	PERCENT OF PERSONS 25 TO 29 YEARS OLD WHO HAVE COMPLETED AT LEAST 4 YEARS OF COLLEGE
Males	
Whites	25
Blacks	12
Hispanics	11
Females	
Whites	21
Blacks	13
Hispanics	9

Source: U.S. Bureau of the Census.

children, and vice versa. By this stricter definition of integration, the distinction between School A and School B disappears. For the city as a whole, we may say that only 0.1 percent of the black population attends school with whites. This is far more descriptive than saying that 50 percent of the city schools are integrated.

This broader concept of integration has tremendous significance for our perceptions of educational desegregation. Ten years after the Supreme Court's historic order to desegregate, the state of Florida boasted that nearly a third of its schools were integrated. Closer scrutiny revealed, however, that only 2.65 percent of Florida's black pupils were attending school with whites. Progress was even slower in other southern states.

Table 10.2 summarizes the extent of school integration across the country in 1980. This table reflects segregation not only of black students, but other minority students as well. The table indicates, for example, the percentage of minority students who attend schools that are comprised almost exclusively (80 to 100 percent) of minority students. Such extreme segregation was experienced by 38 percent of all minority students in 1980. Another 24 percent of all minority students attended schools that were predominantly (50 to 79 percent) minority. While there were significant regional variations, the basic segregation of educational facilities prevailed everywhere. Whether he or she lives in the North or the South, in the city or on a farm, a black, Hispanic, or other minority child is very unlikely to attend a truly integrated school. Racial isolation in the schools is still the hallmark of the American educational system.

One additional note of caution about the concept of integration is necessary. The concept of integration we have offered goes no further than the outer walls of the school, but even an ostensibly integrated school may be severely segregated within. Students may be assigned rooms, teachers, and facilities within the school on an explicitly racial basis. An extreme illustration of such internal segregation was encountered in Milwaukee. Like most other cities,

TABLE 10.2   SCHOOL INTEGRATION, 1980

REGIONAL	PERCENT OF MINORITY STUDENTS IN SCHOOLS WHERE ENROLLMENT IS:		
	80-100% MINORITY	50-79% MINORITY	LESS THAN 50% MINORITY
U.S. total	38	24	38
Northeast	53	18	29
Midwest	43	18	39
West	31	29	40
South	33	28	39
Border states	36	17	47

Source: U.S. Department of Education.

Milwaukee was prodded by the courts to integrate its schools. In part, integration was achieved by busing black pupils to previously white schools. The substance of educational opportunity was little changed, however. The bused-in black pupils were maintained in separate classrooms and bused back and forth to their old schools for lunch. Black students who lived close to the white schools were even required to proceed to the more distant black schools for bus transportation to the receiving schools!

Not all internal school segregation is as explicit and extreme as was the case in Milwaukee. A more popular and subtle form of segregation is embodied in the so-called *tracking systems*, under which the more able students are separated from the rest and provided special opportunities to advance, while the least able students are held back for intensive remedial work. What makes the system so racially discriminatory is the fact that black pupils have received inferior education prior to integration, so that using IQ tests or other achievement examinations to allocate pupils serves to perpetuate racial separation. A still subtler form of segregation within the classroom may prevail where teachers regard black pupils as innately or culturally incapable of attaining success.

Equality of Facilities

The statistics of Table 10.2, together with our observations on the nature of integration, provide a sobering view of our efforts to provide equal opportunity "with all deliberate speed." In light of that background, we may argue that blacks and other minorities still attend school separately from majority whites. How equal, then, are their separate opportunities?

A comparison of educational opportunities at the local level is easily made: Visit any black (or Mexican-American) school and any white (Anglo) school in the same city. You can readily detect enough qualitative differences in their educational environments to judge the relative attractiveness of the minority school. These local observations of school quality cannot be expanded across the country, however. It would be too expensive and time-consuming to visit all the school districts across the nation in order to assess the average quality of black and white schools. Even if we had enough time and money, our judgments would depend on the perspectives and standards of many different observers. Finally, any conclusions we reached would be limited to such statements as "white schools are better (or very much better)," with no clear indication of how great existing inequalities are. Accordingly, we are compelled to seek more objective, easily quantified measures of school quality.

In the most comprehensive survey of educational facilities ever undertaken, the U.S. Office of Education employed sixty-seven separate measures of school quality. These measures ranged from the number of books in the school library to the education of the teachers' mothers. They represented a concerted effort to capture and measure every dimension of the educational environment that might distinguish white schools from black schools. What the Office of Education discovered is that black and white schools differ on a multitude of separate measures but that such individual differences were relatively small. The only clear pattern to emerge from their mountain of statistics was that black schools tended to be most deficient in primarily academic facilities such as science labs, textbooks, and debate clubs.

In assessing these results, the Office of Education recognized many limitations in their approach. They reported that:

> The school environment of a child consists of many things, ranging from the desk he sits at to the child who sits next to him, and including the teacher who stands in front of his class. Any statistical survey gives only the most meager evidence of these environments, for two reasons. First, the reduction of the various aspects of the environment to quantitative measures must inherently miss many elements, tangible and more subtle, that are relevant to the child. The measures must be comparable from school to school; yet the elements which are experienced as most important by the child will likely differ from one school to another, and may well differ among children in the same school.

> Second, the child experiences his environment as a whole, while the statistical measures necessarily fragment it. Having a teacher without a college degree may indicate an element of disadvantage; but in the concrete situation, a schoolchild may be taught by a teacher who is not only without a college degree, but who has grown up and received his schooling in the local community, who has never been out of the State, who has a 10th-grade vocabulary, and who shares the local community's attitudes.

> For both these reasons, the statistical examination of difference in school environments for minority and majority children will give an impression of lesser differences than actually exist.[7]

We are left, then, with a very incomplete assessment of the school facilities available to whites and blacks. All we can say with certainty is that our everyday observations agree with the survey of the Office of Education in concluding that tangible (and intangible) differences in black and white educational facilities exist. We have no summary measure, however, of how large or how important those differences are.[8]

[7]U.S. Office of Education, *Equality of Educational Opportunity* (The Coleman Report) (Washington, DC: Government Printing Office, 1966), p. 37.

[8]For differing views on the importance of school inputs for educational achievement, see Christopher Jencks, et al., *Inequality* (New York: Basic Books, Inc.), 1972; and Anita A. Summers and Barbara L. Wolfe, "Do Schools Make a Difference?" *American Economic Review*, September 1977.

Inherent Inequalities

The Supreme Court provided a way out of this statistical ambiguity in 1954 by determining that segregated facilities were *inherently* unequal. The Court declared that "to separate them [black children] from others of similar age and qualifications solely because of their race generates a feeling of inferiority as to their status in the community that may affect their hearts and minds in a way unlikely ever to be undone."[9] The Court thus relegated the issue of tangible facilities to one of distinctly secondary importance. Even ostensibly "equal" schools for blacks and whites could never generate equal educational opportunity.

There were several specific considerations that led the Supreme Court justices to their landmark decision. They recognized that black pupils in segregated schools would have low self-esteem, knowing they were surrounded by failures and in schools regarded as inferior. Moreover, they would acquire a personal sense of futility knowing that, regardless of their individual attainments, they would always be identified by the community as members of a group viewed as less able, less successful, and less acceptable. Hence, the individual black child would see little reason to develop his individual talents. Community views would also affect the attitudes of teachers. Aware of, and probably sharing, the white community's low regard for blacks, teachers attached to black schools would tend to accept and transmit low expectations. They would not teach as much, or as well, to children deemed less teachable.

Impressive evidence in support of the Court's judgment was assembled by the U.S. Commission on Civil Rights in 1967. The Commission discovered that black pupils of similar backgrounds performed quite differently in varying racial situations. In particular, it found that black educational achievements increased substantially where schools were more thoroughly integrated. In addition to the fact that white schools were generally better, it was observed that black pupils benefited from integration by believing that their opportunities had improved and by seeing others succeeding around them. Discrimination, then, and more especially school segregation, were seen to be major determinants of black achievements and status.[10]

CLASS DISCRIMINATION IN EDUCATION

While blacks do suffer from serious and pervasive discrimination in the educational system, there is no reason to believe that they alone are singled out for substandard treatment. On the contrary, it is clear that other minority groups,

[9]*Brown* v. *Board of Education*, 347 U.S. 483 (1954).
[10]More recent evidence confirms the Court's view. See Congressional Budget Office, op. cit., pp. 10–11.

among them Mexican Americans, Puerto Ricans, and American Indians, confront barriers at least as formidable as do blacks. Accordingly, nearly everything we have said about racial discrimination against blacks applies with equal force to all minority group members. But including other minority groups in our discussion does not completely cover the subject of discrimination. As we are just beginning to perceive, racism has its counterpart in what has become known as *classism*. Poor individuals as a group, irrespective of their ethnic origin, are provided substandard facilities and opportunities in America.

We have already noted that many whites lose out as a result of racial discrimination in education, namely those who are not able to escape predominantly black neighborhoods and schools. But even where blacks are not present, poor whites may be confined to separate and substandard schools. Neighborhoods are even more likely to be homogeneous by income classes than by race; that is, poor families will be located in distinct areas of any city. Moreover, because school expenditures and decisions are determined by administrative bodies composed largely of the nonpoor, schools in low-income neighborhoods are likely to receive less than equal facilities.

Inequality of educational opportunities across income classes tends to be reinforced by the way schools are financed. Slightly over half of all elementary and secondary school expenditures are financed by local property taxes, with most of the remainder financed out of state revenues (only 10 percent of elementary and secondary school expenditures are financed out of federal revenues). This implies that children in poorer states and poorer school districts are provided with fewer resources. And so they are: in 1979–80, for example, average per pupil expenditure varied across states by nearly $2,000 (from a low of $1,741 in Alabama to $3,681 in New York). Within states, disparities across school districts are often just as large. In Georgia, Connecticut, Massachusetts, and California, high-spending school districts spend more than twice as much per pupil as do the school districts with lowest per pupil expenditure.[11] Because expenditures within a school district may also be distributed unequally, educational opportunities are unlikely to be the same for all income classes.

The analogy of class discrimination to racial discrimination goes beyond differences in school facilities. Like blacks, poor white children tend to be surrounded by families that have failed to achieve material success. Poor white children see few demonstrations of personal aspiration and talent leading to higher socioeconomic status. Furthermore, they are aware that society regards material success as a mark of personal worth and thus see themselves and their families as stigmatized by the larger community. They know, too, that their schools are inferior and that completion of their studies will leave them ill-

---

[11]Several state courts have ruled this pattern of school financing to be an unconstitutional denial of Fourteenth Amendment rights, but the U.S. Supreme Court failed to uphold such decisions (March 21, 1973).

prepared to compete in the labor market. As a consequence, they are likely to internalize a sense of futility and inferiority.

The cumulative impact of class discrimination is apparent in the educational attainments of lower-class children. Poor children drop out of high school at over twice the rate of nonpoor children. Even more startling is the fact that a substantial number of poor children leave the educational system even before they enter high school. And those relatively few lower-income children who do manage to make it through until high school graduation cannot depend on their abilities to get them into college. College admissions are still reserved for those who can support themselves or forego several years of employment income.

Table 10.3 provides some perspective on the barriers to higher education imposed by low incomes. This table includes all families with at least one child 18 to 24 years old. Within this group of families, the table indicates the percentage of families within each income class who have at least one child attending college full-time. For example, 49 percent of all high-income ($25,000 plus) families have at least one child in college. Among the lowest-income families (under $5,000), only 12 percent have a child in college. As the first row of Table 10.3 reveals, the likelihood of attending college increases markedly with family income.

Another notable feature of Table 10.3 is the absence of significant racial differences *within* income classes. Look at the group of families with incomes of $15,000–19,999, for example. Within this income class, black and Spanish-speaking youth are actually *more* likely to attend full-time college than (Anglo) white youth. Within other income classes, racial differences are negligible. This suggests that *racial* differences in educational opportunity may, in fact, reflect *class* differences. From this perspective, blacks and other minorities do worse than whites in the educational system because their families' incomes are generally lower.

TABLE 10.3   PERCENT OF YOUTH ATTENDING COLLEGE FULL-TIME, BY FAMILY INCOME AND RACE (1981)

	FAMILY INCOME						
GROUP	UNDER $5,000	$5,000- 9,999	$10,000- 14,999	$15,000- 19,999	$20,000- 24,999	$25,000 AND OVER	All FAMILIES
All youth	12	20	26	31	35	49	41
White	12	20	25	29	34	49	43
Black	12	19	28	34	39	39	29
Spanish-speaking	9	17	16	33	28	45	22

Source: U.S. Bureau of the Census.

The Question of Ability

It is generally assumed by the nonpoor that poor children do not attain higher educational status because they are uniformly less able, but there are some very obvious weaknesses in this assumption. For example, a very talented poor youngster has no control over his family's finances. Hence, if the family cannot afford either to forego his earnings or even to supply him with school clothes and lunches, he will not be able to take advantage of his "free" high school education. Furthermore, there are no scholarship or loan programs for high school students. So, we may anticipate that many talented poor children will never complete high school. Even for those who do attain high school diplomas, college admission will be barred by similar financial obstacles and by a legacy of inferior schooling.

It is not easy to determine how many bright, poor children are denied higher education because of their poverty. IQ tests remain our only standardized measure of ability, and those tests create problems for poor whites similar to those for blacks. Because their schools are substandard, poor whites fall increasingly far behind the nonpoor in educational performance. Hence, they demonstrate decreasing IQs over time, and it is difficult to discern how many originally bright children existed among the poor. And yet, even on the restrictive criterion of IQ tests, we can identify a large number of poor and able high school graduates who never attained a college degree.

As Table 10.4 reveals, the socioeconomic status of one's family has tremendous impact on a child's chances for college education. For any demonstrated level of twelfth-grade IQ, children from higher status families are far more likely to reach college graduation. What is especially noteworthy here is the comparatively small proportion (20 percent) of very able poor students who graduate from college. Children of lesser ability but more prosperous families take the places of the more gifted among the poor. Educational opportunity is distributed neither equally nor evenly on the basis of demonstrated ability.

Class discrimination in education, then, is a strong force in the educational

TABLE 10.4 COLLEGE GRADUATION RATES, BY SOCIOECONOMIC STATUS AND IQ (percent)

SOCIOECONOMIC STATUS	IQ SCORE		
	LOW	MIDDLE	HIGH
Low	1.8	5.4	19.6
Middle	2.1	9.5	27.4
High	2.9	17.9	46.7

Source: Bruce Eckland and Louis Henderson, *College Attainment—Four Years After High School* (Durham, NC: Research Triangle Institute, June 1981).

system and helps to determine the distribution of poverty. Whatever aggregate level of poverty exists, we may confidently predict that the children of the poor will be heavily overrepresented in the poverty statistics. It is also possible that class discrimination has become a stronger force in American society than racial discrimination. The U.S. Commission on Civil Rights, for example, found that schools were severely segregated by socioeconomic class and that the social class composition of schools is a stronger determinant of achievement than race. Moreover, there is mounting evidence that middle-class whites, if forced to choose, would prefer as neighbors middle-class blacks to poor whites. Poor persons, of whatever color, are least accepted by the larger society. This will be of little comfort to poor blacks and other minorities, of course, who are likely to be the subject of both racial and class discrimination.

SEX DISCRIMINATION IN EDUCATION

The educational handicaps of minority and lower-class groups are reasonably easy to document, but the disadvantages that women confront in the educational system are more subtle, at least in the early grades. The sex barriers that characterize primary and secondary educational systems consist of sex-typing certain kinds of curricula. Girls are encouraged to take home economics, foreign languages, and typing, while gently discouraged from taking manual crafts, business courses, and science. The barriers emanate both from school counselors—who want to be "realistic" about occupational goals—and, perhaps more importantly, from parents and peers attuned to certain expectations with respect to male and female roles in society. As the Carnegie Commission on Higher Education has noted:

> Almost from the moment of birth, boys and girls are subject to a wide variety of cultural influences that tend to prepare them for differentiated roles in life. Little girls are typically given dolls or miniature cooking utensils for toys; boys are generally given trucks and electric trains and mechanical toys. School readers show pictures of father going off to work and mother waving good-bye at the window, or of father playing baseball with his sons while mother bakes cookies. Girls play jump rope or tag on the school playground, while boys play ball. At about the seventh or eighth grade, boys take a course in manual training, while girls are taught cooking and sewing.
>
> We are not suggesting that matters ought to be reversed, or that little girls should be forbidden to play with dolls, but rather that there ought to be more freedom of choice. Girls who show signs of a mechanical bent should be given an opportunity to

play with mechanical toys and to enter the course on manual training. Boys should not be barred from courses on cooking and sewing if they are interested.[12]

This kind of acculturation tends to restrict the educational aspirations of female students and to frustrate them when they challenge those restrictions.

More explicit manifestations of sex discrimination in education have been apparent at the postcollege level. As suggested earlier, female college graduates have had difficulty gaining access to the professional schools that confer the necessary credentials for many desirable jobs. Secretarial schools have always been easy to get into, but law schools, medical schools, and business schools have often been a different story. Figure 10.2 depicts the proportion of different educational degrees awarded to women in 1979–1980. As is evident, women accounted for a very substantial percentage of graduate enrollments in educa-

FIGURE 10.2   Women in Education, 1979–1980

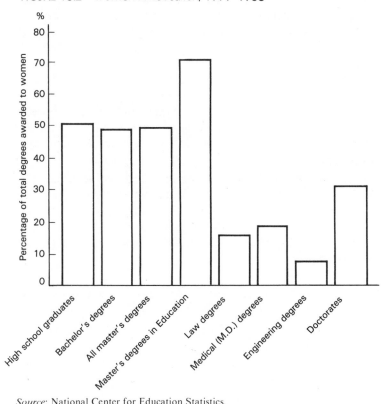

Source: National Center for Education Statistics.

[12]Carnegie Commission on Higher Education, *Opportunities for Women in Higher Education* (New York: McGraw-Hill Book Company, 1973), pp. 42–43.

tion schools, but were poorly represented in law or medicine, and virtually nonexistent in engineering schools.

To a large extent, this pattern of graduate education is the consequence of sex-differentiated roles and expectations nurtured from the crib to the campus. But these forces are reinforced at the graduate-admissions level by a tendency to reject female applicants with superior qualifications in favor of male applicants with lesser qualifications. Together these forces result in the fact that as recently as 1976 only 23 percent of female college graduates went on to graduate school, as compared with 28 percent of male graduates.

The same kind of observation has been made by the Council of Economic Advisers. In a special 1973 study on the economic role of women, the Council noted that although fewer women receive college and postcollege degrees:

> Even more striking are the differences in the courses taken. At both the undergraduate and advanced levels, women are heavily represented in English, languages, and fine arts—the more general cultural fields. They are poorly represented in disciplines having a strong vocational emphasis and promising a high pecuniary return. In 1970, 9.3 percent of the baccalaureates in business and 3.9 percent of the masters in business went to women. In the biological sciences, women had a larger share, taking about 30 percent of the bachelor's and master's degrees and 16 percent of the doctorates. But only 8.5 percent of the M.D.s and 5.6 percent of the law degrees went to women. Most of these percentages, low as they are, represent large gains from the preceding year.
>
> The situation is quite different in the so-called women's occupations. In 1971, women received 74 percent of the B.A.s and 56 percent of the M.A.s given in education. In library science, which is even more firmly dominated by women, they received 82 percent of all degrees in 1971. And in nursing 98 percent of all the degrees went to women.[13]

The implication of this pattern of sex discrimination is that women will enter the labor market with less valuable human capital than men.[14] As a

---

[13] *Economic Report of the President* (Washington, DC: Government Printing Office, 1973), pp. 101–2.

[14] This point was underscored by a 1975 report of the Carnegie Council on Policy Studies in Higher Education that identified underrecruitment of women to appropriate graduate programs as the major obstacle to greater equality of jobs in higher education.

consequence, we anticipate that a disproportionate number of women, especially those trying to raise families on their own, will end up in poverty.

SUMMARY

Discrimination on the basis of race, income class, or sex violates commonly accepted standards of social justice. Where discrimination is pervasive, the freedom of minority groups is severely restricted, as are their opportunities for achievement. Such limitations harm not only those discriminated against, but also the larger community. Talents go undeveloped, potential output is irrevocably lost, and markets are unnecessarily restricted.

In the American educational system, racial discrimination has resulted in a pattern of segregated and inferior schools for blacks and other minorites. Over one-third of all minority students continue to attend virtually all-minority elementary and secondary schools. The inferiority of the education these children receive derives not only from disparities in school facilities but, more importantly, from a sense of isolation and subjugation imposed by the white community. The consequences of this discrimination are manifest in the low educational attainments of minority youth.

As serious and pervasive as discrimination against minorities is, it is not the only kind of discrimination practiced in the educational system. Poor children, in particular, are maintained in schools segregated largely by socioeconomic class and provided with substandard facilities. They and their families are also stigmatized by the larger community for failure to attain material success. As a result, children of poor families drop out of school at alarming rates and generally lag behind nonpoor children in demonstrated achievement. Even those relatively few poor children who do demonstrate high levels of achievement are denied high levels of education. Class discrimination, then, is directly analogous to discrimination against racial or minority groups.

Finally, we must recognize that women are discriminated against in the educational system as well, even if such discrimination is more subtle. To the extent that such discrimination restricts later job opportunities, particularly for those women who end up as heads-of-household, it too contributes to the level and distribution of poverty.

Because educational attainments are a prime determinant of the distribution of poverty, those discriminated against in the schools are most likely to be among the poor. For whatever level of aggregate poverty exists, the children of yesterday's poor, blacks, and female-headed families will be grossly overrepresented in the poverty statistics. Children of poor black families headed by women will be the most disadvantaged, as they may be subjected to all forms of discrimination.

FURTHER READING

On the Nature of Discrimination

DOLLARD, JOHN. *Caste and Class in a Southern Town*. Garden City, NY: Doubleday & Company, Inc., 1957.

FRANKLIN, RAYMOND S., and SOLOMON RESNIK. *The Political Economy of Racism*. New York: Holt, Rinehart and Winston, 1973.

FRIEDMAN, MILTON. *Capitalism and Freedom*. Chicago: University of Chicago Press, 1962, Ch. 7.

KLUEGEL, JAMES R., and ELIOT R. SMITH. "Affirmative Action Attitudes: Effects of Self-Interest, Racial Effect, and Stratification Beliefs on Whites," *Social Forces*, March 1983.

MASSEY, DOUGLAS S. "Effects of Socioeconomic Factors on the Residential Segregation of Blacks and Spanish-Americans in U.S. Urbanized Areas," *American Sociological Review*, December 1979.

On Discrimination in Education

CONGRESSIONAL BUDGET OFFICE. *Inequalities in the Educational Experiences of Black and White Americans*. Washington, DC: Government Printing Office, 1977.

CORCORAN, MARY, and LINDA P. DACHTER, "Intergenerational Status Transmission and the Process of Individual Attainment," in *Five Thousand Families*, Vol. IX, Martha S. Hill, et. al., eds. Ann Arbor, MI: Institute for Social Research, 1981.

GOTTFREDSON, DENISE C., "Black-White Differences in the Educational Attainment Process: What Have We Learned?" *American Sociological Review*, October 1981.

JENCKS, CHRISTOPHER, et al. *Inequality*. New York: Basic Books, Inc., 1972, Ch. 2.

MICKELSON, ROSLYN ARLIN, "Social Stratification Processes in Secondary Schools: A Comparison of Beverly Hills High School and Morningside High School," *Journal of Education*, Fall 1980.

MOSTELLER, FREDERICK, and DANIEL P. MOYNIHAN, eds. *On Equality of Educational Opportunity*. New York: Random House, Inc., 1972.

SUMMERS, ANITA A., and BARBARA L. WOLFE. "Do Schools Make a Difference?" *American Economic Review*, September 1977.

Discrimination in the Labor Market

In 1927, a clothing manufacturer in New York City advertised for help with the following wage offer: "White Workers $24; Colored Workers $20."[1] His offer embodied one of the most flagrant forms of racial discrimination in the labor market; namely, the payment of unequal wages for equal work. Few employers are so blatant today, and certainly no one advertises his discriminatory practices in print anymore. Nevertheless, it is still believed that blacks and other minority workers do not receive equal treatment in the labor markets.

If minority workers are discriminated against in the labor market, they are denied full use of their productive abilities. As a consequence, their incomes will be depressed, and they will be heavily represented in the ranks of the poor. Hence, racial discrimination in the labor market tends to affect both the distribution and extent of poverty. In this chapter, we examine the consequences, forms, and practices of discrimination in the labor market. As in Chapter 10, we begin with a discussion of racial discrimination and then consider the phenomena of class and sex discrimination.

RACIAL DISCRIMINATION
IN THE LABOR MARKET

We know that there are tremendous disparities between the incomes of blacks and whites. In Chapter 2 we noted that one out of three blacks is poor compared

---

[1]Cited by Orley Ashenfelter, "Changes in Labor Market Discrimination Over Time," *Journal of Human Resources*, Fall 1970, pp. 403–30.

to only one out of nine whites. In Chapter 8, we observed that average black family incomes are $10,000 less than white incomes. Moreover, we have observed that racial or cultural theories cannot explain these inequalities. Thus, there are strong grounds for assuming that blacks continue to be the subject of discrimination, despite the lack of advertising to that effect.

It would be mistaken, however, to conclude that all existing income inequalities can be explained by discriminatory practices in the labor market. We know, for instance, that blacks enter the labor market with less human capital than whites as a result of racial discrimination in the schools. Accordingly, a labor market that rewarded all individuals only on the basis of demonstrated achievement would still provide less income for blacks than whites. A very high proportion of blacks also continue to live in the South, where employment levels and wages are generally lower. Hence, income disparities alone do not prove the existence of racial discrimination in the labor market; they simply create a presumption that discrimination will be discovered if sought.

Even if we find that income disparities continue to exist after we have accounted for educational and geographic differences, we cannot assert conclusively that discriminatory practices are rampant in the labor market. If discrimination against blacks ceased altogether, black workers would still be handicapped by past labor market discrimination. They would be less skilled and experienced and lower on seniority ladders, for example. As in the area of education, blacks would remain disadvantaged by past discrimination, even if present discrimination were eliminated.

The observed income disparities between whites and blacks, then, are potentially the result of three forces: nonmarket discrimination, past labor market discrimination, and present labor market discrimination. What we seek to identify in this section is that portion of existing income disparities attributable solely to continuing racial discrimination in the labor market.

Disparities in Earnings

White families have accumulated vast amounts of wealth in the form of property, savings accounts, bond holdings, and stock ownership. Stockholders' equity alone now amounts to over $1,300 billion, while another $4 trillion is tied up in savings, cash, government bonds, and other assets. Black families have comparatively little access to this wealth, as they have been denied equal opportunity to earn and accumulate money in the past. Thus, the average white family has six times as much wealth as the average black family.[2] Such disparities in wealth tend to overwhelm differences in income.

[2] Data on wealth are not very reliable. Estimates of black–white differences in wealth are contained in Henry S. Terrell, "Wealth Accumulation of Black and White Families: The Empirical Evidence," *Journal of Finance*, May 1971; and James D. Smith, ed., *The Personal Distribution of Income and Wealth* (New York: Columbia University Press, 1975). A more recent study suggests that racial differences in wealth may be much smaller; see William P. O'Hare, *Wealth and Economic Status* (Washington, DC: Joint Center for Political Studies, 1983).

For the most part, these differences in wealth do not reflect current labor market discrimination. They do, however, tend to distort comparisons of current white and black incomes. Current income includes money derived from accumulated wealth, especially money received in the form of dividends, interest, and capital gains. Accordingly, *total* income differences between blacks and whites are much larger than differences in *earnings*, that is, income derived from labor market activity. To assess the impact of racial discrimination in the labor market, then, we need to focus on racial disparities in earnings alone.

In 1982, the median earnings of white male workers aged 35-44 was $23,129. For black workers, the average was only $15,127, a mere 65 percent of white earnings. The earnings of Hispanic (Mexican American, Cuban, or Puerto Rican) workers were just slightly lower than those of black workers. In absolute terms, the earnings gap between (Anglo) white and minority workers was approximately $8,000 per year.

How much of this difference was due to discrimination in the labor market? To isolate the impact of racial discrimination on this disparity, we need to identify the influence of other earnings determinants. Education, skills, age, and geographic location all influence a person's earnings. Only by controlling for these other factors can we perceive the independent influence of racial discrimination in the labor market.

We have already noted the tremendous importance of educational attainments for income. Therefore, we must control for the influence on earnings of the nonmarket discrimination suffered in schools. This may be done by observing the comparative earnings of workers with equal educations. If there were no racial discrimination in the labor market, blacks, Hispanics, and whites with equal education should command approximately equal incomes. When this adjustment is actually made, however, the gap in earnings between white and minority workers is only partially closed. Table 11.1 shows that black and Hispanic workers earn less than white workers with equal educational credentials. Although the "adjusted" earnings gap closes somewhat, especially for college-educated workers, a substantial and unexplained earnings differential remains.

TABLE 11.1   MEDIAN EARNINGS, BY RACE AND EDUCATION FOR MEN AGED 35 TO 44, 1982

| | MEAN EARNINGS OF: | | |
EDUCATION	WHITE WORKERS	BLACK WORKERS	HISPANIC WORKERS
High school dropout	$15,903	$10,143	$13,561
High school graduate	21,636	15,884	17,745
Some college	25,136	18,050	21,139
College graduate	27,575	19,242	27,100

Source: U.S. Bureau of Labor Statistics.

To some extent, the earnings gaps remaining between white and minority workers of equal years of schooling might be explained by differences in the *quality* of schooling. Years of schooling do not have the same educational significance for blacks and whites (see Chapter 10). A complete adjustment for nonmarket discrimination would have to control for the significant differences in the *quality* of education received by each group. We must recognize that a typical black high school graduate comes to the job with as little educational preparation as the typical white high school dropout. When this additional control for nonmarket discrimination is imposed, observed labor market disparities shrink further. Black workers of equivalent educational backgrounds, including both quantity and quality of schooling, earn incomes approximately 90 percent as large as their white counterparts.

It appears, then, that most of the earnings disparity between whites and blacks can be attributed to prior (nonmarket) discrimination in the schools. This means that no more than half the observable earnings disparity can be explained by present labor market discrimination. Indeed, the combined influence of other factors, including skills, age, and region, reduce the disparity further. Recent studies of discrimination have estimated that only about one-fourth of existing earnings disparities are directly attributable to discriminatory labor market practices.[3] As a rough approximation, then, we may say that one-half of the $8,000 earnings disparity is due to nonmarket discrimination (education, residence); one-fourth due to past market discrimination (work skills and experience); and one-fourth to current labor market discrimination.

While nonmarket discrimination apparently overwhelms other types of discrimination, some caution is necessary in interpreting these conclusions. First, an annual earnings loss of $2,000 is a substantial setback to black workers. Racial discrimination in the labor market is, thus, a large and important racial barrier, even if outsized by discrimination in education. Furthermore, it cannot be assumed that these proportions are fixed. If, in fact, the quality and quantity of schooling for blacks increases—as they have in recent years—we have no assurance that black educational attainments will continue to be rewarded at the same rate. As more educated black workers emerge, racial discrimination in the labor market may intensify. Much potential discrimination in the labor market is now averted due to the fact that so few blacks are able to compete directly with whites. As black educational attainments—and thus labor market competition—increase, the situation may change dramatically. Accordingly, we

---

[3]See James Gwartney, "Changes in the Nonwhite/White Income Ratio, 1939–67," *American Economic Review*, December 1970; Leonard Weiss and Jeffrey G. Williamson, "Black Education, Earnings and Interregional Migration: Even Newer Evidence," *American Economic Review*, March 1975; James P. Smith and Finis Welch, "Race Differences in Earnings: A Survey and New Evidence" (Santa Monica, Calif.: Rand Corporation, 1978); and Stanley H. Masters, *Black-White Income Differentials* (New York: Academic Press, Inc., 1975). A more descriptive and less analytical study is in U.S. Commission on Civil Rights, *Unemployment and Underemployment Among Blacks, Hispanics, and Women* (Washington, DC: Government Printing Office, 1982).

have no firm basis for predicting a linear reduction of earnings disparities as educational opportunities become more equal. These calculations illustrate where the locus of discrimination is now; they cannot predict where it will be in the future.

Components of Earnings Disparities

While the image is provocative, it is mistaken to picture a thief called Discrimination openly robbing minority workers of $8,000 each year, even though the effect may be the same. Instead, we must realize that this income loss emerges from several dimensions of the labor market process. Minority workers are not robbed of their earnings outright. Very little of the discrimination that takes place in the labor market is of the sort exemplified by the New York garment manufacturer who paid different wages to white and black workers. Aside from being illegal, the visibility of such practices makes them especially vulnerable to public scrutiny and civil rights action. In addition, such overtly inequitable treatment violates the consciences of most employers. Rather, minority workers are hired less often, for fewer hours, for less desirable jobs, and at lower wages (see Figure 11.1). They are also offered less training on the job. The sum total of these different forces leaves the minority worker poorer. A more thorough understanding of discrimination is attained by considering the relative importance of each of these forces.

Because minority workers are less educated, less experienced, and less attractive to most employers than available white workers, they are least likely to be hired. In any given job situation white workers will be hired first and laid off last. Hence, the frequency of employment and the number of hours worked will differ for minority and white workers as the combined result of nonmarket and market racial discrimination. Indeed, a significant part of the observed earnings disparity derives not from the decision to pay minority workers lower wages but from the decision to employ them less often. Table 11.2 shows that black workers are more than twice as likely to be unemployed as are white workers. Black workers also tend to remain unemployed for a longer time.

FIGURE 11.1   Components of Earnings Disparities

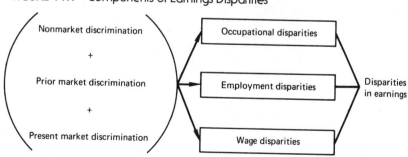

TABLE 11.2   UNEMPLOYMENT OF MALE WORKERS BY RACE, 1983

	WHITES	BLACKS	HISPANICS
Unemployment rate (%)	8.2	19.5	12.3
Average duration of unemployment (weeks)	15.0	18.4	13.4

Source: First quarter 1983 data from U.S. Bureau of Labor Statistics.

Hispanic workers also experience unemployment more frequently, although for shorter periods of time.

Of still greater significance to the observed earnings disparity is the decision to employ black and Hispanic workers at different kinds of jobs. Once again, all forms of discrimination take their toll. Minority workers are denied entrance to many occupations because they lack necessary educational attainments or credentials. They also often lack required work skills and experience. And finally, whites regard many jobs as being inappropriate for blacks and therefore exclude them. Garbage collection and bus driving are regarded as acceptable black or Hispanic occupations; retail sales, management, or even teaching are inappropriate. And only in the most dire of circumstances could most whites imagine trusting themselves to the services of a black doctor or lawyer (not to mention a female one of any race). Accordingly, most minority workers are largely excluded from full participation in the more pleasant and remunerative occupations. Table 11.3 indicates the general nature of existing occupational patterns.

White workers of either sex are much more likely to hold white-collar jobs than are minority workers. The very small percentage of black and Hispanic

TABLE 11.3   OCCUPATIONAL STATUS, BY RACE AND SEX, 1982 (percent)

	MALE WORKERS		FEMALE WORKERS	
OCCUPATIONAL STATUS	WHITE	MINORITY	WHITE	MINORITY
White collar	45.4	31.4	68.5	52.5
Professional and technical	17.0	12.7	18.0	15.7
Managers and administrators	15.6	7.4	8.0	3.9
Sales workers	6.8	2.9	7.4	3.3
Clerical workers	6.1	8.4	35.1	29.7
Blue collar	42.0	48.8	12.1	17.1
Craftsmen	20.8	15.9	2.1	1.5
Operatives	9.5	13.5	8.2	13.5
Transport drivers	5.2	7.6	0.7	0.7
Nonfarm laborers	6.5	11.8	1.2	1.5
Service workers	8.4	17.1	18.1	29.7
Farm workers	4.1	2.7	1.2	0.6

Source: U.S. Bureau of Labor Statistics.

workers in managerial and administrative jobs is especially noteworthy. Apparently, minority workers seldom have the opportunity to be the boss.

Occupational disparities are further aggravated by the fact that minority workers who do gain access to the better occupations end up in the lowest and least desirable jobs *within* each occupational group. Within the professional, technical, and managerial class, for example, white workers tend to be lawyers, doctors, engineers, and social scientists. Black workers, on the other hand, are more likely to be funeral directors, welfare workers, and teachers in segregated schools. The same situation exists in the other occupational categories, sometimes in even more extreme form. For example, among clerical workers are grouped both white insurance adjusters and black postal clerks, among salesworkers both white stockbrokers and Puerto Rican sales clerks. In other words, the tremendous disparities evident in occupational distributions reveal only a relatively small proportion of the job barriers that actually confront minority workers.

At the bottom of the occupational ladder, the respective concentrations of blacks and whites are, of course, reversed. As Table 11.3 reveals, two-thirds of all black workers are concentrated in the lower occupational categories, and, again, the disparities in actual jobs are great. Black women are maids in private homes or maids in hotels and office buildings. Black men are bootblacks, elevator operators, porters, and janitors. The better service and blue-collar jobs, including fire fighters, police, bartenders, and teamsters, are largely reserved for whites. The fact that minority workers are employed less often and for fewer hours is of relatively little significance in comparison with this uneven distribution of occupational opportunities.

Job disparities *within* occupational categories are reflected in earnings. Table 11.4 displays the weekly earnings of whites, blacks, and Hispanics working in the same occupational category. Within the professional and technical occupations, for example, the typical majority white worker earns $443 per week, substantially more than blacks ($352) or Hispanics ($386) working in the same broad occupational category. These disparities reflect the fact that minority workers hold different *jobs* within a given occupation, are likely to be more concentrated in certain *industries*, and may be paid less for the same work.

Another disparity between majority and minority workers relates to training. Workers in the U.S. economy get most of their skill training on the job. This on-the-job training provides the basis for both job security and later advancement. In general, the more training an employer "invests" in a worker, the faster the worker is likely to advance on the job. The additional human capital acquired also makes a worker more attractive to other employers.[4]

The amount of training actually received by whites is nearly double that received by minority workers. White workers report that they are more likely to

[4]The impact of OJT training on wage offers is discussed in Bradley R. Schiller, "Corporate Kidnap of the Small-Business Employee," *The Public Interest*, Summer 1983.

TABLE 11.4   WEEKLY EARNINGS, BY OCCUPATION AND RACE, 1981

	MEDIAN WEEKLY EARNINGS OF FULL-TIME MALE WORKERS		
	WHITE	BLACK	HISPANIC
White collar			
Professional and technical	$443	$352	$386
Managers and administrators	471	391	381
Sales workers	372	249	286
Clerical workers	335	286	280
Blue collar			
Craftsmen	$364	$314	$304
Operatives	304	267	231
Transport drivers	319	258	261
Nonfarm laborers	247	220	225
Service workers	$245	$214	$190
Farm workers	$185	$154	$191

Source: Earl F. Mellor and George D. Stamas, "Usual Weekly Earnings: Another Look at Intergroup Differences and Basic Trends," *Monthly Labor Review,* April 1982.

receive on-the-job training and to get it for a longer period of time.[5] As a consequence, observed disparities in occupations and earnings may understate eventual income differences.

Who Discriminates?

It is not easy to visualize so much discrimination taking place in the labor market. It is even more difficult to picture those persons or groups who actually engage in discrimination. Very few of us can readily identify anyone as an outright racist. The whole notion of purposeful maltreatment simply runs counter to the way we are accustomed to viewing ourselves or the market place. Nevertheless, employers, unions, employees, employment agencies, and training programs are all implicated in the charge of labor market discrimination. To understand how so many individuals and groups are involved, we must return to the nature of discrimination.

Much market discrimination is unintended. Even persons free of prejudice or animosity may engage in discriminatory patterns of behavior. While such unintentional practices make fewer headlines, their impact on minority employment opportunities is no less important. Traditional company recruitment practices provide a simple illustration. Most companies, large or small, rely heavily on existing employees for new recruits. If new jobs open up, present employees usually are able to locate friends or relatives who want the new positions, and a word-of-mouth recruitment system is remarkably efficient.

[5]Saul D. Hoffman, "On-the-Job-Training: Differences by Race and Sex," *Monthly Labor Review,* July 1981.

Present employees know the company, the jobs, and the applicants; therefore, they are in a position to match jobs and people accurately. Word-of-mouth recruitment is also inexpensive; no outside agencies need be contacted, and advertisement costs are kept to a minimum. Large companies are so impressed with this recruitment system that they offer bonuses to employees who bring in new workers.

Word-of-mouth recruitment practices, although efficient, tend to exclude minority workers from better jobs. Would-be minority applicants do not have a network of friends in better employment positions. Accordingly, they are seldom aware of developing opportunities and are rarely brought to the attention of recruitment personnel. Even in the absence of willful discrimination, they are effectively cut off from new jobs.

Recruitment outside the firm does not always yield much better results. Companies are generally unfamiliar with the people and skills available in minority residential areas, especially ghetto areas. They do not know who, how, or where to recruit. As a result, they tend to rely on traditional sources and agencies of recruitment more readily accessible to whites. Would-be minority applicants also experience a certain hesitancy in approaching unfamiliar companies or employment agencies. Knowing that prejudice exists and having possibly confronted explicit discrimination themselves, minority job-seekers are often reluctant to risk embarrassment or harassment. They rely, instead, on familiar sources and companies with established reputations in the community for fair treatment. Recent converts to equal employment opportunity have difficulty communicating their new intentions.

While these institutionalized patterns of behavior constitute a barrier to truly equal employment opportunity, we cannot ignore the impact of overt discrimination. Not all discriminatory practices are innocent. Some persons and groups willfully exclude minority workers from employment opportunities. Here we can only review the most obvious and widespread examples.

The Unions

Labor unions are a popular target for attack on many fronts, the subject of racial discrimination included. Unions are widely believed to constitute the greatest barrier between minority workers and improving employment opportunities. Labor unions are large, highly visible, and often contain outspoken racist members. They also tend to control access to the better-paid jobs for which minority job-seekers are presently most qualified. High-status employment areas of lesser union strength, among them clerical, technical, and professional work, tend to require higher educational credentials. Hence, unions are in a position to provide the fastest route to improved economic status.

The history of labor unions is not very encouraging. While the American Federation of Labor (AFL) was founded on the principles of racial and worker solidarity, its practices quickly departed from that philosophy. As early as 1895, nine years after its inception, the AFL compromised on the issue of racial equality by admitting deliberately discriminatory unions. By 1899 the AFL was even admitting unions whose constitutions explicitly forbade black membership, thereby forsaking even the pretense of racial equality. This development was particularly damaging to black workers, because the AFL was strongest in those areas where black employment skills were concentrated—namely the crafts, such as carpentry, blacksmithing, and mechanical arts. Indeed, at the time of the Civil War black workers dominated craft employment in the South, outnumbering white craftsmen five to one. As the craft union movement grew, however, blacks lost their foothold in the job market. Black craftsmen were forced out of their jobs and denied access to new ones. Apprenticeship programs were also closed, thereby eliminating future opportunities for employment.

While racial prejudice was clearly at the root of much union discrimination, there is abundant evidence that economic motivations were dominant. The nascent unions knew that their strength and welfare depended on their ability to control job entry. Any potential craftsman was viewed as a direct economic threat. The AFL unions not only sought to eliminate existing and potential competition from blacks but also worked vigorously to restrain all immigration from abroad. The Chinese were viewed as "people of vice and sexual immorality who were incompatible with our moral concepts."[6] Japanese and Koreans were no less undesirable. Even European immigrants were viewed as a threat to economic security and organizational strength. Hence, it is probably fair to conclude that the AFL was egalitarian in its discriminatory practices; that is, it discriminated against all potential competition with little regard to race, creed, or color! Where racial arguments were employed, their primary purpose was to camouflage narrower economic interests. Nevertheless, black workers were most abused, since they were the largest and closest competition.

The Congress of Industrial Organizations (CIO) emerged in 1935 in a changed economic climate and with a different constituency. Whereas the AFL had focused on craft labor, the CIO directed its attentions to the mass of workers on assembly lines and in less skilled jobs. These jobs generally required less training and experience and were concentrated more in the North. Not only were blacks significantly represented in these jobs, they also constituted an enormous threat to future union strength. If excluded from the industrial unions, black workers could be used by employers as strikebreakers to undercut union power. The same possibility did not exist in craft unions because specific skills were required for available jobs. Hence, the CIO had a powerful economic incentive to lower racial barriers to union entry. This, combined with the egalitarian outlook of its leaders, especially John L. Lewis, led the CIO to establish nondiscriminatory membership policies.[7]

[6]Cited by Herbert Hill in Arthur M. Ross and Herbert Hill, eds., *Employment, Race, and Poverty* (New York: Harcourt Brace Jovanovich, Inc. 1967), p. 389.

[7]The tendency of craft unions to be more discriminatory continues today. See Orley Ashenfelter, "Racial Discrimination and Trade Unionism," *Journal of Political Economy*, May 1972; and

The AFL-CIO merger in 1955 did not revolutionize union practices. While the new union was founded on stronger antidiscrimination principles, it did little to alter the actual practices of local affiliates, especially the older AFL locals. Local unions retain a broad range of autonomy, and the national leadership has little power or incentive to discipline them on the subject of racial equality. Consequently, black workers continue to be excluded from many unions and relegated to inferior jobs or separate seniority lines when admitted. Experienced black workers are oftentimes required to undergo long and low-paid apprenticeship courses as a condition for union entry; inexperienced black workers find that they cannot enter apprenticeship programs at all.

Employers

Like unions, business management tends to reflect the interests and attitudes of its members: Some employers harbor racial prejudices and stereotyped views of minority workers. Even more prevalent, however, is a general reluctance to engage in actions that are controversial or merely tangential to primary business pursuits. Employers are hesitant to challenge traditional hiring practices or to confront what they regard as the community's racial attitudes. Hence, employers will often ignore potential minority workers, not as a result of their own prejudice, but because they fear that such hiring will trigger the prejudices of white employees or existing customers.[8] Employers have very little incentive to stir up racial troubles or even to bother determining whether such troubles would actually emerge. Profits, politics, recreation, and even the community chest command more attention and commitment. As a result, only the most cautious antidiscriminatory actions are undertaken, and then usually only as a result of economic or social pressures, such as boycotts or legal action.

Another barrier to more affirmative action on the part of business management arises from the nature of collective bargaining. Where management does, in fact, decide to hire minority workers on a more equal basis, the unions are likely to demand reciprocal concessions. Unions tend to view management's initiatives as an encroachment on their own prerogatives. Altered hiring practices are interpreted as a concession to management, so the union seeks compensation in other areas, chiefly in wages or working conditions. Thus, the cost of affirmative action escalates, and management is even less likely to press for the elimination of discriminatory employment patterns.[9]

Duane E. Leigh, "Racial Discrimination and Labor Unions," *Journal of Human Resources*, Fall 1978. The general impact of unions on racial inequality is examined in E.M. Beck, "Labor Unionism and Racial Income Inequality: A Time-Series Analysis of the Post-World War II Period," *American Journal of Sociology*, Vol. 85, 1980.

[8]The productivity of white males may also decline if newly-hired minority workers upset traditional on-the-job social relations; see Barbara Bergmann and William Darity, Jr., "Social Relations, Productivity, and Employer Discrimination," *Monthly Labor Review*, August 1981.

[9]Large, highly unionized firms in concentrated industries apparently do discriminate more than other firms. See Walter Haessel and John Palmer, "Market Power and Employment Discrimination," *Journal of Human Resources*, Fall 1978.

Just how cautiously management may proceed in the area of race relations was amply demonstrated in Birmingham, Alabama, during the early 1960s. While managers in several steel companies there made some progress in formal hiring and promotion practices, they were reluctant to tamper with the vestiges of Jim Crow. White and Colored signs were removed from drinking fountains and bathhouses, but twin facilities were maintained. Naturally, no workers took it upon themselves to integrate the newly desegregated facilities.

Finally, even "objective" hiring practices of employers may have discriminatory effects. We have already observed how word-of-mouth recruitment and traditional advertising may tend to exclude minority workers. Another obstacle emerges from the use of employment tests and other credentials as hiring criteria. All too often, test and educational credentials used to screen out prospective employees exclude a disproportionate number of minority workers. Moreover, such tests may have no direct relationship to job performance. Under such circumstances, the tests simply reduce an employer's hiring costs by reducing the number of extended interviews. In the process, however, many minority workers lose potential job opportunities. Such nonfunctional tests were outlawed by the U.S. Supreme Court in 1972 (*Griggs* v. *Duke Power Company*), but have not been eliminated completely.

Even if all such tests were eliminated, minority workers would still suffer from "statistical discrimination." In reality, employers do not know for sure which job-seekers will turn out to be the best employees. Tests and educational credentials are used to help reduce such uncertainty. If all such screening criteria are eliminated, employers may rely more on racial characteristics. Because white workers have, on average, more education, skill, and experience than minority workers, an employer is statistically "safer" in hiring white workers. In other words, screening out minority workers on the basis of their lower *average* qualifications may be an efficient recruitment technique, particularly if no surer screening mechanisms are available. In this case, minority workers are excluded from equal consideration on statistical grounds, not because of employer prejudice.[10] Of course, to the minority job-seeker, the end result is the same.

CLASS DISCRIMINATION
IN THE LABOR MARKET

Minority racial groups are not the only workers who suffer discrimination in labor markets. Racial discrimination has a counterpart in class discrimination. In this case, individuals from low-income backgrounds are consistently denied equal access to better jobs and pay.

[10]The concept of "statistical" discrimination is discussed in Edmund S. Phelps, "The Statistical Theory of Racism and Sexism," *American Economic Review*, September 1972; and Dennis J. Aigner and Glen G. Cain, "Statistical Theories of Discrimination in Labor Markets," *Industrial and Labor Relations Review*, January 1977.

Employers, like the larger society, tend to have low estimates of the capabilities of job applicants who are poorly dressed or from "bad" neighborhoods. There is an underlying conviction that poverty reflects personal inadequacy (Flawed Characters). As a result, poor applicants are viewed differently than others and must exhibit exceptional talents to obtain competitive jobs. If their talents are only equal to, say, middle-class applicants, then prejudice is likely to deny employment to the poor. Prejudices are reinforced, of course, by the use of academic achievement tests that often have little or no relation to the content of the available job.

These discriminatory practices are often institutionalized in the recruitment procedures of companies. As we noted earlier, corporations tend not to recruit in poverty areas. They know virtually nothing about available talent in poor neighborhoods and expend little effort to increase their knowledge. As a consequence, poor job-seekers and company recruiters seldom make contact. The same kind of isolation results from the word-of-mouth recruitment practices previously mentioned. Like blacks generally, poor whites tend to have comparatively few friends or acquaintances employed at higher-status jobs. They thus have little knowledge of or access to good jobs that are opening up. What jobs they hear of are those they have always encountered: dirty, low-paid, and menial.

Class discrimination in the labor market, then, means that poor job-seekers have less chance to obtain employment than nonpoor job-seekers of equal ability. Racial discrimination has the same effect for blacks and other minority groups, sex discrimination the same effect for women. In all cases, discrimination takes place as a result of individual prejudices and institutionalized practices. The poor, like blacks, have many personal characteristics and backgrounds unfamiliar to middle-class employers, employment agencies, and even unions. Conduct, speech, and dress are among those factors that create communication barriers. Employers tend to see these differences as indicators of ability rather than as the result of socioeconomic environment. It is assumed that the poor will not be as able or dependable on the job. Workers are not sought from poorer areas and, when they come forth, are unfavorably considered.[11]

SEX DISCRIMINATION IN THE LABOR MARKET

The same forces that tend to constrain the earnings of minorities and lower-income classes also operate to limit the employment and income opportunities of women. Here again, we must take into account the fact that women enter the labor market with less human capital than men do, especially when measured in terms of advanced degrees. They also tend to be trained for different kinds of

[11]Some of the intergenerational effects of inequality are explored in John A. Brittain, *The Inheritance of Economic Status* (Washington, DC: The Brookings Institution, 1977).

work, as a result of both societal pressures and overt discrimination in the educational system. These handicaps help explain why women exhibit less labor force participation, inferior occupations, and lower pay. But such handicaps do not provide a complete explanation, because female workers additionally suffer from limited access to jobs for which they are otherwise qualified.

As we noted in our discussion of racial discrimination (see Table 11.3), occupational segregation is a major source of earnings disparities. This tendency is especially important for women as well, as they tend to be relegated to a limited number of occupations and an even more limited number of jobs within each occupation. The statistics in Table 11.5 provide a clue as to how high the sex barriers are when one begins to examine the labor market in some detail. Within the "professional and technical" occupational category, for example, we discover that there are clearly "female jobs" and "male jobs": 97 percent of all registered nurses are women, while only 2 percent of our engineers are women. The same kind of imbalance is evident throughout the list.

Nor is this the end of the story. Even within the more detailed occupations of Table 11.5, men and women tend to be employed at different kinds of jobs, in different industries, or in different work settings. Consider just one example, that of waiters and waitresses. Women comprise a whopping 89 percent of that category, but how many of them are employed in the best restaurants (where prices and tips are highest, incidentally)? Very few.

These male-female job disparities *within* occupational groups result in sharply different wages for men and women. The median weekly earnings of full-time female workers ($227 in 1981) is only two-thirds of male workers ($347). The same kind of differential exists within most occupations.[12] Like minorities, women are also less likely to receive OJT training that will increase their responsibilities and wages.

A popular explanation for these job and pay disparities is the lesser labor force attachment of women. Most women who do work either start their careers after having children or interrupt their careers for that purpose. The job interruption that typically accompanies childbirth translates into lost job experience and thus less human capital development, at least from a labor market point of view. Can't this "natural" barrier to female productivity explain occupational and income differentials?

Partially, but *only* partially. As the President's Council of Economic Advisers has observed:

One important factor influencing the (earnings) differential is experience. The lack of continuity in women's attachment to the labor force means that they will not have accumulated as much experience as men at a given age. The relatively steeper

---

[12]Nancy F. Rytina, "Earnings of Men and Women: A Look at Specific Occupations," *Monthly Labor Review*, April 1982.

TABLE 11.5   A NONLIBERATED LABOR FORCE (percent)

	THE JOBS THAT WOMEN HOLD	PROPORTION OF JOBS HELD BY WOMEN	THE JOBS THAT WOMEN DON'T HOLD	PROPORTION OF JOBS HELD BY WOMEN
Professional and technical	Librarians	82	Engineers	2
	Registered nurses	97	Lawyers and judges	5
	Elementary teachers	84	Doctors	9
	Dieticians	92	Clergy	3
Managers and administrators	Restaurants, cafeterias, and bars	34	Public agencies	6
Salesworkers	Demonstrators	91	Sales representatives	7
Clerical and kindred workers	Secretaries	97	Mail carriers	8
	Bank tellers	86	Shipping clerks	15
	Telephone operators	95	Dispatchers	17
Craftsmen	Bookbinders	58	Electricians	2
	Decorators	58	Telephone linemen and service	3
Operatives	Dressmakers	95	Taxicab drivers	6
	Laundry and dry cleaning	70	Truckdrivers	2
Service	Practical nurses	96	Police officers	4
	Waitresses	89	Bartenders	21

Source: Council of Economic Advisers, *Economic Report of the President* (Washington, DC: Government Printing Office, 1973), Table 33.

rise of men's income with age has been attributed to their greater accumulation of experience, of "human capital" acquired on the job.

(But) a differential, perhaps on the order of 20 percent, between the earnings of men and women remains after adjusting for factors such as education, work experience during the year, and even lifelong work experience.[13]

Accordingly, we cannot dismiss occupational and earnings differentials between men and women on the basis of "natural" responsibilities of childbirth. Discrimination is clearly at work here: The pay and job status of women workers

[13]*Economic Report of the President* (Washington, DC: Government Printing Office, 1973), pp. 104–6. See also Nancy F. Rytina, "Tenure as a Factor in the Male-Female Earnings Gap," *Monthly Labor Review*, April 1982; and Paula England, "The Failure of Human Capital Theory to Explain Occupational Sex Segregation," *Journal of Human Resources*, Summer 1982.

are being constrained by exclusionary employment practices. Moreover, we must take care to note that the same kind of negative feedbacks that constrain the human capital development of blacks affect women, too. Why should a woman postpone childbirth or pursue a lengthy and difficult course of study if it appears that she will not receive commensurate rewards in the labor market? Role differentiation and labor market discrimination tend to reinforce each other.[14]

SUMMARY

Minority racial groups, women, and the poor generally start out in the labor market at a distinct competitive disadvantage, largely as a result of discrimination in the educational system. Their handicaps do not end there, however. In the labor market itself, these groups do not even have an equal opportunity to make the best of their disadvantaged beginnings. Prejudice and institutional employment practices combine to handicap them still further.

Racial and class discrimination in the labor market takes many forms. Some employers and unions willfully exclude blacks. Others, perhaps less prejudiced, rely on recruitment procedures that have the same effect on minority racial groups, women, and the poor. Doubts about the capabilities of individuals who fall into any of these categories also limit employment and promotional possibilities. Notions of what kind of work is "proper" for blacks and fear of employee or community disapproval restrains even unprejudiced, but profit-maximizing, employers from providing equal opportunity. The cumulative impact of these practices is evident: Members of minority or poor populations end up working less often, for fewer hours, at less attractive jobs—and, ultimately, for less income.

FURTHER READING

BRIGGS, VERNON M., JR., WALTER FOGEL, and FRED H. SCHMIDT.   *The Chicano Worker.* Austin, TX: University of Texas, 1977.

CORCORAN, MARY, and GREG J. DUNCAN.   "Work History: Labor Force Attachment, and Earnings Differences Between the Races and Sexes," *Journal of Human Resources*, Winter 1979.

DACHTER, LINDA P.   "Race/Sex Differences in the Effects of Background on

---

[14]This point and additional criticism of the *Economic Report*, cited above, are contained in Barbara Bergmann and Irma Adelman, "The Economic Role of Women: A Review," *American Economic Review*, September 1973.

Achievement," in *Five Thousand American Families*, Vol. IX, Martha S. Hill, et. al., eds. Ann Arbor, MI: Institute for Social Research, 1981.

DARRITY, WILLIAM, JR. "The Human Capital Approach to Black-White Earnings Inequality," *Journal of Human Resources*, Winter 1982.

MARSHALL, RAY. "The Economics of Racial Discrimination: A Survey," *Journal of Economic Literature*, September 1974.

NATIONAL RESEARCH COUNCIL. *Women, Work, and Wages: Equal Pay for Jobs of Equal Value.* Washington, DC: National Academy Press, 1981.

SOWELL, THOMAS. *Markets and Minorities.* New York: Basic Books, 1981.

U.S. COMMISSION ON CIVIL RIGHTS. *Unemployment and Underemployment Among Blacks, Hispanics, and Women.* Washington, DC: Government Printing Office, 1982.

Income Maintenance Policies

Income transfer payments are amounts of money transferred from one person to another through the medium of government taxes and payments. Given their apparent simplicity, they are often proposed as the most compelling and obvious solution to poverty. Simply give the poor enough money, it is argued, and poverty will disappear. Among others, economist Milton Friedman and urbanologist Irving Kristol have questioned whether our public commitment to end poverty is sincere in light of our failure to provide the obvious remedy.[1]

The apparent simplicity of income transfer solutions to poverty is deceptive, however. We could, of course, provide enough money to close the poverty gap, the difference between what the poor now have (including existing income transfers) and what they need to maintain minimum standards of living. In 1982 that gap was only $43 billion, less than 2 percent of the nation's total output.

The transfer of another $43 billion to the poor—were it politically feasible—could create significant problems, however. First, exclusive reliance on income transfers as a "solution" to poverty serves to perpetuate the poverty problem. If an expansion of income transfers is adopted as an alternative to expansionary aggregate demand policies and increased efforts to expand and equalize educational opportunities, there will be as many people in need of public assistance next year as there were this year. In other words, income transfers do not reduce "latent poverty" (Chapter 2). The added income makes life easier for the poor, of course, but otherwise leaves their educational and employment opportunities unchanged. Income transfers are, therefore, best

---

[1]Recall that other observers argue that we *have* eliminated poverty with income transfers, particularly in-kind transfers; see Chapter 2.

viewed as an interim form of support, especially for those who are in a position to benefit from increased education or employment opportunities.[2]

Even on a temporary basis, however, income transfers give rise to problems. Suppose that we guaranteed everyone an income equal to the 1982 poverty standard. This would amount to approximately $9,862 for a family of four (or approximately $11,000 in 1984 dollars). Any family earning less than this amount would receive an income transfer payment to make up the difference, thus bringing everybody up to the established minimum standard. We would clearly eliminate the existing poverty problem with this approach, but we would create a few new problems in the process. Persons just above the poverty line—for example, those working at dead-end, low-paying jobs—would have strong incentive to abandon employment and join the ranks of the nonworking poor. The decision to work is largely a response to the financial and psychological rewards associated with employment. People in dull, dirty, low-paying jobs get little of either. By quitting their jobs, declaring themselves poor, and accepting a guaranteed transfer payment income, they would gain much more leisure at minimal financial or psychological cost. Similarly, people already counted as poor would have an incentive to substitute public transfers for whatever employment income they already possessed. This is the kind of behavior former Treasury Secretary William Simon had in mind in 1975 when he characterized our transfer programs as a "haven for the chiselers and rip-off artists."[3] Accordingly, we must recognize that the provision of income transfers may conflict with established work incentives, and consequently that both the observed size of the poverty population and the need for income transfers may be sensitive to the particular form our income transfer policies take.

These basic problems of income transfer have led to a proliferation of income maintenance programs. Some programs provide income for persons on the basis of need alone, while others provide transfers on the basis of previous contributions. When you pay Social Security taxes, for example, you are providing income transfers for the elderly while establishing your right to receive such transfers in old age. Other programs demand no such contributions. To receive benefits from state general assistance programs, you need only be poor and unable to obtain employment or other support. In this case, money is transferred from the taxpaying public directly to those in need.

Those income maintenance programs that provide assistance on the basis of need alone are usually referred to collectively as "the welfare system." Although many people tend to think of welfare as one big, centrally adminis-

---

[2]If the education and employment opportunities are slow in coming, however, the "interim" support may have to continue for a long time. In the interim the children of the poor will at least benefit from improved nutrition and shelter.

[3]August 12, 1975, address to the Junior Achievement conference in Bloomington, Indiana. Simon's characterization was strongly challenged by many, including Senator George McGovern (*Washington Post*, August 13 and 14, 1975).

tered program, the realities of welfare are very different. First, the welfare system is composed of two distinctly different kinds of assistance. Some programs provide *cash assistance* to the poor, while others provide *in-kind assistance*— things like housing, food, and medical services. Furthermore, within each classification there are a variety of programs, each with its own characteristics, regulations, and objectives. We begin our analysis of income maintenance policies by examining welfare programs.

WELFARE: THE CASH ASSISTANCE PROGRAMS

Table 12.1 provides a summary view of the major programs that provide cash assistance to the poor. The three programs listed in the table are directed to very different population groups. The federal Supplemental Security Income (SSI) program was established for the aged, the blind, and the permanently disabled. It was introduced in July 1973, and took the place of three previous programs.[4] As of 1983 it was providing cash assistance to about 4 million people at an estimated annual cost of approximately $7 billion. By contrast, the federal–state Aid to Families with Dependent Children (AFDC) program was serving more than 11 million people in the spring of 1983, at an annual cost of roughly $11 billion. The third program, General Assistance (GA), is operated solely under state and local auspices to provide help to those who are poor but do not fit one of the other two categories.

Inadequacies

The statistics provided in Table 12.1 suggest that we are giving a lot of money to a lot of people. Hence, it is not too surprising that in the minds of most

TABLE 12.1   CASH ASSISTANCE PROGRAMS, 1983

PROGRAM	NUMBER OF CURRENT RECIPIENTS	AVERAGE BENEFIT PER RECIPIENT (per month)	TOTAL ANNUAL PAYMENTS (billions)
Supplemental Security Income (SSI)	4,019,000	$183	$ 7.3
Aid to Families with Dependent Children (AFDC)	11,164,000	$ 99	$11.1
General Assistance (GA)	1,001,000	$144	$ 1.4
Total	16,184,000		$19.8

Source: U.S. Department of Health and Human Services.

[4]The SSI program was enacted as part of the 1972 Social Security Act Amendments and consolidated the Old Age Assistance (OAA), Aid to the Blind (AB), and Aid to the Permanently and Totally Disabled (APTD) programs.

hard-working taxpayers welfare conjures up visions of the easy life—a can of beer on a hot afternoon, color television at night. As we noted earlier, former Treasury Secretary Simon characterized welfare programs as a "haven for the chiselers and rip-off artists," while former President Nixon referred to welfare as a "free ride." But it is clear from actual welfare experience that very few welfare families are even tolerably comfortable, much less riding high. The typical AFDC family (mother and two or three children), for example, received only $3,600 of cash assistance in 1983, approximately half the amount the government has determined such families need. A budget that small simply does not go far, no matter how thinly it is spread. Just recall how little food, shelter, and clothing is provided by the much larger poverty budget. It would be a strange individual who forsook any but the poorest paying and most loathsome job for such a "free ride."

Table 12.2 shows a recent monthly budget for an AFDC family of four in California, one of the more generous states. In computing the needs of an AFDC family, the state legislature scrutinized each individual potential expense, using a procedure identical to the one we used earlier to construct hypothetical poverty lines. These figures, however, are real; they represent the standard of living for a California AFDC family in 1983. Note that they were allowed no more than $180 for rent, no telephone, and only $19 per month for recreation and education! In less generous states, of course, the situation was far worse.

In light of the pittance available to AFDC recipients, it seems most unlikely that wage earners, even low paid ones, would rush to the welfare rolls. To guard against this remote possibility, however, stringent property limitations have been established for those who seek public assistance. You cannot turn to welfare, at least not for long, just because you run out of money. To enter and

TABLE 12.2   MONTHLY BUDGET FOR AFDC FAMILY IN CALIFORNIA, 1983

CONSUMPTION ITEMS	AMOUNT ALLOWED
Food	$216
Clothing	75
Personal and incidental	13
Recreation and education	19
Community participation	—
Telephone service	—
Transportation	6
Household operations	33
Intermittent needs	11
Rent (maximum)	180
Utilities (maximum)	35
Total	$588

Source: California Department of Human Resources; updated.

remain on the welfare rolls, you must also dispose of nearly all property. A welfare family may possess no more than $1,000 in personal property exclusive of home and car. Some states have even lower asset limits than this federal standard.

A discussion of welfare programs must begin, then, from the observation that financial dependence on public assistance is not comfortable. Families turn to public assistance only after they are impoverished and no other support is available. When on welfare, families will be maintained below levels society otherwise deems minimally adequate.

Inequities

In addition to providing inadequate levels of income maintenance, the welfare system is also beset with inequities. Notice first that only 16 million people received cash assistance in 1983, even though over 30 million people were counted as poor. Clearly, the welfare system provides some help to many, but none at all to others. The question is: Who is denied help and for what reasons?

Conspicuously missing from the welfare rolls in nearly every state are male-headed poor families. As we noted above, the SSI program aids the aged, the blind, and the disabled, while the AFDC program is supposed to provide help to families with children. But of the 24 million poor people in families with children (see Figure 2.3), only 11 million were receiving AFDC assistance (Table 12.1). Thus, being poor in a family with children is not sufficient qualification for receiving AFDC support; a further distinction is made between the deserving and the undeserving poor. In this case, the deserving are those whose fathers or husbands are dead, deserted, or otherwise absent from the home. The presence of a male adult in the home is taken as prima facie evidence that the family is capable of its own support. AFDC payments are largely reserved for fatherless homes, regardless of whatever needs male-headed poor families may have.[5]

Even among those families poor enough to receive welfare payments, there are tremendous disparities in the amount of support provided. Notice in Table 12.1, for instance, how differently recipients of SSI and AFDC are treated: SSI recipients receive on average nearly twice as much aid as AFDC recipients. This disparity arises in part from taxpayers' sympathy for the aged and disabled, combined with their distrust of younger poor families. The distrust of AFDC families stems largely from the assumption that they could support themselves if they so chose. Not only are the adults who benefit from AFDC relatively young

---

[5] An exception to this rule is the AFDC-UF program, which provides benefits to poor families with unemployed fathers, but the program is too small and restrictive to merit attention here. In the spring of 1983, only 291,000 persons were receiving AFDC-UF benefits. For a summary of who receives various transfer benefits, see Sheldon Danziger, Robert Haveman, and Robert Plotnick, "Income Transfer Programs in the United States: An Analysis of Their Structure and Impact," a study for the Joint Economic Committee of the U.S. Congress, May 1979.

but their marital status—which the program itself constrains—is suspect. Public distrust of the program is heightened by the fact that large numbers of blacks, Hispanics, families headed by women, and illegitimate children participate in the program. Even more distressing to taxpayers is that the program's growth appears impervious to advances in the economy. Thus, provision of AFDC benefits usually begins against a background of public mistrust and resentment.

Further inequities in the cash assistance programs arise from the different levels of benefits received by families in identical situations. Although the "average" AFDC family of four received over $3,600 in cash assistance in 1983, actual benefits varied widely across states: Some AFDC families in Alaska and California received over $7,000 per year in welfare payments, while similar families in Mississippi received less than $1,500. Table 12.3 indicates how actual and maximum benefits varied in other states.

Disparities in support reflect far more than differences in the cost of living. In essence, they reflect the ability and willingness of taxpayers in each state to provide for the needy. At present, federal, state, and local governments must contribute to the financing of AFDC. If the county or state cannot or will not provide adequate "matching" funds, the federal contribution is proportionately diminished. Welfare payments in Mississippi, for example, are low, both because there is little public or private money in the state and because white Mississippians do not want to spend what little there is in providing for the poor, many of whom are black.[6]

TABLE 12.3   AFDC PAYMENTS IN SELECTED STATES, 1981

| STATE | MONTHLY BENEFIT FOR 4-PERSON FAMILY | |
	MAXIMUM ALLOWED	AVERAGE PAYMENT
Texas	$201	$141
Mississippi	$251	$120
Alabama	$480	$148
Arkansas	$273	$142
Tennessee	$217	$148
New York	$515	$438
California	$601	$515
Wisconsin	$662	$601
Vermont	$842	$563
Alaska	$634	$581
Utah	$640	$634

Source: U.S. Department of Health and Human Services.

[6]See Larry Orr, "Income Transfers as a Public Good," *American Economic Review,* June 1976; and Bradley R. Schiller, "Income Transfers as a Public Good: Comment," *American Economic Review,* December 1978.

Work Disincentives

In view of the inadequacies and inequities of our cash assistance programs, it is not surprising to learn that welfare recipients are upset with "the system." Not surprisingly, no one else is particularly happy with it either. Liberal critics of the program are dissatisfied with AFDC's coverage, its benefits, and the "red tape" and humiliation associated with the receipt of public assistance. Taxpayers generally are unhappy with the spiraling costs of the program and continue to view recipients with disfavor and suspicion. And finally, all critics unite in pointing out that the welfare system tends to undermine the motivation to work.

The work incentive problem arises from the way in which a family's welfare benefits are calculated. When a family applies for welfare, it is obliged to report any income at its disposal. A woman with small children, for example, might earn $150 a month by babysitting for neighbors. Up until 1967 welfare authorities subtracted any such income from the family's needs—as determined by those same authorities—and provided the difference. Suppose the welfare authorities concluded that Ms. Jones and her three children needed $400 a month: They paid her only $250, knowing that she could provide the rest.

Although the foregoing procedure for calculating welfare benefits might appear reasonable, it destroyed all monetary incentives to work. To appreciate the dynamics of this situation, imagine that Ms. Jones was offered regular part-time employment—as a nurse's aid, for example—at $5 an hour for ten hours a week. Ms. Jones may be reluctant to leave her small children in the care of others, but she could certainly use the money. Consequently, she is inclined to accept the new job rather than continue babysitting, especially if transportation problems (she has no car) and child-care arrangements can be worked out. But what will happen to her actual income if she takes this step toward self-improvement? Absolutely nothing. The welfare authorities simply noted that she is earning $200 a month rather than $150, reckoned that she is better providing for her own needs, and reduced her welfare payment to $200. Her family's income remained at $400 whether or not the family head found employment and regardless of how hard she strove for self-improvement. From Ms. Jones' perspective, work clearly did not pay.

The reduction in welfare benefits that took place when Ms. Jones accepted the nurse's aid job amounted to an implicit tax on her earnings. Indeed, the *marginal tax rate* turns out to be 100 percent in this case—Ms. Jones loses one dollar in welfare benefits for every additional dollar she earns. Faced with such a high tax rate, how many people would seek additional employment? Very few, which is the heart of the work incentive problem.

The Social Security Amendments of 1967 alleviated the work incentive problem somewhat by reducing the marginal tax rate. The significance of this change is illustrated in Figure 12.1. Consider the case of Ms. Jones again. If she

FIGURE 12.1   Work Incentive Provisions under 1967 AFDC Reforms

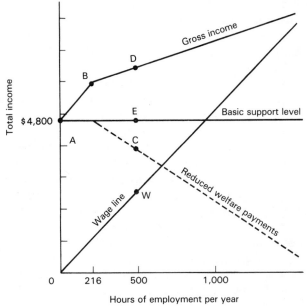

Hours of employment per year

does not work at all, she will receive $4,800 a year ($400 a month) from welfare, a situation designated by point A. Now suppose she is offered the nurse's aid job, for 500 hours a year (ten hours a week). If she accepted the job under the old AFDC system, she would move to point E, working more but with no change in total income. Under the 1967 regulations, however, she moved to point D and increased her well-being by working. Point D is obviously more desirable than E, as it represents more income for the same amount of effort. Hence, whatever Ms. Jones' feelings about work, she was more likely to take a job under the post-1967 system than the old one. In this sense, the revised system provided a greater incentive to work.

How did Ms. Jones get to point D under the post-1967 system? First, the welfare authorities recognized that there are certain costs associated with working, things like transportation expenses, additional clothes, and added meal costs. In Ms. Jones' case, these expenses amounted to $60 a month (or $720 a year). To assure that Ms. Jones took home at least enough income from her new job to cover these costs—and thus to eliminate the possibility of her incurring a net loss from working—the welfare department "disregarded" that much income in calculating her welfare benefits. Whereas they would have deducted $720 from her welfare checks under the old system, they now deducted nothing, thus enabling her to receive both the $4,800 in welfare benefits and the first $720 she earned. To give Ms. Jones still more incentive to work, the welfare authorities also disregarded an additional $30 per month ($360 per year). Ms. Jones could then earn a total of $1,080 in wages before experiencing any reduction in welfare benefits. In effect, the marginal tax rate, the rate at which welfare benefits are reduced as earnings increase, on the first $1,080 of earnings dropped from 100 percent to 0 percent. As a result, Ms. Jones could work 216 hours per year earning $1,080 and move to point B without welfare department interference.

Only as Ms. Jones' earnings exceeded $1,080 a year did the welfare department begin to take notice of her added income and reduce her welfare check. Accordingly, beyond point B, Ms. Jones' total income rose more slowly than her increased earnings. But it did rise, because the welfare department no longer reduced her benefits by a dollar for every additional dollar she earned. That is, they no longer imposed a 100 percent marginal tax on earnings beyond point B, but instead allowed her to keep something for herself. Under the revised AFDC system the marginal tax rate was 67 percent, so that the welfare department reduced her benefit check by only sixty-seven cents for every additional dollar she earned. The remaining thirty-three cents increased Ms. Jones' total income, thus providing a financial incentive to work. The incentive was still modest, to be sure, but nevertheless greater than the one that existed prior to the 1967 reform.

The total income of Ms. Jones and her family at point D is easily computed. The post-1967 welfare benefit formula was:

$$\text{Welfare benefit} = \$4,800 - (0.67 \times \text{Earnings in excess of } \$1,080)$$

If Ms. Jones worked all year (500 hours) at her new job, she received the following amount: her wages ($2,500 at point W) plus a welfare check reduced by two-thirds of her wages in excess of $1,080. In this case, she received a welfare check in the amount of $3,853 (point C). Her total income at point D was thus $2,500 from working plus $3,853 from welfare, or $6,353. By her own modest efforts, then, she managed to substantially increase her family's economic status.

Conflicting Welfare Goals

It is comforting to know that Ms. Jones could increase her family's income from $4,800 to $6,353 a year by working ten hours a week as a nurse's aid. It might, however, be nicer still if the welfare department would let her keep a little more of the money she earns from making beds, emptying bedpans, and sterilizing bandages. After all, the life of a nurse's aid is not exactly glamorous and Ms. Jones obviously needs the money. So why not lower the marginal tax rate from 67 percent to, say, 25 percent, or even zero? That would clearly solve the work incentive problem while giving Ms. Jones a real chance to make a few bucks.

The difficulty with this solution to the work incentive problem is that it conflicts with other goals. Three distinct goals are commonly associated with welfare systems: income provision, work incentives, and cost minimization. To the extent that we want to protect people from the indignities of poverty, we should provide a high income floor (or guarantee). If we also desire to encourage employment and self-improvement, we must impose low marginal tax rates (allow a recipient to keep a substantial share of her earnings above the minimum). And if we desire to hold program costs down to some reasonable level, we must limit the coverage of the program to those in need. All these objectives are worthwhile, just as the means for achieving them are clear. Nevertheless, they are mutually exclusive. We cannot move in all three directions at once.

Suppose that we actually eliminate the marginal tax rate on Ms. Jones' earnings, thus allowing her to keep everything she earns. In that case, her total income would rise to $7,300 ($4,800 in benefits plus $2,500 in wages). Still no life of luxury, but improving. Now suppose that the hospital technicians form a union and pay scales are increased. Ms. Jones is offered a raise to $6 an hour, provided that she works 1,500 hours a year (thirty hours a week). Because we no longer reduce her welfare benefits as her earnings increase, this stroke of good fortune will give Ms. Jones the opportunity to take home a total income of $13,800. Terrific! But should we still be providing $4,800 in welfare payments to someone who earns $9,000 on her own? How about someone earning $15,000? $20,000? Or, to make a long story short, where should we draw the line? Clearly, if we do not impose a marginal tax rate at some point, everyone will be eligible for full welfare benefits and we will preclude our third goal, that of cost minimization.

The conflict between the goals of income provision, work incentives, and cost minimization can be summarized in a simple equation:

$$\text{Break-even income level} = \frac{\text{Income floor}}{\text{Marginal tax rate}} + \text{Disregarded income}$$

The break-even income level refers to the amount of money a person can earn before losing all welfare benefits. In Ms. Jones' case, the break-even point under the post-1967 AFDC system was:

$$\$8,280 = \frac{\$4,800}{.67} + 1,080$$

Beyond that level of earnings, she would have been on her own. If the marginal tax rate were 100 percent as under the pre-1967 system, the break-even point would be $4,800 ($4,800/1.00), meaning that people who earned $4,800 on their own would get no assistance from welfare. Under our aborted proposal to lower marginal tax rates to zero, the break-even point would rise to infinity ($4,800/0), and we would all be on welfare.

As is apparent from the arithmetic above, a lower break-even income level can be achieved only by sacrificing a high income floor or low marginal tax rates. Hence, cost minimization can be fulfilled only be sacrificing income provision or work incentives. More generally, fulfillment of any two objectives necessitates sacrificing the third.

The Goal Compromise

Obviously, the compromise we strike between the goals of income provision, work incentives, and cost minimization is not going to please everyone. More important, however, we should note that the same compromise is not necessarily appropriate for all population groups. For those people incapable of working, a sacrifice of income provision for the sake of enhancing work incentives would be ridiculous. On the other hand, high-income guarantees for those who are capable of working might seem unnecessary. Hence, it would make sense to strike a different compromise of welfare goals for two distinct groups, those who can work and those who cannot.

Unfortunately, it is not always possible to draw such a neat distinction. A ninety-two-year-old woman confined to a wheelchair would seem to have very few employment opportunities; for her, income provision would be more appropriate than work incentives. But what about the father of four children who loses his job? Or the mother who is left with a five-year-old child when her husband skips town with the next-door neighbor? Or what about the coed who got pregnant and is now trying to raise a child on her own? Are work incentives irrelevant in these cases? Our collective response, as reflected in welfare regulations, has been "no."

Although it is often difficult to distinguish the potentially employable from the rest of the poor, we attempt to approach this distinction by segregating needy families into different welfare classifications. This is why we have a separate welfare program (SSI) for the aged, the blind, and the handicapped, a program that provides higher income guarantees and smaller work incentives. In the process, of course, many younger families temporarily unable to find or accept employment end up at the margins of deprivation. This is especially true for those impoverished families headed by unemployed or underemployed males that are denied welfare benefits because of their assumed employability.

WELFARE: THE IN-KIND PROGRAMS

As noted earlier, the welfare system incorporates two kinds of programs, those that provide cash income and those that provide income in kind. In recent years, the in-kind programs have been growing much more quickly than the cash-assistance programs. As we saw in Chapter 2, these in-kind programs have complicated our measures of the poverty population and have also altered the balance of competing welfare goals. In the following paragraphs, we review a few of the major in-kind programs, then look at their impact on welfare adequacy, cost, and work incentives.

Food Stamps

Food stamps are the most familiar of in-kind welfare benefits. Food stamps are simply coupons ("stamps") that allow a person to buy food. The stamps may be "spent" at the grocery store, where they are accepted at face value. The grocer, in turn, cashes the stamps in at a local bank, which itself redeems them at face value from the government. In effect, then, food stamps are a direct substitute for cash. Food stamps are not fully equivalent to cash, however, since they may be used only for food purchases.

Food stamps are distributed to poor families on the basis of need. The value of stamps given to a family depends on its income and family size. The maximum monthly benefit in 1983-1984 was $253 for a four-person family without other income. Average benefits are much lower—around $150 per month (about 40 cents per meal per person). The value of food-stamp transfers is automatically increased each year to account for higher food prices.

Medicaid

Even larger than the food-stamp program is Medicaid, the program that provides medical services to the poor. Under Medicaid an eligible person can use the services of a doctor or hospital just like anyone else. The difference is that the Medicaid patient simply passes the bill on to the government, rather than paying for it directly or submitting it to a private insurance company. Obviously, the amount of benefit a poor family gets from Medicaid depends on how often it requires medical treatment. In 1982 nearly all public welfare recipients made some use of Medicaid, as did many others who had incomes just above the poverty standard. The average value of the services received exceeded $1,000 per year for a family of four.

Housing Assistance

In addition to food and medical services a poor family can also receive housing assistance. For the most part, such assistance is provided in the form of public housing, usually large housing projects owned and operated by the government. In a public housing project the tenants enjoy cheap (subsidized) rents, although not a great deal more in terms of quality of environment. Nevertheless, the fact that they are paying less than the market value of their apartments means that they are effectively receiving an income transfer, which on average works out to approximately $1,000 a year. Fewer than a million families receive such transfers every year.

In addition to public housing projects, there are also housing assistance programs for low-income people who are renting or even buying their apartments and homes in the private market. In these programs, the rent or mortgage payment is reduced, with the government (the Department of Housing and Urban Development, or HUD) making up the difference.

These three in-kind welfare programs, taken together, provide substantial noncash benefits available to poor (and near-poor) families are substantial. Were a family of four eligible for the average benefits available from food stamps, Medicaid, and housing assistance, it could receive an in-kind subsidy valued as high as $3,700 a year. This would be in addition to the average *cash* benefit of $4,800 a year available from AFDC. The combination of both cash and in-kind assistance has the potential, then, to lift a family out of poverty. Table 12.4 depicts the total costs and average benefits associated with the major in-kind programs.

The Goal Conflict

In-kind welfare programs substantially raise the standard of living for the poor; they do so, however, at the expense of certain identifiable costs. Obviously they involve a substantial amount of public expenditure—over $27 billion in 1979. Less obvious, but perhaps more important, is the impact of these in-kind programs on the goal compromise we observed earlier. As we noted, the cash assistance programs, particularly AFDC, sacrifice more of the income-provision goal in order to better fulfill the work-incentive and cost-minimization goals. That compromise has been tampered with by the introduction of food stamps, Medicaid, and housing assistance.

Although it might seem that the in-kind programs are a way of meeting all three of our welfare goals simultaneously—of filling in the gaps left in our earlier compromise—such an assumption is merely whistling in the dark. The three goals remain irreconcilable, and the provision of in-kind assistance serves only to strike a new compromise, not to render our separate goals more compatible.

TABLE 12.4   IN-KIND WELFARE PROGRAMS, 1982

PROGRAM	NUMBER OF RECIPIENTS (millions)	AVERAGE BENEFIT PER RECIPIENT PER MONTH	TOTAL ANNUAL COST (billions)
Food stamps	21	$40	$10.2
Medicaid	40	58	17.4
Housing assistance	2.5	40	1.2
School lunch program	15	7	2.2
Total			$27.1

Source: U.S. Departments of Health, Housing and Urban Development, and Agriculture.

The impact of in-kind programs on our policy compromise can be seen in Figure 12.2. In this figure we reconstruct the opportunities available to Ms. Jones under the AFDC program as it was structured from 1967 to 1981 ("AFDC only" line). As we noted earlier, Ms. Jones had an incentive (albeit limited) to take a job under AFDC, as she could increase her standard of living (move to points B and D) by so doing.

The new and higher line in Figure 12.2 represents the opportunities available to Ms. Jones and her family from the *combined* provisions of AFDC, food stamps, Medicaid, and housing assistance. As is evident, Ms. Jones' family enjoyed a much higher standard of living when it got not only welfare checks, but lived in subsidized housing and get free medical services and food stamps as well. Even if Ms. Jones chose not to work at all, her total real income was $4,800 in welfare benefits *plus* $3,000 in in-kind benefits. This income of $7,800 is represented by point A* in Figure 12.2. This is far superior to the cash (AFDC) income available at point A.

There is another change in Figure 12.2. Notice what happens to her total gross income as she works more hours. Her gross income rises slowly at first, then not at all for awhile (where the gross income curve flattens out). Then it begins rising again until it reaches point M. Ultimately (at point M), her gross

FIGURE 12.2   Effect of In-Kind Benefits on Income and Work Incentives

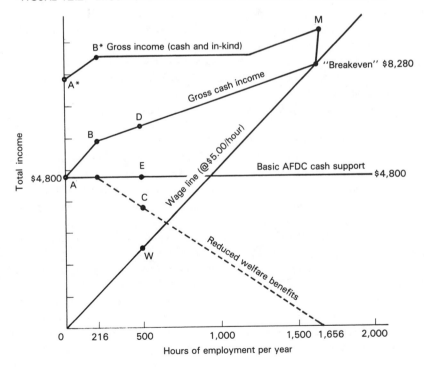

income actually *falls* as her work effort increases! Not only does Ms. Jones now feel less *need* to work as a result of her greater public subsidy, but she now confronts less *incentive* to work. The attainment of greater income provision has been achieved at the sacrifice (opportunity cost) of work incentives. That is not to say that the new compromise is any better or worse than the old one, but simply to point up the fact that the old goal conflict still exists.

The reduction in work incentives came about from an increase in the marginal tax rate. In the post-1967 system, Ms. Jones' welfare benefits declined rapidly when she worked more. This was not due to any change in AFDC benefit calculations: AFDC still allowed her to keep 100 percent of the first $1,080 she earned and 33 percent of everything above that. Now, however, she loses some of her in-kind benefits when her earnings increase.

Recall that the value of a family's food-stamp allotment depends on a family's income. Families with higher incomes get fewer stamps. Hence, part of what Ms. Jones earns is effectively taken away in the form of food-stamp losses; this acts as a tax on earnings. The same is true of housing assistance: When Ms. Jones' earnings increase, she will have to pay a larger share of the market value of her rent. These provisions are perfectly compatible with the equity concept of reserving welfare assistance for the neediest. However, they also diminish the net rewards associated with employment.

In Figure 12.2 it is assumed that the *combined* "tax" on earnings imposed by food-stamp and housing subsidy regulations amounts to 33 percent. When Ms. Jones worked 216 hours she earned $1,080. AFDC authorities disregarded these initial wages, i.e., imposed no "tax." Now, however, Ms. Jones loses $360 worth of food stamps and housing assistance when she earns $1,080. Her gross income increases more slowly than her wages. As a result her gross income is only $8,520 at point B*.

To the right of point B* work incentives diminish further. Once her wages exceed $1,080, Ms. Jones starts losing AFDC benefits. The *combined* marginal tax rate is now 100 percent—67 percent in AFDC "taxes" and another 33 percent from food stamps and housing assistance. The gross income line flattens out to the right of B*; further work effort does not result in higher real income.

Gross income does not start rising again until Ms. Jones has lost her food stamps and housing assistance. It rises at that point because Medicaid—her only remaining in-kind benefit—imposes a zero tax rate.

The greatest blow to work incentives occurs at point M, the point at which Ms. Jones' earnings rise above Medicaid eligibility ceilings. Only those who have an income less than 133 percent of the relevant poverty standard are eligible for Medicaid assistance. If Ms. Jones' income rose above that limit, she would have had to pay her family's medical bills herself, thereby losing $1,000 (on average) in Medicaid benefits. Accordingly, her total income (including the value of in-kind assistance) drops by $1,000 at point M. How many people would work an extra hour or day if they were going to be rewarded with that kind of income loss? Clearly, the higher standard of living that in-kind welfare benefits make possible also diminishes the incentives to seek employment.

WELFARE REFORM

The Carter Proposals

In view of the inadequacies, inequities, and work disincentives associated with a mix of cash and in-kind welfare programs, welfare reform has been widely sought. In 1977 President Carter observed that "the welfare system is neither rational nor is it fair; it is antiwork and antifamily. It is unfair to the poor and wasteful of taxpayers' dollars." To remedy this situation, Carter proposed "a complete and clean break with the past."[7] He proposed to replace the welfare system with a sweeping reform plan, entitled the Program of Better Jobs and Income (PBJI).

The cornerstone of PBJI was its classification of poor people into two groups, depending on their employment potential. Each group was to be provided with a different mix of income support, as follows:

Tier 1:
   Families not expected to work (i.e., the aged, blind, disabled, and single-parent families with children under seven years)

   Tier 1 families would be provided with a basic income guarantee of $4,200 per year (for a family of four), and a marginal tax rate of 50 percent. Thus, the break-even level of income would be $8,400.

Tier 2:
   Families expected to work (i.e., two-parent families, single-parent families with older children, single individuals, childless couples)

   Tier 2 families would be provided with a basic guarantee of only $2,300. But the marginal tax rate would be zero on the first $3,800 of earnings, thereby permitting a family to attain a poverty standard of living ($6,100) by working. Thereafter, a marginal tax rate of 50 percent would be imposed, creating a break-even of $8,400 for these families also.

The basic objective of the PBJI proposal was to minimize work-incentive problems while assuring all families an adequate level of income support.

[7]Presidential statement. Plains, Georgia, August 6, 1977.

Attainment of this objective depended on two critical assumptions: (1) that the employable poor could be distinguished from the nonemployable poor (PBJI's two tiers), and (2) that the people in Tier 2 would be able to find jobs. We have already observed that the first assumption is doubtful in many cases. Poor families move in and out of the labor force repeatedly, and for a variety of reasons (see Chapters 4 and 5). "Employability" is not a permanent characteristic of a family or its members. Hence, the separation of poor families into two "employable" and "unemployable" groups requires high administrative costs and invites subterfuge.

The assumption that all "employable" families will find work—and thus survive with their minimal welfare support—is potentially even more troublesome. Millions of individuals are poor because too few jobs are available (see Chapter 4). For his welfare reform to succeed, President Carter had to guarantee jobs. To do so, he proposed to create 1.4 million jobs in public service employment. These jobs would be temporary and pay the minimum wage.

President Carter's reform proposals failed to get Congressional approval. Among the criticisms leveled at the Carter proposal were that it was too expensive; that its work requirements were not strong enough, especially for single-parent families; that it did not provide enough jobs; and that its benefit levels were too low. There was also a lot of doubt whether the distinctions between employable and nonemployable families could be maintained.[8]

The Reagan Reforms

President Reagan was more successful in reforming the AFDC system. The Reagan reforms, however, were very different from what Carter had proposed. The welfare reforms of 1981 sharply limited the income of welfare recipients, greatly reduced work incentives, and imposed mandatory work requirements.[9] In the process, the Reagan Administration completely altered the earlier compromise between goals of adequacy, work incentives, and cost.

Three features of the pre-1981 welfare system greatly disturbed the Reagan Administration. The first was the high level of income welfare recipients could attain. As illustrated in Figure 12.2, a welfare recipient could get $7,800 in cash and in-kind benefits without working and even more with minimal labor supply. Because this was more income than millions of workers received, it violated the Administration's concept of vertical equity; people working hard to support themselves should have more than those living on welfare.

Horizontal equity was the second concern. As noted earlier, the amount of welfare a person could get depended on where she lived; some states were

---

[8]For a detailed analysis of President Carter's plan, see Sheldon Danziger, Robert Haveman, and Eugene Smolensky, "The Program for Better Jobs and Income—A Guide and Critique," A study prepared for the Joint Economic Committee of the U.S. Congress, October 1977.

[9]The Reagan reforms were contained in a budget bill, the Omnibus Budget Reconciliation Act (OBRA) of 1981.

generous, others stingy. Within states, too, there was great variation in benefits among similarly-situated families. The rules for determining work expenses and child care costs invited such inequities. According to 1967 legislation, the welfare authorities could "disregard" $30 of income per month *plus* work and child-care expenses. The intent of this provision was to encourage recipients to work by guaranteeing them a net return (over and above expenses). It also implied, however, that a recipient could achieve a high "disregard"—and a high gross income—by claiming large work expenses. This system—analogous to the itemized deductions middle-class taxpayers can claim—invited fraud and abuse. At a minimum, it created tremendous variation in the amount of benefits received by different AFDC families.

Finally, there was simply the cost of the whole system. Welfare benefits kept increasing, despite economic conditions. The Reagan Administration was determined to reduce welfare costs, while continuing to provide assistance to the "truly needy."

Income and Asset Limitations

Stricter limits on the income and assets of welfare recipients was the Administration's first objective. They did this in four ways by:

1. *Imposing a ceiling on gross income.* The maximum income a welfare family can receive is 150 percent of the state's need standard. States may include in-kind benefits in computing the value of gross income.

2. *Standardizing work expenses.* Welfare recipients can no longer claim unlimited (itemized) work expenses and child-care costs. The maximum disregard allowed for these expenses is $75 and $160 per month respectively.

3. *Limiting eligibility for the $30 per month disregard.* This disregard is now available only during the first four months a person is on welfare.

4. *Setting a limit on asset holdings.* A welfare family can possess no more than $1,000 in assets, exclusive of their home and car.

The impact of these changes is illustrated in Figure 12.3. The dotted lines replicate the income opportunities that existed before 1981 for a person who could earn $5 per hour (Figure 12.2). The solid lines illustrate the Reagan ceilings. In this case, we assume that the $4,800 per year that Ms. Jones received at point A equaled her state's need standard.[10] The Reagan cash income ceiling is therefore $7,200 (150 percent of $4,800). Once Ms. Jones reaches this level of income, she can no longer add to her income by working. At point R the new income ceiling is effective. To keep her below that ceiling, the welfare department cuts her AFDC benefits by one dollar for every additional dollar she earns. This abrupt imposition of a 100 percent tax rate leads to a rapid decrease in her welfare benefits, starting at R*. Additional work effort beyond that point (1,008

[10]Actual benefits are often below the need standard, as illustrated in Table 12.2.

FIGURE 12.3   The Reagan Reforms

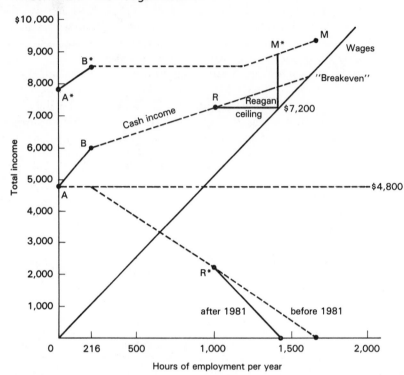

hours of work per year) does not enhance total income. If Ms. Jones nevertheless works 1,440 hours she will lose her AFDC eligibility entirely, and perhaps
her Medicaid as well (M*).

The income ceilings and implied tax rates of the 1981 reforms clearly
reduced work incentives. A welfare mother like Ms. Jones simply has no
economic incentive to earn more than $2,400 per year (half of her basic AFDC
grant).

Workfare.   In place of work incentives, the 1981 reforms created mandatory work provisions. According to *workfare*, a welfare recipient can be
forced to perform community work in return for welfare benefits. In this way,
recipients can "earn" their benefits. These workfare provisions are intended to
eliminate any "free rides" while giving welfare recipients an opportunity to
acquire work experience and skills. Refusal to accept a workfare job could also
lead to loss of welfare benefits.

Rather than creating a national program, Congress gave the states the
option of implementing the workfare program. Many states, in turn, passed on
to their counties the decision of whether to impose mandatory work requirements. The appeal of workfare was its potential to discourage continued welfare

receipt while producing valued public projects. Critics argued, however, that the costs of creating and supervising workfare jobs were too high, especially in comparison to welfare savings. Many also worried that the workfare requirements could be enforced arbitrarily and unjustly, particularly when the number of available workfare jobs exceeded the number of adult AFDC recipients.[11] As a consequence, workfare was used only sparingly in its first two years.

Negative Income Taxes

In view of the complexities and disappointments of the current welfare system, better alternatives are still sought. A popular alternative is the "negative income tax." A negative income tax (NIT) is a tax system wherein people automatically receive transfers ("negative taxes") from the government if their incomes fall below established levels. The "system" consists of (1) a guaranteed income floor, and (2) a marginal tax rate, which together determine who will receive income transfers and how much. What distinguishes such systems from our current welfare programs are two features: universality and simplicity.

The universality of NIT plans arises from the fact that their benefits would be available to everyone on the same basis of need; their simplicity derives from the consolidation of all welfare programs. As we have noted, the current patchwork of public assistance programs necessitates a case-by-case determination of eligibility, need, and grant levels. Not only is such a determination expensive and frustratingly slow; it often leads to administrative abuse. Under a negative income tax program, case-by-case determinations would be unnecessary and administrative abuse unlikely.

Another consequence of present administrative arrangements is that welfare regulations are confusing and vary by state. Recipients have little access to information regarding the rules that govern them or the benefits to which they are entitled. Generally, they are compelled to rely on caseworkers for this information, making them totally dependent on the capability and benevolence of local authorities.

NIT programs would overcome most of these deficiencies by standardizing eligibility criteria and by making assistance available as a matter of right. Every poor family would receive identical aid based on the number of family members. Access to financial assistance would be as simple and direct as income taxes now are, and similar verification procedures would be utilized to certify eligibility. Local authorities would have no discretionary control over the behavior of recipients, whose identity would be confidential.

Although NIT-type proposals are attractive, they are no panacea for our welfare problems. The conflict between the goals of adequacy, work incentives,

---

[11] The potential of workfare to increase family problems is discussed in Patricia Spakes, "Mandatory Work Registration for Welfare Parents: A Family Impact Analysis," *Journal of Marriage and the Family*, August 1982.

and cost minimization remains. There is simply no way to achieve all three goals within the context of any single program. NIT programs generally appeal to people who worry more about income adequacy or work incentives than about program cost.

To determine the effects an NIT might have on work and other behavior, the federal government sponsored several NIT experiments. The experiments offered recipients various combinations of income guarantees and tax rates, then observed recipient behavior. In general, the experiments have shown that recipients reduce their work effort when offered high income guarantees or confronted with high marginal tax rates. The effects are modest, however, especially for male household heads. On average, the labor supply of husbands declined by 5 percent as a result of the experimental NIT, while the labor supply of wives fell by 22 percent. The work effort of female heads of families was reduced by 11 percent.[12] Although modest, these effects underscore the potential conflict between the goals of income adequacy and work incentive.[13]

Another problem that NIT-type programs must confront is the immediacy and variability of families' income-maintenance needs. Families whom we count as "poor" aren't necessarily in need of income maintenance all year round. Their low income for the year may reflect adequate income part of the year and no income for the rest. By the same token, families whose *annual* income ranks them among the nonpoor may have experienced short-term deprivation and needed assistance. One of the reasons our present welfare system is so complex and costly is that it is responsive to such variation; thousands of families move on and off welfare every month. By contrast, NIT-type systems, modeled after our regular tax system, envision longer accounting periods and less responsiveness. Unfortunately, families who experience sudden income losses can neither eat last year's income nor afford to wait until assistance comes later, on a retroactive basis. Hence, NIT-type proposals are likely to be amended in practice and end up with more administrative complexities than their authors envision.

---

[12]Michael C. Keeley, et al., "The Estimation of Labor Supply Models Using Experimental Data," *American Economic Review*, December 1978.

[13]For a discussion of the NIT experiments and their significance, see U.S. General Accounting Office, *Income Maintenance Experiments: Need to Summarize Results and Communicate the Lessons Learned*, April 1981. Other studies include Joseph Pechman and P. Michael Timpane, eds., *Work Incentives and Income Guarantee* (Washington, DC: The Brookings Institution, 1975), the symposium published in the *Journal of Human Resources*, Spring and Fall issues, 1974, and John L. Palmer and Joseph Pechman, eds., *Welfare in Rural Areas* (Washington, DC: The Brookings Institution, 1978). For alternative models, also see Mark Killingsworth, "Must a Negative Income Tax Reduce Labor Supply? A Study of the Family's Allocation of Time," *Journal of Human Resources*, Summer 1976, and Ronald Hoffman and Bradley R. Schiller, "Work Incentives of the Poor: A Reconsideration," *Review of Economics and Statistics*, August 1970, or Frank Levy, "The Labor Supply of Female Household Heads," *Journal of Human Resources*, Winter 1979.

SOCIAL SECURITY

Social Security is by far the largest income transfer program in the United States. Unlike welfare, however, Social Security benefits are not reserved for those in need. Tax contributions, not need, establish eligibility for benefits. Anyone who has paid Social Security payroll taxes a prescribed number of years is eligible to receive Social Security benefits at retirement age. Thus, the program is neither intended nor operated as an antipoverty mechanism. The majority of the 35 million individuals who receive Social Security retirement benefits have never experienced poverty. Yet, they receive more than $140 billion in annual payments, triple the size of annual public assistance payments (cash and in-kind).

What we call "Social Security" is really a mixture of three distinct programs. Its formal title is the Old Age, Survivors, Disability and Health Insurance (OASDHI) Program. The health program funds Medicare benefits for the aged, while the disability program provides assistance to people with long-term, work-inhibiting disabilities. The third and most familiar program provides retirement benefits.

Social Security's three basic programs are financed by payroll taxes. In 1984, all workers in "covered" employment had to pay a tax of 7 percent on their earnings, up to a taxable ceiling of $37,800. Employers had to "contribute" an identical amount. Because Congress has scheduled increases in the tax rate and tied the tax ceiling to the inflation rate, annual payroll taxes increase each year.

The payroll taxes collected each year finance the Social Security benefits of persons already retired. There is no fund of money accumulating for future returns. The whole system is on a pay-as-you-go basis. When it appeared in the early 1980s that the current benefits would exceed tax receipts, Congress had to adjust tax rates, coverage, and benefit computations. Congress also raised the age of full ("normal") retirement eligibility from 65 to 67 for people born after 1959.[14]

The benefits received by a retiree reflect a combination of insurance and welfare principles. The insurance aspect results from the fact that people who pay more taxes when working get higher benefits when retired. The welfare aspect results from restrictions on that relationship. There are minimum and maximum limits on benefits and other progressive features in the benefit-computation formula. These assure low-wage workers a disproportionately high retirement benefit while reducing the "return" to high-wage earners.

Because of its progressive redistribution features and sheer size, Social Security is a major antipoverty program. For 9 million aged Americans, Social

[14]For a summary of the 1983 Social Security reforms and their effects, see John A. Svahn and Mary Ross, "Social Security Amendments of 1983: Legislative History and Summary of Provisions," *Social Security Bulletin*, July 1983.

Security benefits provide the difference between a poverty income and a higher standard of living. Another 3 million Social Security recipients remain poor but still get vital support from Social Security.

The impact of the Social Security program testifies to its potential effectiveness as an antipoverty mechanism. The program has done a remarkable job of reducing the number of aged poor and of alleviating the condition of those who remain poor. Nevertheless, there are many observers who argue that we could further reduce poverty by increasing Social Security benefits. Across-the-board increases in benefits would extend to the poor and nonpoor alike, of course. Thus, if we wanted to aid the aged poor while holding down program costs (and payroll taxes!), minimum benefit levels would have to be raised faster than average benefit levels.

There are strong objections to raising minimum benefit levels faster than average benefit levels or, for that matter, raising any benefit levels at all. The primary objection is that the Social Security system should retain as much of its insurance character as possible, and not become a straightforward welfare program. What is feared is that the further substitution of welfare (income redistribution) objectives for insurance objectives will undermine the popular support that the Social Security system enjoys. Thus, Congress walks a thin line when it seeks to aid the aged poor while maintaining broad public support.

A second objection to increased benefits arises from fears about the system's financial viability. As we have noted, current benefit payments depend on current payroll taxes. Higher benefits thus require higher tax rates or an alternative source of financing. Critics argue that tax rates are already so high that they are eroding work incentives and inflating production costs. Critics also fear that dependence on alternative financing sources (e.g., general revenues) would destroy Social Security's unique character and its political credibility.

INCOME MAINTENANCE AND POVERTY

Together, our welfare and Social Security programs transfer substantial sums of money and alleviate much poverty. Table 12.5 shows just how much poverty has been reduced by these income transfer programs. In the absence of Social Security and welfare programs, 22 percent of all U.S. families would have been poor in 1980 (column 1 of Table 12.5). Social Security and other nonwelfare transfers, however, cut the poverty rate to 14.2 percent. Most of this antipoverty effect is concentrated among older families, of course. The cash welfare programs cut the poverty rate even further—only 13 percent of all families remained poor by official standards. If in-kind benefits (e.g., Medicaid) are also included, the poverty rate drops even further. Thus, the income transfer system is very effective in reducing the incidence of poverty.

TABLE 12.5   THE IMPACT OF INCOME TRANSFERS ON POVERTY, 1980 (PERCENT)

GROUP	PERCENTAGE OF POPULATION IN POVERTY		
	BEFORE TRANSFER INCOME	AFTER SOCIAL SECURITY AND NONWELFARE TRANSFERS	AFTER CASH WELFARE TRANSFERS
All persons	21.9%	14.2%	13.0%
Aged females	67.9	27.1	24.3
Nonaged males	9.8	7.2	6.8

Note: Welfare transfers include AFDC, Supplemental Security Income, and General Assistance; nonwelfare transfers include Unemployment Insurance, Worker's Compensation, Government Employee Pensions, Veteran's Pensions and Railroad Retirement..

Source of data: Sheldon Danziger, "Budget Cuts as Welfare Reform," *American Economic Review*, May 1983.

The income transfer system would eliminate still more poverty if benefits were increased further and distributed more widely. Higher welfare benefits are not, however, what society has in mind when it talks of eliminating poverty. Public-opinion polls consistently record the view that too many people are already on welfare, and receiving too much money. Taxpayers seek not only to alleviate the plight of the poor but to eliminate the *need* for welfare. If the elimination of poverty is achieved only by greater transfer payments, there is no prospect of diminishing welfare rolls and costs; income transfers will have to be continued forever. Meaningful reduction of both poverty and welfare costs necessitates that welfare families be given greater opportunity to provide for themselves. To what extent does the welfare system yield this kind of long-run benefits?

The greater financial resources provided to families under our income transfer programs most certainly do have some long-term effect. The payments at least enable families to avert starvation and function normally. In some cases, they even provide enough money for children to stay in school, properly fed and clothed, and for parents to seek a job. Adequate financial assistance may even help hold a family together. All this doubtlessly contributed to personal and economic development. Higher standards of living also raise morale, aspirations, and initiative. As former Senator Fred Harris of Oklahoma pointed out during Congressional deliberations on welfare reform: "If you provide an adequate level of income, people are in fact encouraged to work, and initiative and incentive are increased, while incomes below what is necessary for decent health, housing, and living standards destroy initiative and make it difficult for succeeding generations to break the welfare cycle."[15]

[15]Senate Committee on Finance, *Hearings on H.R. 16311* (Washington, DC: Government Printing Office, 1970), p. 158.

As important as these many contributions to personal and economic well-being are, however, they must still be evaluated within a more general economic context. Greater nutrition, stability, and initiative are necessary but not sufficient conditions for economic independence. To achieve independence, one must also have access to a meaningful job. Yet, welfare systems themselves do nothing to alter the number or types of jobs available. They were neither intended nor designed to expand employment opportunities. In essence, welfare programs strive only to provide income maintenance for families until and unless other economic opportunities emerge.

The inherent limitations to welfare programs render them relatively ineffective as long-term solutions to poverty. Yet, abolishing them would totally ignore the plight of the poor. And even in the best of economic and racial situations, many individuals will be temporarily or permanently incapable of self-support. Yet we must not confuse welfare reform with expansion of opportunity, nor should we indulge in the fiction that more generous assistance today will eliminate the need for assistance tomorrow. We must expand and improve the welfare system to provide for those in need. But to reduce the number of people who need assistance, we must expand opportunities for financial independence.

SUMMARY

There is no coherent *system* of income maintenance in the United States. Instead, we rely on a variety of diverse income transfer programs, designed and implemented independently of each other. Despite these patchwork origins, however, current public assistance and Social Security programs do provide much aid for the poor. Social Security eliminates poverty for millions of individuals, while Social Security and public assistance together relieve the hardships of impoverishment for still more persons.

Analysis of income maintenance programs may proceed from two distinct perspectives. We may inquire first how efficiently and equitably current programs now perform their intended transfer functions. However, it is also necessary to ask how appropriate *any* kind of income maintenance system is as a long-run solution to poverty.

While current income maintenance programs provide much assistance, they do so with much inequity and little efficiency. Public assistance programs are particularly inequitable in their disregard of the needs of poor families with working fathers. These *working poor* are excluded from assistance due to a misplaced concern for work motivation and a general desire to contain public expenditures. Also maltreated are those who are eligible for categorical assistance programs but reside in impoverished or unsympathetic states. Even after receiving assistance, they remain pitifully below acceptable standards of living.

To a large extent, proposed public assistance reforms promise to correct some of these deficiencies. A negative income tax plan would move slightly further in the same direction with more universality and less implied control over behavior. Even these programs, however, would have to contend with the competing objectives of income provision, work encouragement, and cost minimization.

The Social Security program is the largest and most popular income transfer program. Yet, its ability to eliminate, rather than perpetuate, poverty depends on its ability to depart from insurance principles. The small departures that have been made in the past have yielded significant benefits for the aged poor. Still further increases in minimum Social Security benefits could virtually eliminate poverty among the aged, but are resisted in order to retain the insurance character of the program and to assure continued financial viability.

Existing and foreseen income maintenance programs do have the potential of alleviating poverty. They are not a solution to the poverty problem, however, as they fail to provide more than a marginal impetus to financial independence. They can meet the need for income support, but they cannot eliminate the need itself. If relied on exclusively, public assistance programs would perpetuate poverty and the need for extensive public assistance expenditures. This is not consistent with the needs of the poor, the objectives of the taxpaying public, or the requirements of a viable economy. Income maintenance policies must be complemented by the policies that provide opportunities for economic independence.

FURTHER READING

ANDERSON, MARTIN.   *Welfare.* Palo Alto, CA: Hoover Institute, 1978.

BISHOP, JOHN H.   "Jobs, Cash Transfers and Marital Instability: A Review and Synthesis of the Evidence," *Journal of Human Resources,* Summer 1980.

CONGRESSIONAL BUDGET OFFICE.   *Welfare Reform: Issues, Objectives, and Approaches.* Washington, DC: Government Printing Office, 1977.

DANZIGER, SHELDON, ROBERT HAVEMAN, and ROBERT PLOTNICK.   "How Income Transfer Programs Affect Work, Savings, and the Income Distribution: A Critical Review," *Journal of Economic Literature,* September 1981.

DANZIGER, SHELDON, and ROBERT PLOTNICK.   *Has the War on Poverty Been Won?* New York: Academic Press, 1980.

MUNNELL, ALICIA H.   *The Future of Social Security.* Washington, DC: The Brookings Institution, 1977.

PAGLIN, MORTON. *Poverty and Transfers in Kind*. Palo Alto, CA: Hoover Institute, 1979.

PECHMAN, JOSEPH, and P. MICHAEL TIMPANE, eds. *Work Incentives and Income Guarantees*. Washington, DC: The Brookings Institution, 1975.

U.S. CONGRESS, COMMITTEE ON WAYS AND MEANS. *Background Material on Poverty*. Washington, DC: Government Printing Office, October 1983, Section 5.

13 Employment Policies

If meaningful and long-term solutions to the problem of poverty are to be implemented, public policy will have to venture beyond income maintenance. Simply providing money to the poor has little potential for stimulating financial independence. The only possible lasting solution to the problem of poverty is to assure that decent jobs are available to all who seek them. Under such circumstances, poverty and the need for income maintenance will be at a minimum.

The government has several alternatives at its disposal for expanding employment opportunities. At the most general level, it may seek to increase the demand for labor by stimulating aggregate demand. A variety of fiscal and monetary measures are available for that purpose. On the other hand, government policy may concentrate on the supply of labor. Rather than stimulate new demand, government policy may focus on training unemployed workers for jobs already available. Or the government might take still more direct action by creating jobs itself, via public employment programs. Still another possibility is to make labor markets more efficient in matching available workers with vacant jobs.

To some extent, each of these policy alternatives has been implemented, but they have received markedly different degrees of attention. In the 1930s a heavy emphasis was put on public employment. After World War II the government placed primary reliance on aggregate economic policies to provide the necessary job opportunities. Only in the late 1950s and early 1960s did an awareness emerge that other approaches were also necessary to provide a requisite number of jobs; at that time, a variety of training programs was introduced. The whole sequence started again in the 1970s. First there was an expansion of public employment programs, especially in the mid-1970s. Then the primary importance of aggregate demand policies was emphasized, along with an increasing concern for aggregate supply. This concern led to a preference for training over public jobs and a search for new ways to improve the match between job-seekers and job vacancies. This chapter reviews the nature, history, and potential of each of these alternatives for eliminating poverty.

AGGREGATE DEMAND POLICIES

Most people believe that the United States could have averted the Great Depression were we as knowledgeable in 1930 as we are now about the workings of the economy. This belief stems from the conviction that economists can now manage the economy to a degree formerly unheard of. Present-day arguments between economists concentrate, not on the issue of whether the level of demand can be affected, but on how much success can be achieved by such policies.

The claims of modern economists inspire hope for the plight of the poor. If we really can manage aggregate demand we can provide enough jobs for the unemployed, the underemployed, and the discouraged poor. Anyone who has even skimmed through an introductory economics textbook can provide an outline for action. Fiscal policies can expand demand through increased government expenditures, consumer tax cuts, or enlarged investment and depreciation allowances. Monetary policy may provide a stimulus to demand by making access to credit easier and cheaper. Together, such policies could move millions of persons out of poverty.

But the question of why this has not yet been done remains. Either our claims to precision are exaggerated or we lack the necessary resolve. Both of these factors are evident.

Our resolve to expand aggregate employment opportunities visibly weakens when other objectives appear to conflict. As discussed in the appendix to Chapter 4, the goal of full employment is readily sacrificed whenever inflation threatens. Inflation hurts the middle class more than unemployment does. Hence, full employment and reductions in poverty take a back seat to anti-inflation policies whenever these goals appear to conflict. There is also a widespread conviction that the goals of price stability and full employment are inherently incompatible.

In the late 1950s full employment was defined as the attainment of less than 5 percent unemployment. When Walter Heller, President Kennedy's economic advisor, publicly aspired to reach full employment of 4 percent, he was chided for recklessness. As unemployment sank below even 4 percent in the mid-1960s, some began to wonder whether we had not previously underestimated our abilities and unnecessarily relegated millions of individuals to poverty. The public never became wholly convinced, however. When the rate of inflation did spurt at the end of the sixties, it was concluded immediately that the rise in prices was due to our efforts to create full employment. Indeed, both the Nixon and Ford administrations argued repeatedly that "full employment" should be redefined as an unemployment rate of 5 or 5.5 percent. The Carter Administration first adopted 4.9 percent as its definition of "full employment," then raised it to 5.5 percent. The Reagan Administration made full employment appear still more attainable by setting it at 6.5 percent. Not one of these administrations succeeded in reaching its increasingly easy goals, however. Each time "full employment" came into view, rising prices, or fear thereof, led to U-turns in economic policy.

Fear of inflation has not been the only obstacle to more effective aggregate demand policies. In the general euphoria of our discovery that we could manipulate aggregate demand, we neglected some simple truths. The way in which aggregate demand is stimulated has significant impact on the economy. A large reduction in interest rates, for example, will stimulate the housing and lumber industries, where interest charges are a major component of total cost. Investment credit allowances, on the other hand, will benefit manufacturers of steel, airplanes, and heavy machinery, with little impact on housing production. More generally, tax cuts expand the private sector while increases in government spending expand the public sector. Indeed, every fiscal or monetary action will affect the distribution of output, as well as its volume. There really is no such thing as a neutral aggregate demand policy, that is, one that does not alter the mix of output, relative prices, or the distribution of income.

What this suggests is that we might be able to do a better job of providing jobs for the poor if we examined the content of our aggregate demand policies more carefully. Some policies will provide more jobs for the poor, with little effect on prices, while others will do just the reverse. The trick is to find the right ones. This will require that policymakers explicitly incorporate antipoverty objectives into their aggregate demand planning and look more closely at the impact of alternative policy strategies. Unfortunately, the public's general apathy toward questions of race and poverty has permitted policymakers to ignore these requirements. Indeed,the general public believes that most poor people could find jobs "if they wanted to." As a result, policymakers tend to attribute their failures to the inherent unattainability of full employment rather than to their own errors of policy design and implementation. This syndrome has aptly been dubbed "blaming the victim."

However, even truly enlightened full employment policies will not provide decent jobs for all who need them. As unemployment levels drop it becomes increasingly difficult—and socially expensive—to reach those who still need employment. Accordingly, expansionary fiscal and monetary policies alone cannot wholly eliminate poverty among those who are presently or potentially in the labor force. But it is even more important to emphasize that without determined full employment policies all other efforts to eliminate poverty are rendered impotent. In 1975, for example, more money was spent on welfare, training, education, and other antipoverty efforts than in earlier years. Nevertheless, the number of people in poverty grew by 2.5 million because unemployment levels were allowed to rise. The demand for labor, especially labor provided by the poor, must be kept at high levels if the poor are to gain financial independence. All other efforts are secondary.

TRAINING POLICIES

While the necessity for maintaining a high level of demand for labor is clear, we must also recognize other approaches to full employment. One such approach is to train unemployed workers to fulfill unsatisfied demand. As every freshman economist knows, both supply and demand forces operate in the labor market. Hence, to many observers it seems as logical to adapt supply to demand as to proceed the other way around. Indeed, training programs for unemployed workers enjoy much greater acceptance than policies designed to expand and redirect labor demand toward the poor. What accounts for their popularity and how effective are they?

The potential of training programs to increase total employment is suggested by job vacancies. Help wanted ads continue to appear even in periods of high unemployment. People move from job to job with great frequency, creating a kind of musical chairs situation in the labor market. In addition, there are always businesses either expanding or contracting, thereby creating or eliminating available jobs. Thus, at any point in time some jobs are vacant and employers must advertise that fact. How fast those vacancies are filled depends on how many workers are looking for jobs and what their talents are. Where millions of workers are unemployed, vacancies are quickly filled. In periods of lower unemployment, employers must wait longer and look further before obtaining needed labor.

Almost as important as the number of available workers are the skills they possess. If employers are seeking skilled craftsmen, millions of unemployed day laborers will contribute little to the fulfillment of job vacancies. Skills possessed by job-seekers must bear some resemblance to the requirements of available jobs. Nevertheless, it should not be concluded that an existing mismatch of job requirements and skills of the unemployed constitutes an insurmountable barrier to full employment. On the contrary, rarely is a worker hired who is ready to perform his or her job with no orientation or training. Employers can and do provide available workers with needed skills. Government programs to train or retrain the unemployed can provide the same service.

Even though private employers frequently engage in some form of orientation or training, they seek to keep training expenses to a minimum. They much prefer to hire persons who are already skilled and experienced. That option is not always available. Those who are not yet hired are likely to possess fewer skills. The amount of training employers will have to provide thus varies inversely with the level of unemployment. If aggregate demand is strong, employers will incur the added expenses willingly.

Government programs to train the unemployed have a slightly different orientation. To some extent, they merely relieve private employers of the burden and expense of training. This may be done by providing training directly or by subsidizing the training efforts of private industry. But training programs directed at the poor have an additional objective: They seek to improve the competitive position of the poor in the labor market. Although the two training functions overlap, they have very different implications. Training designed to create skills in demand leads directly to increased employment; training designed to increase the competitive position of the poor serves to redistribute existing unemployment.

The first full-scale government training program was established in 1962 under the Manpower Development and Training Act (MDTA). Persistently high rates of unemployment in the period 1958–61 coupled with fears of advancing automation led many observers to conclude that a basic mismatch existed between people and jobs. The only way to approach fuller employment, it seemed, was to provide the unemployed with the new skills demanded by advancing technology. Accordingly, Congress provided for a national effort to retrain displaced and unemployed workers in new skill areas.

In the years since the establishment of the MDTA program, the federal government has introduced and operated scores of training programs, with various services and for different target groups (the young, the old, the skilled, the unskilled, welfare recipients, high school dropouts, etc.). Four programs are particularly significant, because they illustrate different approaches to skill training.

The CETA Program

The Comprehensive Employment and Training Act (CETA) of 1974 was the centerpiece of employment policy in the 1970s. A unique feature of CETA was its transfer of program responsibilities from the federal government to state and local governments. Local "prime sponsors" received CETA funds from the federal government to run employment and training programs tailored to local needs.

The CETA program included a broad range of employment and training services. In part, this reflected the decentralized nature of the program. Even more important, however, is the fact that CETA funds were allocated by Congress under six different subprograms, defined by target group and type of service. The subprograms (separate titles of the Act) gave Congress some continuing control over the content of the overall CETA program. When

President Carter, for example, decided that public service employment (PSE) should be expanded, he was able to do so by persuading Congress to allocate more funds to the appropriate titles. Local prime sponsors then had the choice of expanding PSE or foregoing some federal grants. In its peak years of operation, CETA was spending over $4 billion a year on PSE programs.

Another feature of CETA was its increasing focus on "disadvantaged" (low-income and minority) workers and youth. In its final year (fiscal 1983) over 95 percent of CETA participants were disadvantaged. This focus maximized the program's antipoverty effectiveness. To further assure that disadvantaged workers could participate in CETA, the program paid participants a stipend while enrolled in education and training classes. Although small, these stipends enabled people with little other income to acquire needed skills.

From 1974 to 1982 the CETA program served over 30 million people. In 1981 alone, nearly 4 million participants were enrolled at a cost of $8 billion. One-third of this cost was associated with the public sector employment part of the program.

The CETA program was terminated in 1983, at the urging of the Reagan Administration. In part, the cutbacks and subsequent termination of CETA were simply part of the Reagan Administration's general retrenchment of social spending. There were additional motivations for the termination of CETA, however.

The chief criticism of CETA was its heavy emphasis on public sector employment. These PSE jobs were viewed as extraordinarily expensive "make-work" jobs, that taught few skills, seldom led to private-sector employment, and were too easily corrupted by local political interests. Critics also argued that CETA undermined the work ethic by paying people to rake leaves or attend classes. Although defenders of the program pointed to its success in serving the truly needy, they were unable to demonstrate that the public service employment programs were having any lasting impact on skills or employment.[1]

JTPA

CETA was replaced by the Job Training Partnership Act (JTPA) of 1982. Like CETA, JTPA provides for a variety of employment and training services. There are important differences, however, in JTPA's focus, content, and administration.

Under CETA, employment and training funds were allocated to local prime sponsors, often bypassing state governments. In the process, a whole new bureaucracy was created. JTPA eliminated this level, by distributing funds

---

[1] For a review of CETA performance, see Sar Levitan and Garth Mangum, eds., *The "T" in CETA* (Kalamazoo, MI: Upjohn Institute, 1980); and Laurie Bassi, "The Effect of CETA on the Post-Program Earnings of Participants," *Journal of Human Resources*, Fall 1983.

directly to governors to allocate within their own states. At the same time, JTPA gave local Private Industry Councils veto power over JTPA expenditures. This cemented the "partnership" dimension of the program, and provided some assurance that the program would be responsive to business needs.

Whereas CETA provided a mix of training and public sector employment, JTPA focuses exclusively on training. No funds are available for PSE jobs and no more than 15 percent of program funds may be spent on administration costs. Furthermore, the U.S. Labor Department must establish performance standards for training programs and demonstrate to Congress every two years that the training programs are cost-effective. JTPA is seen as a long-term solution to subemployment, rather than as a short-run response to cyclical unemployment.

The focus of JTPA was broadened to include "dislocated" workers as well as the "disadvantaged" workers who were the target of CETA. Dislocated workers are those who have lost jobs because of plant closings and permanent layoffs, and who have little chance of returning to their old jobs. They need not be low-income or minority status, as are disadvantaged workers. Title III of JTPA (see Table 13.1) is devoted exclusively to dislocated workers. The Act tries to get dislocated workers back into employment by providing skills, (re)training, job search assistance, and other services. If successful, these services can help prevent dislocated workers from slipping into poverty.

TABLE 13.1   JTPA TITLES AND FUNDS, FY 1984

JTPA TITLE	FY 1984 FUNDING	PROJECTED ENROLLMENT
Title I: Job Training Partnership; describes administration features and responsibilities	N/A	N/A
Title II: Training Services for the Disadvantaged; authorizes adult, youth, and summer youth programs for low-income minority workers	$2.6 billion	7.8 million
Title III: Employment and Training Assistance for Dislocated Workers; authorizes programs for experienced workers unemployed because of plant closings and permanent layoffs	$240 million	105 thousand
Title IV: Special Target Groups; authorizes the Job Corps program for youth; programs for veterans, farmworkers, and other special groups	$740 million	163 thousand

Source: Office of Management and Budget.

The WIN Program

A frequent criticism of JTPA and other "mainstream" programs is that they fail to serve adequately the neediest individuals. The number of available training and employment slots is always less than the number of unemployed workers. Hence, some deliberate choices must be made about whom to serve. Under these circumstances, program administrators often prefer to serve those individuals who are most job-ready. The least needy individuals are likely to provide the greatest "success" stories for program administrators. Unfortunately, this tendency to "cream" from the pool of potential program participants leaves many of the neediest job-seekers to fend for themselves.

The failure of "mainstream" training programs to provide adequate help to the neediest led to the creation of another major training program, the Work Incentive Program (WIN). What distinguished WIN from the outset was the fact that it serves only those who are receiving public assistance: Program participation is specifically limited to adult recipients of AFDC assistance. Moreover, all adult recipients are *required* to register for WIN services, unless exempted for reasons of health or the care of preschool children. This provision resulted from the widespread conviction that welfare recipients seek to avoid employment (see Chapter 8). On a more positive note, the program attempts to provide the supplemental services necessary for successful program completion. These range from day-care services and work orientation to medical examinations, transportation allowances, counseling, and job placement. In addition, because of WIN's link to welfare, there are no financial barriers to program participation. WIN enrollees continue to receive the same public assistance they had prior to entry. Thus, the program offers a package of services designed to move people from welfare to employment.

Although WIN seemingly offers all the ingredients for successful movement into employment, the program has not been regarded as a success. This view of WIN is not based so much on demonstrated program outcomes—WIN has achieved modest employment success—but more on the disappointment that WIN does not materially reduce welfare rolls.[2] In any case, the institutional training components of the program have virtually been scrapped. The emphasis in WIN is now on direct placement. What this means is that AFDC recipients are referred to employment counselors who try to find jobs for them immediately, rather than train them for jobs they might later fill. Such placement services can be valuable, at least to the extent that they improve communications between job-seeking welfare recipients and employers who might hire them. Unfortunately, the change in WIN was introduced just about the time national unemployment rates started soaring, leaving the employment counselors with little good news to report. Over the long run, we cannot expect WIN to be very successful until unemployment rates fall and employers start looking for less qualified help.

[2]For a description of WIN activities and outcomes, see Bradley R. Schiller, "Lessons from WIN: A Manpower Evaluation," *Journal of Human Resources*, Fall 1978.

Job Tax Credits

The three employment programs discussed so far all entail direct government expenditure and administration. As a result, they are highly visible and inevitably viewed as part of the public sector. The tax system, however, offers alternative approaches for employment and training policy. Rather than raising money through taxes to pay for government outlays, we can support training programs with tax credits. Tax credits permit companies to keep some of the taxes they would otherwise have to pay. These tax savings can then be used to finance desired employment and training activities.

The Targeted Jobs Tax Credit (TJTC) of 1978 illustrates the potential of this approach. The TJTC was designed to increase the employment and training of specific ("targeted") groups, including disadvantaged youth, ex-convicts, veterans, and welfare recipients. Companies hiring from these groups could claim a tax credit equal to 50 percent of the wages in the first year, and 25 percent of second-year wages. These credits reduce the cost of hiring labor and thus encourage more hiring and training of the poor.

Although tax credits have a lot of appeal, they have important limitations. To be effective, the tax credits must stimulate a net *increase* in the employment and training of disadvantaged workers. Otherwise, the credits become just a general subsidy to firms that were already employing disadvantaged workers. This was the case in the early years of the TJTC program, as indicated by the fact that three-fourths of the credits were certified retroactively, after employment decisions had already been made.

Tax credits are also weakened by an inherent goal conflict. The more specifically they are targeted on certain groups or activities, the more complex they become. This increases the administrative cost of using them, especially for small firms. Workers, too, are often reluctant to reveal their "disadvantaged" status to prospective employers.[3]

PUBLIC SERVICE EMPLOYMENT

It was suggested in Chapter 9 that underdeveloped skills or education are not a prime cause of poverty. It was argued instead that education and training credentials simply render an individual more competitive in the job search. Credentials provide a person with early access to job vacancies, but do not guarantee that such vacancies will exist. The experience with government training programs tends to support this view. For the most part, training programs are unable to place people in jobs unless labor market conditions

[3]The conflict between general and targeted tax credits is discussed in Dave M. O'Neill, "Employment Tax Credit Programs: The Effects of Socioeconomic Targeting Provisions," *Journal of Human Resources*, Summer 1983.

warrant. If there are no jobs waiting when training is completed, the net effect of training is to create a slightly more skilled pool of *unemployed* workers. Training programs are not able to significantly increase employment, particularly when unemployment is rampant.

Frustration with the results of government training programs has led most observers to the conclusion that more jobs must be created. But there are great differences of opinion about how this should be done. For decades it was assumed that expansionary fiscal and monetary policies could create all the desired jobs. But the resulting expansion of the public sector and attendant inflation were viewed by many as a deterrent to economic growth. Aggregate economic policies now reflect a concern both for the overall level of aggregate demand as well as for supply-side incentives.

One of the most controversial components of employment policies is public service employment. As we observed earlier, CETA's emphasis on public service employment was a principal cause of its ultimate demise. Public service employment is a very special kind of job creation. It involves the government directly in the employment process. It gives the government explicit control over what will be produced and who will be employed to produce it. At times this control may be advantageous; public services are not well provided for in the market context. Even though all taxpayers anguish over the lack of sanitation, transportation, education, protection, and recreation services, few are willing to pay for them. Nor can these public services be provided and paid for on an individual basis.[4] Accordingly, there is an output void that can be filled only by explicit government provisions.

The control that public service employment bestows over the structure of demand can also be used to advantage. Generalized aggregate demand policies, such as tax cuts, have widespread impact, some of which may be undesirable. Public service employment programs, on the other hand, can channel new labor demand to those areas or population groups most in need. Hence, maximum impact can be achieved with minimum disruption elsewhere in the economy. This advantage is especially important when average unemployment rates are low and unemployment is concentrated among specific minorities or in particular areas.

Public service employment, then, may fulfill two objectives: providing needed services and expanding employment opportunities. How well it fulfills these objectives depends on how much money is allocated for this purpose and how well those funds are spent. The Emergency Employment Act of 1971 provided for a maximum of 200,000 jobs over a period of two years. While that number was not insignificant, it represented only a small dent in the ranks of the unemployed, who, at the time, numbered over 5 million. The Works Progress Administration (WPA) of the 1930s employed about 2 million individuals at any

---

[4]This dilemma of public goods, or *externalities*, is discussed in most recent economics textbooks.

given time. Even President Carter's expanded use of CETA public service employment appears modest by comparison.

Whatever the potential benefits of public sector employment, it instinctively produces an image of make-work activity. People continue to think of the WPA as a major leaf-raking force. Even members of Congress—themselves beneficiaries of public service employment—are prone to distinguish between "real" work and public service jobs. Yet, the WPA constructed 651,000 miles of roads, 16,000 miles of water lines, 35,000 public buildings, 11,000 recreation facilities, and much more. What relatively little leaf-raking did take place was the consequence of hasty implementation rather than a dearth of public needs. Today the situation is no different. There is an abundance of useful and needed work to be done, and well-designed programs can do it. We might start by cleaning up our air and water.

What is, perhaps, equally curious about the make-work accusations is that they are applied only to public service employment. Very few people wonder or care whether a stockbroker, psychologist, or college professor does any "real" work. Indeed, we pay farmers enormous sums to avoid real work. Yet when the spotlight turns to the employment of poor persons, the public takes on a special concern for the nature and content of the work performed. Such concern implies a double standard, subjecting the output of the poor to more scrutiny than that of the affluent.

Another misapprehension about public service employment is that it requires the government to do all the administrating. This was done in the 1930s, but it is not the only approach possible. Where the government perceives that a service can be provided usefully, it may contract with private firms to carry out the actual hiring and production activity. The federal government can just as easily pay the Boeing Company to build sewage treatment plants as to build aircraft frames. This approach cuts right across the distinction between public and private employment. It may also render public service employment programs more acceptable politically. The government can even channel public service funds through community organizations, thereby reaching a higher proportion of those in need.

Although the potential of public service employment is impressive, it has not won broad acceptance. CETA vastly expanded the use of public service employment, especially during President Carter's economic stimulus program of 1977–78. However, critics have argued that many of the jobs "created" by CETA simply substituted for state and local jobs that would have been funded with nonfederal revenues. In the most blatant cases, cities "laid off" workers one day and "rehired" them the next day with CETA money. In the process, no new jobs were created. When such "fiscal substitution" occurs, public service employment is simply a disguised form of general revenue sharing.[5]

[5]For a discussion and estimates of "fiscal substitution," see Michael Wiseman, "Public Employment as Fiscal Policy," *Brookings Paper on Economic Activity* (Washington, DC: The

Public service employment programs are also opposed because they enlarge the size of the public sector. When the government creates more public jobs, it acquires greater control over our economic decisions. Moreover, a larger public sector implies that fewer resources will be available for the production of private goods and services. Hence, even proponents of public service employment argue that such jobs should be temporary, with a planned transition to private employment. This transition is dependent, however, on adequate private sector demand and some training while in public service employment. Neither expectation has been completely fulfilled.

A COORDINATED APPROACH

The possibilities for converting public jobs into private employment highlight the basic interdependence of the three routes to fuller employment and economic security. Aggregate demand policy, training programs, and public service employment are not mutually exclusive alternatives. Instead, they must be perceived and implemented as complementary dimensions of a single, coordinated manpower policy. High aggregate demand reduces the need for, and improves the outcome of, training programs. Public service employment has the same effects. Each approach makes the others more effective.

To some extent, two or more of the manpower approaches are combined in a single program. Take the WIN program, for example. While billed as a government training program, WIN incorporates aspects of public service employment. Program activities require the talents of caseworkers, counselors, and trainers, all of whom are performing needed public services. In addition, many graduates of the program become coaches or counselors themselves or are employed as aides in other government programs. Hence, the WIN program not only offers training but provides new job slots as well. Expenditures on the program also tend to expand aggregate demand. Other programs, including local manpower training programs, operate in a similar fashion.

In attempting to assess the potential effectiveness of employment policies for eliminating poverty, then, one must perceive the whole of manpower activity. We must recognize that no single approach will bring about full employment or eliminate poverty—at least not without enormous social costs. Government training efforts illustrate the point most vividly. Government training programs enrolled over 4 million individuals in 1981, at a federal cost of nearly $10 billion. Nevertheless, they failed to make a significant dent either in unemployment or

Brookings Institution, 1976); George Johnson and James Tomola, "The Fiscal Substitution Effect of Alternative Approaches to Public Service Employment," *Journal of Human Resources*, Winter 1977; and Michael Borus and Daniel S. Hammermesh, "Estimating Fiscal Substitution by Public Service Employment Programs," *Journal of Human Resources*, Fall 1978.

poverty. Restrictive fiscal and monetary policies undercut all other manpower efforts.

The critical role of aggregate demand policies in a general manpower policy is underscored by another consideration. Training and public service employment programs necessitate large and direct public expenditures. Many dimensions of fiscal and monetary policy involve no such outlays. Prevailing attitudes toward government expenditure are unlikely to yield training and public service employment programs of sufficient size to overcome the deficiencies of inadequate aggregate demand policies.

The end product of a coordinated employment policy should be an abundance of jobs—jobs that provide decent wages and advancement opportunity. The benefits of such jobs are as obvious as is the necessity for them. They will provide the incomes necessary to lift families out of poverty, to keep them together, and to give them promise of a secure future. Their benefits will reach to the children of the poor, who will have the means and incentive for staying in school. Employment policy has the potential, then, of minimizing both present and future poverty.

SUMMARY

The major components of employment policies are fiscal and monetary actions, training programs, and public service employment. While each of these components has its own character and purpose, they are all interdependent. No one component can succeed without support from the other two. At the same time, effective action in any one area enhances the potential for success in the others. One reason government manpower policy has not been more effective in the past is that these components have been viewed more as alternatives than as complements.

Government training programs have a short but well-funded history. Nevertheless, they have failed to fulfill their objectives. They are founded on the premises that good job vacancies exist and that the poor can be equipped to fill them. The WIN program reflects the degree to which this premise has been accepted. Every conceivable effort, including compulsory enrollment, was undertaken by WIN to prepare welfare recipients for work. Still, the program was not able to overcome the obstacles of slack aggregate demand and an absence of large public service employment opportunities. Training did not lead to jobs because jobs did not exist. CETA had more success in increasing employment, largely because it was part of an expansionary fiscal policy. In other words, employment and training programs have succeeded only when coordinated with full-employment macroeconomic policies.

Public service employment has been regarded as the unwanted stepchild of employment policy. It suffers from distorted memories of the 1930s and widespread fears of make-work and government expansion. Yet, public service employment could be an important component of manpower policy. Not only does it create more jobs, but it can fulfill important public service needs. Moreover, the performance of these public services can be undertaken by the private sector with government financing, thus breaking down the distinction between private and public work. Recent public service employment programs have been criticized, however, for poor design and administration. Fiscal substitution and lack of training have been recurrent problems.

Coordinated and comprehensive manpower policies could sharply diminish existing and future poverty. Jobs—in abundance and of good quality—are the most needed and most permanent solution to the poverty problem.

FURTHER READING

ADAMS, CHARLES F., JR., ROBERT COOK, and ARTHUR J. MAURICE. "A Pooled Time-Series Analysis of the Job-Creation Impact of Public Service Employment Grants To Large Cities," *Journal of Human Resources*, Spring 1983.

DAVIS, FRANK G. "What to do About Urban Poverty: The Black Ghetto Case," *Journal of Economic Issues*, September 1982.

LERMAN, ROBERT. "The Public Employment Bandwagon Takes the Wrong Road," *Challenge*, January 1975.

NATHAN, RICHARD P., et al. *Public Service Employment*. Washington, DC: Brookings Institution, 1981.

NATIONAL COMMISSION FOR MANPOWER POLICY. *CETA: An Analysis of the Issues*. Washington, DC: Government Printing Office, 1978.

PERRY, CHARLES R., et al. *The Impact of Government Manpower Programs*. Philadelphia: University of Pennsylvania Press, 1975.

SNYDER, ALAN HAROLD. "The Job Training Partnership Act of 1982: Two Birds with One Stone," *National Bar Association Law Journal*, Vol. XI, No. 2, 1982.

ULMER, MELVILLE E. "The Pitfalls and Promises of Public Employment," *Challenge*, January 1975.

U.S. DEPARTMENT OF LABOR. *Employment and Training Report of the President*. Washington, DC: Government Printing Office, annual.

14

Equal
Opportunity
Policies

Earlier chapters have documented the disadvantaged status of minority groups in America. Not only do such groups command fewer resources now, but they have less chance to acquire resources in the future. They have less opportunity to attain higher educational levels or even good quality schooling at lower levels. Even with appropriate educational credentials, they are not permitted to make maximum use of their attainments in the labor market. Such discrimination—both in schools and in the labor market—creates institutional barriers between people and jobs. Those barriers, in turn, alter both the size and composition of the poverty population.

In Chapter 11, a distinction was drawn among three different categories of discrimination. These were present market discrimination, prior market discrimination, and nonmarket discrimination. Social policies may be directed toward the elimination of any one or all of these categories. At the same time, however, we must recognize that each form of discrimination may require a different kind of policy. Furthermore, the antipoverty effectiveness of alternative policies may vary considerably.

The necessity for adaptive policy is easily illustrated. Consider, for example, the alternatives of eliminating present discriminatory practices or eliminating the effect of prior discrimination. There is no way to forbid discrimination that has already taken place. Consequently, efforts to combat previous discrimination must focus on the effects of that discrimination. Such remedial policies may take many forms, including government training programs to provide skills and education earlier denied; public service employment to create new opportunities; affirmative action to redistribute jobs or training; and even monetary compensation for denied educational and employment opportunities. But the potential of such actions is limited. As long as discriminatory practices continue, the need for remedial action will grow. Truly effective policy must focus on current discriminatory practices as well.

To some extent, continuing discrimination can be reduced by illuminating the nature and sources of prejudice. More direct action may include outright legal prohibitions, withdrawal or redirection of government funds, or public disclosure of discriminatory actions. Government may choose to use all of these approaches or none of them. It may also choose to engage in actions that foster discrimination. The focus of this chapter is on the extent to which government bodies are either abetting or combatting discrimination in schools and jobs.

EQUAL EMPLOYMENT OPPORTUNITY POLICIES

Public concern with the employment status of black workers came to the forefront just prior to World War II. Frustrated with their inferior employment status in a generally depressed labor market, black workers threatened to march on Washington, D.C., in the spring of 1941. To forestall that march, President Roosevelt issued an executive order creating the first federal Fair Employment Practices Committee (FEPC). The stated purpose of the FEPC was to provide the machinery necessary to enforce the general provisions of the Thirteenth, Fourteenth, and Fifteenth Amendments to the Constitution, amendments which were thought to forbid discrimination in the labor market. The FEPC was to monitor and correct any such discriminatory practices.

The power of Roosevelt's FEPC was extremely limited. Nevertheless, it confronted persistent and decisive opposition in Congress. Congress twice dismantled the FEPC, finally burying it in 1945. While Roosevelt's FEPC never had a chance to function effectively, its members nevertheless saw great potential for meaningful action. In their final report, the FEPC staff claimed that racial discrimination in employment could be ended if and when the federal government took decisive action.

No further equal employment opportunity action was taken until 1951. At that time, President Truman created a committee similar to the old FEPC. That committee, too, had few powers and continued to exist quietly throughout the eight years of the Eisenhower administration.

The federal effort to promote equal employment opportunity first began to look serious in 1961. That was the year President John Kennedy issued an executive order committing the government to action. According to Kennedy's executive order, the federal government assumed specific responsibility to "promote the full realization of equal employment opportunity." The government pledged not only to eliminate discrimination within its own agencies and departments but to assure equal opportunity in all private firms that performed work for the federal government. Failure to eliminate discrimination, the government warned, would result in the termination of federal contracts. This threat was the first real power such a committee attained. An Office of Federal Contract Compliance—now called the Office of Federal Contract Compliance Programs (OFCCP)—was established to carry out the executive order.

The EEOC

A parallel move toward equal employment opportunity took place in Congress shortly afterwards. The historic Civil Rights Act of 1964 incorporated provisions to forbid discrimination in the labor market. Title VII of that act explicitly outlawed discrimination by corporations, unions, or any other labor market participants. The enforcement of that prohibition was delegated to the newly created Equal Employment Opportunity Commission (EEOC).

Because the enforcement machinery and effectiveness of the EEOC and the OFCCP differ greatly, it is necessary to consider them separately. The Equal Employment Opportunity Commission has only limited enforcement power. It is directed by Congress to "endeavor to eliminate any discriminatory employment practice by informal methods of conference, conciliation, and persuasion." It may not impose sanctions, issue cease and desist orders, nor even make public the fact that discrimination is being practiced. It depends largely on the goodwill of the offender to bring about equal employment opportunity once a complaint is filed. Punitive or remedial action is rarely sought through the courts, and until recently it required the initiative of the victims of discrimination. But in 1972 the EEOC itself gained Congressional authorization, for the first time, to initiate court action to halt discriminatory practices.

The potential effectiveness of the EEOC has been weakened, however, by its procedural orientation. Before the EEOC can take any action at all, it must receive a sworn complaint from an individual. Once the complaint is received, the Commission seeks to determine whether the allegation is reasonable. If the complaint appears well-founded, the Commission then approaches the offending employer, union, or employment agency for "conference, conciliation, and persuasion." If conciliation is not attained, the complainant and the EEOC may seek redress in the courts.

This dependence of the EEOC on individual complaints has several drawbacks. First, it is tremendously expensive and time-consuming to review and process each complaint; indeed, the agency's backlog of unprocessed complaints totaled 99,000 in December 1977, overwhelming its staff lawyers and constraining its effectiveness. The EEOC has since instituted what it calls a "rapid charge processing system" which reduced the backlog to about 20,000 complaints in 1981.

A second procedural drawback is the lack of incentive: An aggrieved person has to report discriminatory actions. The complaint procedure subjects an individual to potential union or employer retaliation, costs him much time and money, and yields little practical benefit. At best, a complaining individual is apt to gain employment or promotion with a chastened and possibly resentful employer.

Much more effective action would be possible if the EEOC had the power to initiate broader investigations and seek more comprehensive resolutions. Realizing this, a former chairman of the EEOC, Lowell Perry, argued that "the one-to-one approach is not going to make a dent in our problem" and initiated investigations of "systemic" discrimination. What this means is that the EEOC would study the hiring and promotion policies of an entire company vis-à-vis minority goups, rather than just the experiences of individual complainants. In this way one action could bring relief or compensation to a much larger number of workers. In one of the first suits developed for this purpose, the EEOC was successful in persuading American Telephone and Telegraph Company (AT&T) to pay nearly $50 million in compensation to its female employees who had been denied equal job opportunities. Despite this early success, the EEOC has made limited use of this systemic approach. Although the EEOC has had over 300 attorney positions in its General Counsel office alone, the EEOC itself admits that only 30 to 40 percent of its attorneys have been sufficiently trained in trial work.[1] In addition, the EEOC has had to cope with its backlog of individual complaints and a continuing flow of 80,000 to 100,000 new cases per year. At the urging of President Carter, EEOC procdures were streamlined and given new leadership in 1977. These administrative changes improved EEOC performance, but gave it no new powers. Nevertheless, the EEOC was able to achieve a landmark "conciliation agreement" with General Electric in 1978. According to this agreement, General Electric agreed to spend $31.9 million to redress prior discrimination and provide improved job and training opportunities for minorities and women. Overall in 1980 and 1981, the EEOC helped attain over $37 million in benefits for victims of employment discrimination.

The OFCCP

Stronger powers of initiative and enforcement have always been available to the Office of Federal Contract Compliance Programs. The OFCCP may itself initiate investigations to determine whether discriminatory practices exist. It may also impose sanctions, such as contract termination, where discrimination is discovered. Furthermore, OFCCP may require employers to take "affirmative action" to remedy past discrimination. These sanctions may be applied to all businesses that sell or service products to the government. Thus, the potential power of the OFCCP is as vast as the government's position in the economy. As of 1983, all companies with more than 50 employees and selling at least $50,000

[1]U.S. Commission on Civil Rights, *The Federal Civil Rights Enforcement Effort—1977* (Washington, DC: Government Printing Office, 1977).

worth of goods and services to the federal government were required to nego-
tiate affirmative action plans with the government. The OFCCP also attempted
a voluntary initiative for smaller businesses but this option was not implemented
because of a feared increase in paperwork ("red tape") requirements. In an
unrelated Title VII case (*Spray* v. *Kellos-Sims*), however, the Supreme Court
ruled that smaller businesses affecting commerce could also be subjected to
discrimination laws.

While the potential power of the OFCCP to eliminate discriminatory
practices and rectify past injustices is great, that power has been rarely used.
Politics are partly to blame. An employer beset by the OFCCP always has
recourse to other authorities. Should he command the attention and sympathy
of Congressmen or other executive offices, OFCCP sanctions may be sus-
pended. Bureaucratic interests also undermine the OFCCP's power. The Department of Defense, for example, regards weapons procurement as more vital
to its mission than guidelines for equal opportunity. Hence, it may devote
relatively little attention to compliance with OFCCP edicts and may even
inveigh against contract cancellations that threaten orderly procurement. Accordingly, the power of the OFCCP remains largely on paper. Until 1979, not a
single contract had been terminated or cancelled to enforce equal opportunity
Moreover, the first big enforcement case, against Uniroyal (the nation's thi·
largest rubber manufacturer, with $36 million in federal contracts in 197?
based on the company's failure to cooperate with an OFCCP investi?
discrimination (begun in 1968!), not because of discrimination r
Reagan Administration has made virtually no use of this power, ⱶ
to rely on conciliation and negotiation rather than litigation.

Quotas and Guidelines

A more affirmative kind of action has been taken by
regard to the nation's labor unions, especially the const
saw in Chapter 11, blue-collar unions have the potential
workers with immediate remunerative employment. I/
ment is a major force in the construction industry, purcl
total output, and could exert considerable leverage to
tory barriers. In pursuing such an effort, the Nixon
establish guidelines for minority recruitment in the
attempt, in Philadelphia, proposed to raise the propo
from 5 percent in 1970 to 25 percent in 1975. That a
phia plans" elsewhere have not been successful, ho
dous political strength and do not like interference
"plans" and "goals" look too much like quotas,
threats of contract termination. Furthermore, th

1970s raised anxious questions about whose jobs would have to be sacrificed to make room for newly hired black workers, the same kind of "reverse discrimination" fear that later surfaced in other industries (including universities). Faced with the prospect of unemployment, union ranks solidify against the threat of increased competition. The government has also been unwilling to carry out threats of contract termination, which would also cause losses for employers.

While the short history of federal activity in the area of employment rights is not encouraging, it has not been wholly without impact. The enactment of legislation and the issuance of executive orders are important, even if they are not religiously enforced. They at least establish the principle that discrimination is not acceptable. They also lay the groundwork for stronger enforcement powers later. From this perspective, federal equal employment policies appear to be a timid beginning rather than an outright failure.

One of the most important side effects of federal legislation and pronouncements has been to stimulate private efforts, particularly legal actions against discriminatory employers. Federal action has established a legal basis on which private individuals can build. Accordingly, much of the responsibility for implementing and enforcing equal employment opportunity has been taken over by individuals and the courts. And in a score of cases—including the major EEOC suit against AT&T in 1974—individuals have won substantial sums of money from their employers to compensate for the income they were denied as a consequence of discriminatory practices in hiring and promotion. In the most controversial decision yet reached, a federal judge in Richmond, Virginia, ruled in January 1975 that workers at a tobacco plant who had been denied promotions because of race or sex discrimination could jump to the higher rungs of the company's job ladder, in the process "bumping" more favored workers down the ladder. That ruling (later appealed) is so drastic in its implications that it is sure to increase employers' efforts to dismantle discriminatory barriers.

Reverse Discrimination

The employment successes that have been achieved with various forms of affirmative action have not eliminated discriminatory barriers. They have been enough, however, to arouse growing hostility to any form of "special" opportunities for women and minority workers. Three-fourths of all Americans oppose "equal" employment opportunity programs that give special "preferences" (quotas, guidelines, etc.) to certain groups. In large part, this hostility reflects the threat that affirmative action poses for already privileged positions. But this is not the only basis for decrying "reverse discrimination." Critics point to the basic contradiction between "special" hiring preferences and equal opportunity. Others point out that the existence of affirmative action tends to cover the real achievements of minority workers. Such achievements are too easily dismissed as the outcome of affirmative action.[2] Such thoughts help explain why only a bare majority of minority and women workers favors "special" preferences.

The critics of affirmative action have taken their case to court. In one such complaint, Brian Weber, a white male employee of Kaiser Aluminum, sued Kaiser and his union, the United Steel Workers, for reverse discrimination. Weber had been rejected by a craft training program that reserved half its places for minorities. In the absence of such a privileged "set-aside," Weber argued, he would have been accepted for training. Lower courts agreed with Weber, noting that Kaiser could not use racial quotas except as a remedy for past discrimination at Kaiser. Since Kaiser itself did not admit to such prior discrimination, there was no legal basis for the special quotas. In 1979, the Supreme Court overruled the lower courts, however, arguing that preferential access to training is permissible when used to remedy "manifest racial imbalance."

The Court broadened the basis for quotas in *Fullilove* v. *Klutznick* (1980). In this case a white contractor challenged a provision of the 1977 Public Works Act authorizing 10 percent of government funds to be "set aside" for minority employers. This provision clearly gave minority contractors preferential treatment even where neither past discrimination nor racial imbalance existed. The Court upheld the set-aside provision, however, arguing that such quotas were not an unjust burden to place on whites (even if they had not consciously committed discrimination) and were permissible ". . . as long as remedial classifications serve important governmental objectives, and are substantially related to the objectives."

In another case the Supreme Court made a decision that seemed to stretch the concept of affirmative action to its limits. Winnie Teal, a black female employee of the Connecticut Department of Public Welfare had applied for the post of permanent welfare supervisor. She was required to take a written examination, which she failed. In fact, 46 percent of the blacks who took the exam failed, compared with only 26 percent of the whites. The department then hired eleven blacks, or 22.9 percent of the total black applicants, and thirty-five whites, or 13.5 percent of the total white applicants. It appeared, then, that the department had given blacks a decided advantage in hiring. Nevertheless, Winnie Teal sued the department, arguing that she had been discriminated against on the basis of race. In July 1982, the Court agreed with her, ruling that no step in the hiring process could manifest "disparate impact." This ruling (*Connecticut* v. *Teal*) appeared to proclaim that blacks had to be guaranteed a proportional share of jobs, regardless of qualifications or seemingly fair hiring criteria.

[2] See Thomas Sowell, "'Affirmative Action,' Reconsidered," *Public Interest*, Winter 1976; see also James R. Kluegel and Eliot Smith, "White Beliefs about Blacks' Opportunity," *American Sociological Review*, August 1982.

These and other court decisions were challenged by the Reagan Administration. In 1983, William Bradford Reynolds, chief of the Justice Department's Civil Rights Division, publicly characterized affirmative action as a "racial spoils system" that violated basic American concepts of fair play. As Reynolds saw it, "Thus we come full circle—fighting discrimination with discrimination . . . an urgent need has been pressed and those intent on finding a quick fix rather than a lasting solution have reached for the loaded weapon—the so-called remedial use of racial discrimination."[3] The Reagan Administration rejected this approach, and sought to eliminate quotas as an affirmative action tool. In pursuing this policy, the Justice Department sided with white Boston firemen in their challenge to affirmative action. The case arose as a result of budget cuts that forced lay-offs within the Boston Fire Department. Based upon the department's "last hired–first fired" seniority rule, minorities would have been laid off first and disproportionately. The NAACP argued, however, that a layoff of black firemen would destroy the gains of earlier affirmative action. When lower courts agreed to shelter the blacks from seniority-based layoffs, the white firemen took their case to the Supreme Court. The case was declared moot, however, when Boston provided the money needed to rescind the layoffs.

Sex Discrimination

The conflict between the goals of equal opportunity (nondiscrimination) and affirmative action (reverse discrimination) has not been confined to racial issues. The same conflict has arisen in attempts to eliminate both past and present sex discrimination in hiring, occupational status, pay rates, pensions, and maternity leave.

Sex discrimination battles have been fought on different battlefields. The first was the field of "equal pay for equal work." The Equal Pay Act of 1963 required employers to pay men and women equal pay for equal work. The courts enforced this act by providing compensatory damages to women whose pay was below that of men performing "identical" work in "similar" conditions.

Critics have argued, however, that this concept of equal pay is too restrictive. Because of occupational discrimination, few women hold jobs identical to men's. To assess "fair" wages, it is argued, "comparable" jobs, not identical ones should be considered. By this standard, women should get equal pay for jobs *comparable* to men's. Comparability is measured in various ways, including skills, responsibility, mental and physical effort, importance, and the extent of training required. The Supreme Court gave impetus to comparable worth cases when it ruled that female prison guards had the right to sue over pay discrimination even though they weren't performing tasks identical to male prison guards (*County of Washington* v. *Gunther*, 1981).

[3]William Bradford Reynolds, "Legitimizing Race As a Decision-Making Criterion: Where Are We Going?" lecture at Amherst College, April 29, 1983.

Although the concept of comparable worth has obvious appeal, it suggests a radical departure from market economics. The forces of supply and demand have a major impact on the wages for different jobs. Wage differentials also encourage people to take jobs that society values highly. To the extent that wages are set instead by computations of comparable worth, labor markets will be less efficient. Critics also question whether anyone really has the ability to make conclusive and objective computations of the "worth" of different jobs.[4]

EQUAL EDUCATIONAL OPPORTUNITY POLICIES

Governmental policy in the field of equal educational opportunity is more difficult to characterize than in the field of employment opportunity. Politics and bureaucracy again take their toll, of course, and there is, again, much complacency and inertia. What renders this subject especially complex, however, is the degree to which equal educational opportunity responsibilities are shared by different levels of government. Educational policy has traditionally been a prerogative of the separate states. The federal government provides less than 10 percent of all educational expenditures and administers no schools. Consequently, it has less power to create equal opportunity in the schools. It cannot terminate contracts or open new job slots as it may do in the labor market. In general, it must instead rely on, and cooperate with, the states and the courts to abolish discrimination in the schools. Only in higher education, particularly among large, research-oriented universities, does federal grant money account for a significant enough share of total income to make direct federal action a more serious threat.

The most obvious form of discrimination in the educational system is school segregation. While discrimination can take place even in the absence of segregation, not even a pretense of equal opportunity is possible as long as segregated schools are maintained. The Supreme Court itself made this observation, as we saw in Chapter 10. To what extent, then, are governmental bodies endeavoring to abolish segregation?

De Jure vs. De Facto Segregation

A distinction is commonly made between two kinds of segregation. The first, *de jure*, refers to a situation where blacks and whites are legally constrained to attend separate schools. The second, *de facto*, refers to a situation where school segregation results, not from edict, but from circumstance. Such a case

---

[4]For more views on comparable worth, see U.S. Congress, Committee on Post Office and Civil Service, *Hearings* on "Pay Equity: Equal Pay for Work of Comparable Value," U.S. Congress, September 16, 21, and 30, and December 2, 1982.

occurs where blacks and whites live in different neighborhoods, thereby making school integration difficult.

While the distinction between *de facto* and *de jure* segregation is often useful, it does have unfortunate consequences. It creates a distinction that few victims of discrimination can appreciate. As Judge J. Skelly Wright noted in a 1967 ruling on District of Columbia schools: "Racially and socially homogeneous schools damage the minds of all children who attend them . . . whether the segregation occurs in law or in fact." The distinction between *de jure* and *de facto* also gives rise to a false aura of innocence. *De jure* segregation is commonly seen as the consequence of evil intent, while *de facto* segregation is seen as the innocent by-product of socioeconomic forces—especially in the housing market. Such a view obscures the fact that government bodies can and do set the pattern for much *de facto* segregation. Segregation of the schools is rarely, if ever, a completely natural and unplanned circumstance.

Governments have two kinds of effects on *de facto* segregation. They may directly affect residential housing patterns, thereby enlarging or diminishing the foundation for *de facto* segregation; or they may alter the distribution of schools within established housing patterns, thereby facilitating or obstructing greater integration of the schools.

Housing Patterns

To a large extent existing residential patterns are the outcomes of millions of individual housing decisions, but free choice is not the only force operative in the housing market. The government, through its building and loan programs, has also participated in the establishment of segregated neighborhoods, and thus, must bear a significant responsibility for the *de facto* school segregation that results from neighborhoods isolated by race and class.

The Federal Housing Authority (FHA) has been a major factor in the housing market since its creation in 1938. It had a particularly important role in establishing the housing patterns of the post-World War II housing boom, patterns that still predominate today. The power of the FHA to alter housing choices lies in its ability to insure or guarantee loans on residential construction. FHA support oftentimes determines whether a house can be purchased, at what location, and at what cost. A measure of its influence is easily grasped. In 1965 alone, the FHA, together with the Veterans Administration (VA), insured or guaranteed some $150 billion in mortgage loans, providing money for more than 15 million housing units. During the housing boom of the late 1940s and 1950s, the FHA helped finance one-third of all new housing. Today's suburbs are, in large part, the product of FHA financing.

Given the power of the Federal Housing Authority in the housing market, its ability to foster or contain segregation is clear. For the most part, it has chosen to encourage and extend rigid racial and class segregation. The FHA

Underwriting Manual of 1938 declared that "if a neighborhood is to retain stability, it is necessary that properties shall continue to be occupied by the same social and racial groups." Agency valuators, considering whether or not to make FHA loans, were warned to protect against "inharmonious racial groups." The FHA even composed and distributed a model racially restrictive covenant, prohibiting "the occupancy of properties except by the race for which they are intended." The FHA deemed it necessary and proper that it create and maintain racially and socially homogeneous neighborhoods.

In 1962, President Kennedy issued an executive order on equal opportunity in housing, which brought to an end the explicitly segregationist practices of the FHA, but that order came too late and has too little force. The new FHA policy of nondiscrimination is limited largely to new housing. Thus, the established patterns of housing segregation are virtually unaffected. Furthermore, FHA loans now cover less than 20 percent of new construction. Of even greater significance is that the issuance of FHA guarantees still depends on the decisions of private lenders. FHA loan insurance is available only to those persons who are eligible to get loans from private banks. Thus, FHA policy reflects the racially and socially restrictive practices of most commercial lenders.

Poor families of whatever color are further handicapped by the FHA's focus on middle-class families. Because loan applicants must be eligible for commercial loans, FHA insurance and guarantees benefit few, if any, poor families. In 1981, for example, over 80 percent of the families using FHA guarantees to purchase a new house had incomes over $25,000; only 2 percent had incomes below $17,000.

Federal efforts designed explicitly to improve the living conditions of the poor have likewise failed to promote residential integration. Public housing projects are a vivid example. Public housing is almost always located in the poorest areas and most often segregated by race. Thus, it tends to intensify racial and economic isolation. The U.S. Commission on Civil Rights reports that, of the quarter of a million public housing units built in the nation's twenty-four largest metropolitan areas, only seventy-six units have been located outside the central city. The result is not only residential segregation but *de facto* segregation of schools as well. The Commission has cited some illustrations:

In San Francisco, for example, six projects totaling more than 2,300 units, each predominantly Negro, are grouped on one piece of land called Hunter's Point. The schools in the area that serve the housing projects all are more than 90 percent Negro. In Cincinnati, two nearby projects—Lincoln Court and Laurel homes—total almost 2,300 units. Together the projects are 99.7 percent nonwhite, and house 2,616 school-age children. Schools serving the development, many of them built specifically for that purpose, are all predominantly nonwhite.

The most extreme example, perhaps, is Robert Taylor Homes, a project in Chicago. Opened in 1961–62, it contains 4,415 units, 75 percent of them designed for large families. Of the 28,000 tenants, some 20,000 are children. The entire occupancy is Negro and schools were built in the area to serve the project alone. Indeed, classes for lower grades are conducted in project units, by agreement between the school board and the housing authority, as a way to relieve overcrowding in the nearby schools.[5]

While the federal government cannot be held responsible for all *de facto* school segregation, it is clear that its housing policies have encouraged racial and economic isolation. The government's housing policies have also intensified popular prejudice and fear, thereby further obstructing the attainment of residential and school integration.

School Patterns

While public and private housing decisions have created a foundation for school segregation, residential patterns alone do not maintain segregated schools. School authorities have broad discretion in defining the number and nature of school boundaries to be superimposed on residential patterns. Hence, local school authorities have the power to combat the segregation that exists in housing. Once again, however, this power has often been employed to intensify rather than to combat racial and economic isolation.

The power of local school authorities to encourage or resist school segregation is embodied in a variety of public decisions. Housing patterns alone do not define neighborhoods, much less school zones. Instead, the definition of a neighborhood is partly determined by the decisions of where and how to locate public schools. The number of schools to build, their size, and their geographic location are all decisions that help to shape neighborhoods. Building one large school between racially segregated housing areas, for example, does more to promote school integration than constructing two separate schools within racially homogeneous communities. Also important for the pattern of school integration is the number of grades to be served by each school and the actual specification of attendance zones. These decisions, too, can abet or overcome residential segregation.

To a large extent, of course, existing school patterns reflect historical, rather than current, decisions. This fact does not exonerate school authorities from responsibility, however. Residential patterns are continually changing and schools are continually being built or rezoned. Hence, school authorities have

---

[5]U.S. Commission on Civil Rights, *Racial Isolation in the Public Schools* (Washington, DC: Government Printing Office, 1967), pp. 37–38.

discretion to alter the distribution of pupils or facilities and to counteract past decisions. They have broad latitude to promote or impede integration as they see fit. Unfortunately, they have often chosen either to neglect the potential for integration or, worse still, to purposefully extend segregation. Local school authorities have used the following tactics successfully to achieve precisely these results:

Gerrymandering.   Gerrymandering refers to the purposeful restructuring of school attendance zones to foster school segregation. It is the oldest, simplest, and most blatant tactic available to local school authorities. Its visibility, however, has led to a decline in its use, especially where legal suits have arisen. The Hawthorne Elementary School in Kansas City provides a rare illustration. There, black families began to expand westward into the school zone of the previously all-white Hawthorne School. School authorities managed, however, to keep integration just beyond the reach of black children, simply by moving school lines westward as fast as black families moved into the area.

The potential for gerrymandering is broadened when a school system is expanding or contracting. When a system is shrinking, some schools must be closed, and their students reassigned to other schools. In the process, entirely new attendance zones can be created. Those new zones can be designed either to foster or impede school integration.

Optional Zones.   A tactic not far removed from gerrymandering is the use of optional attendance zones. An optional zone is a limited geographical area in which students are permitted to choose the school they will attend. In effect, optional zones are a more subtle and flexible tool to achieve either greater integration or segregation. Two illustrations cited by the U.S. Commission on Civil Rights convey the potential of this tool. In San Francisco an optional zone existed for two decades between the Geary Elementary School, predominantly white, and the Emerson School, predominantly black (see Figure 14.1). During that time, the residents of the optional zone were mostly white. By 1960, however, the great majority of the zone's residents were black. Continuation of the option thus threatened to enable black children to attend the white-majority Geary School. In 1961 the option was rescinded; residents of the zone were, thereafter, included in the attendance area of Emerson. Racial isolation was enforced.

In the South, *free choice* provisions are the counterpart of optional attendance zones. Students are permitted or required to state a preference for the schools they wish to attend. Priority is given to those preferences, however, that are based on residential location, established school ties, or other correlates of race. Just how free choice can operate as a subterfuge for purposeful segregation was illustrated in Atlanta. Its Kirkwood School was all-white but located in an area becoming all-black. Free choice provisions required that some blacks be

FIGURE 14.1   Optional Attendance Zones

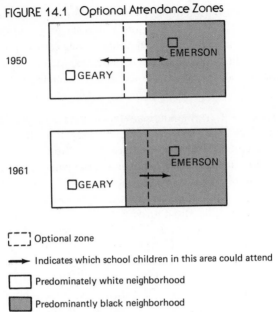

1950

1961

[_] Optional zone

➤ Indicates which school children in this area could attend

☐ Predominately white neighborhood

■ Predominantly black neighborhood

Source: U.S. Commission on Civil Rights. *Racial Isolation in the Public Schools* (Washington, DC: Government Printing Office, 1967), p. 53.

permitted to attend Kirkwood. To forestall integration, however, the superintendent of schools sent a letter to the parents of Kirkwood pupils, notifying them of the impending influx and reminding them of their free choice options. The parents responded promptly. Kirkwood, which had been all-white in 1964, was all-black when it reopened in 1965. All the white children had transferred elsewhere.

School Construction.   As noted earlier, the selection of a school site can have tremendous impact on the pattern of school segregation. Schools located within all-white or all-black residential areas solidify racial isolation. Schools located in fringe areas have the potential—if not subsequently gerrymandered—of accelerating integration. Unfortunately, site selection all too often conforms to segregationist practices. Of the 371 schools constructed in sixteen cities from 1950 through 1965, over 80 percent opened nearly all-white or all-black.

San Francisco's Hunter's Point community has already been mentioned as an example of federally financed residential segregation. The same area illustrates another dimension of school construction that can be manipulated for racial purposes, namely, school size. The abrupt influx of families into the Hunter's Point area necessitated more classroom space. To acquire that space, three of Hunter's Point's predominantly black schools were enlarged to a capacity of 1,000 pupils each. At the same time, however, a new school,

Fremont, was constructed within an adjacent white area. The Fremont school, however, provided space for only 450 pupils. Hence, it could not handle any of the overflow from Hunter's Point. The decision on school size reinforced existing segregation. Fremont retained its all-white character.

Grade Structure.   Even when faced with established school locations and size, school authorities are not powerless to alter racial attendance patterns. One extremely subtle but very effective means for overcoming these obstacles is to redefine grade structures. Enlarging the number of grades a school will serve has the effect of shrinking its attendance zone. On the other hand, schools that serve only a few grades must reach out in all directions to include a sufficient number of pupils. The Meigs School in Nashville illustrates how the technique can be employed. Most Nashville schools are organized on a 6-3-3 or an 8-4 grade pattern. The Meigs School, however, is an exception. It is located in a small black area and is structured to serve grades one to twelve. It is the only school in Nashville so structured, and it was all-black in 1965. The Dunbar Junior-Senior High School in Lexington, Kentucky, and the J.N. Ervin School in Dallas have been structured similarly and for the same purpose.

Selling the Schools.   School and government officials in Shaw, Mississippi, provide a final example of mechanisms for circumventing desegregation. In 1966, an all-white school board foresaw the inevitability of court-ordered desegregation in the public school system. To avoid this fate, the school board authorized the sale of selected public schools to private academies—for a price of one dollar each. The private academies, of course, had more freedom to discriminate. This situation continued until 1983, when the school board acquired 3-2 black majority, and voted 3 to 2 to buy back the schools. This has created a major legal and constitutional battle because a large amount of money has since been spent on renovations.

The many options local school boards have for creating or restructuring school-attendance patterns greatly weaken the distinction between *de jure* and *de facto* segregation. In 1974, the federal courts explicitly noted the difficulty of maintaining this distinction in Boston. Boston had never been segregated by law. However, Judge W. Arthur Garrity, Jr., observed that in the purchase and construction of new facilities, the assignment of staff and students to individual schools, and the use of open enrollments, the Boston School Committee was "at all times displaying an awareness of the potential racial impact of their actions. . . . The defendants have, with awareness of the racial segregation of Boston's neighborhoods, deliberately incorporated that segregation into the school system."[6]

---

[6]Opinion of Judge Garrity in *Morgan* v. *Hennigan*, cited in U.S. Commission on Civil Rights, *Fulfilling the Letter and Spirit of the Law* (Washington, DC: Government Printing Office, 1976).

Busing

To reduce the segregation of Boston's school system, Judge Garrity ordered mandatory busing of pupils between white and black schools. In view of the extensive segregation of both neighborhoods and schools, busing was perceived as the shortest route to equality of educational opportunity. Proponents of busing argued that buses are the only sure access to equality of facilities and may help promote more complete social integration. The legal basis for using school buses to promote equal educational opportunity had been firmly established by the U.S. Supreme Court in 1971 (in *Swann* v. *Charlotte-Mecklenberg*).

The reaction to interracial busing in Boston and other cities was initially hostile and even violent. Visions of masses of white children being bused into black ghettos stir the fears of most white parents. Such visions obstruct an oftentimes reasonable and expedient solution to established segregation patterns. Anxiety is also expressed for the stamina of children who must be bused daily to their classrooms. What is seldom realized is that busing of children to school is a common phenomenon in the United States. Nationally, slightly more than 50 percent of all school children are bused to school. Most are bused simply because such transprotation is most convenient. Only 3.6 percent of all public school pupils are bused for desegregation purposes. Ironically, still others are bused to extend and enforce racial segregation.

The cities of San Francisco and Cincinnati again offer convenient illustrations. The Anza Elementary School in San Francisco was built in a white area about eight blocks from the predomninantly black Golden Gate Elementary School. At the same time, classrooms at Golden Gate were overcrowded and pupils were being bused fifteen blocks to another school. Yet, when Anza was completed, its enrollment was nearly all-white. Black pupils from Golden Gate continued to be bused to the more distant Pacific Heights School.

Cincinnati school authorities were even more blatant. There, black students were bused out of a predominantly white area to a nearly all-black school 5.5 miles on the other side of Cincinnati. The explanation for busing focused on overcrowding, yet there was available space in closer schools, schools with predominantly white enrollments. The U.S. Commission on Civil Rights asked local school authorities to explain Cincinnati's unusual busing pattern. The response is as illuminating as it is evasive:

... the neighborhood—the concept of relationship of having children attend the school that is in the immediate proximity of the school, those closest to it. Now in this particular case all we did different from that is we picked them up and moved them some place else for a school, but in terms of parents we also tried to get the parents to maintain this relationship rather than dividing them up, into five different places and splitting them in five different spots. That's the only difference.[7]

In other words, the school board felt it necessary to keep all black students together, regardless of where or how they attended school.

The question of busing—especially when it is proposed for purposes of facilitating integration—touches a very sensitive nerve in most Americans. Three out of four Americans oppose mandatory busing, even though most still claim to support school integration. Indeed, the hostility to busing is so strong that many white families have fled the cities or schools where mandatory busing has been imposed.[8]

Why is the opposition to busing so fierce? In part, the opposition to busing reflects fears for the safety and stamina of children. As noted above, however, this fear may be exaggerated. A more important concern may be the expectation that the quality of education will decline when mandatory busing is imposed. In part, this concern may simply manifest latent racial prejudices. In addition, however, white parents realize that their children already have a monopoly on better schools. To share these limited resources with bused-in black students implies a reduction in education services. To be bused into a formerly black school implies an even larger reduction in educational services. Also, the turmoil and confusion that accompany the implementation of busing plans is almost sure to disrupt the educational process for at least some time.

Finally, busing is almost always perceived as a direct threat to the cherished notion of a neighborhood school. Even the Cincinnati school board felt obliged to defend its peculiar busing arrangement on the basis of the neighborhood school concept. It is worth reflecting for a moment, then, on what a neighborhood school really is and why it is so revered.

Neighborhood schools are usually deemed desirable for two reasons. They are close to home and thus conveniently accessible. They also serve to foster community cohesiveness. Children who reside close together and attend a common school have more opportunity to interact and are thought to establish more enduring relationships. These two benefits, proximity and social integration, are the mainstays of neighborhood school support.

What is curious about arguments for neighborhood schools is not their potential benefits but their historical perspective. Arguments against economic or racial integration usually proceed from the assumption that integration is destroying the neighborhood school. There are two problems with this perspective. First, children have, historically, traveled quite far to school and continue to do so. More proximate schools have resulted from increasing population

[7]U.S. Commission on Civil Rights, *Racial Isolation in the Public Schools*, p. 56.

[8]See Charles T. Clotfelter, "School Desegregation, 'Tipping,' and Private School Enrollment," *Journal of Human Resources*, Winter 1976.

density rather than from an increased awareness of any "neighborhood" benefits. One could also question whether this higher density actually has fostered better community and personal relationships. Second, we have already demonstrated that there is considerable flexibility in defining a neighborhood school. School attendance zones themselves can create neighborhoods, and deliberate manipulation of school zones can even affect residential choice. Families will want to live near the schools they know they can attend.

Neighborhood schools, then, are not historically sacrosanct. They may not even be the most desirable. As they are now conceived, they serve two specific goals. It would not be completely alien, therefore, to broaden our objectives. Schools could be structured to promote a sense of community in a larger and integrated society rather than to promote cohesiveness in a narrower and often isolated residential tract. Indeed, the narrow neighborhood concept has been repeatedly sacrificed to other social objectives. Every major city, for example, has at least one citywide school reserved for students of outstanding ability. In these cases, productivity and individual development are deemed more important than neighborhood cohesiveness. No one has argued that the attending students are in any way deprived. A high percentage of white parents send their children to distant private schools for exactly the same reasons. And finally, society has all too often demonstrated a willingness to subordinate neighborhood socialization to the goal of racial segregation in the schools. Neighborhood schools are deemed inviolate only when integration threatens.

The opposition to busing, then, is firmly based in both prejudice and privileged position. To overcome this opposition, school authorities would have to provide credible evidence that busing does not reduce the quality of education. School authorities may even have to "bribe" white students to stay in the public schools with improved facilities and programs. In other words, busing for desegregation purposes is most likely to succeed when school authorities recognize the origins of white opposition and respond to them in tangible ways.

To date, the experience with desegregation busing is mixed. There is no convincing evidence that either black or white students have materially benefited from desegregation, much less from forced busing. However, the kinds of benefits expected are both long-run and somewhat intangible. A major objective of the desegregation process is to reduce racial identities and barriers, to develop a more cohesive society. In the process, the quality of the broad educational experience is expected to improve. But none of these things happens automatically, or even very fast. Even under the best of circumstances—when political and financial resources are mobilized to implement desegregation smoothly—the gains from desegregation and busing may be slow to materialize.[9]

The continuing opposition to school busing has succeeded in limiting

[9]For a review of the experience with school segregation and busing in forty-seven school districts, see U.S. Commission on Civil Rights, *Desegregation of the Nation's Public Schools: A Status Report* (Washington, DC: Government Printing Office, 1979).

its use. Although the United States Supreme Court has decided that busing is an acceptable mechanism for achieving more equal opportunity (*Swann* v. *Charlotte-Mecklenberg Board of Education*, 1971), it is up to local administrators and courts to determine the extent and nature of its actual use. Moreover, the Supreme Court ruled in 1974 that school busing plans may not be imposed across school district lines unless it can be shown that the segregation was intentional and materially affected neighboring districts (*Milliken* v. *Bradley (Detroit)*, 1974). In addition, the court has emphasized (in Austin, Indianapolis, and Omaha cases) that all court-mandated desegregation must be based on *de jure* segregation. Specifically, plaintiffs must demonstrate that school authorities *intentionally* acted to segregate schools before the courts may impose desegregation remedies. The cumulative effect of these decisions is to restrict opportunities for desegregation (and busing in particular), especially where cities and their suburbs are racially and economically segregated.

Just how far we have progressed toward racial isolation across city–suburb lines is apparent in Washington, D.C. (71 percent black), Newark (54 percent), East St. Louis (69 percent), Atlanta (51 percent), Cleveland (59 percent), and other large cities. As a consequence, racial and low-income minorities are forced to confine their struggle for equal opportunity to the limited resources of their own school districts; one effect of this limitation has been to foster increased antagonism between inner-city minorities and adjacent low-income, white neighborhoods.

The U.S. Congress has also attempted to limit busing and other desegregation tactics. In nearly every year, Congress has sought to restrict the ability of the government to provide funds for forced busing or to cut off any federal funds to school districts that failed to comply with desegregation orders.

Fiscal Disparities

As we have observed, one of the arguments for school busing is that it will help reduce inequalities in educational facilities. Interestingly enough, the opponents of busing also argue that a more equal distribution of educational resources would eliminate the need for busing, and often offer to redistribute some resources, to provide "quality education for everybody," when pro-busing forces seem to be gaining strength. It seems reasonable to assume, then, that nearly everyone recognizes that educational resources are not equally distributed, that some children are provided with a lot more school resources than others.

Much of this problem derives from the way schools are financed. As we noted in Chapter 11, local communities continue to provide the bulk of their own school resources. In 1982 the federal government supplied only 9 percent of all educational expenditures and the state governments contributed 43 percent;

local governments provided the remainder. This means that the quantity and quality of educational resources in a community depends largely on the ability of the local populace to pay taxes. In substantive terms this means that wealthier white enclaves in the suburbs can provide educational opportunities for their children that few cities can ever hope to match.

It is easy to see how such disparities arise. In the suburbs the ratio of property values to school age children is far higher than in the cities. Indeed, population density is ten times larger in urban ghettos than in surrounding areas. This means that residents of the city must support far more school children per square mile than people in the suburbs. Furthermore, the wealthier residents of the suburbs are better equipped to support public schools. They have the property and income on which school revenues depend.

The economics of local school financing encourages school districts to attempt to maximize their tax base while minimizing enrollment size. That is, they seek to include the wealthier and exclude the poorer, especially those with many children. The results are staggering. In California, for example, the poorest elementary school district had only $438 of assessed property per pupil in 1977. The richest district had over $2.4 million of property per pupil. This lead to a lower tax rate for those most able to pay, an outcome of great benefit to the wealthier but of great disadvantage to the poor.

Given the nature of school financing, suburban communities have a tremendous incentive to insulate their school systems from the poor. They have little desire to impose higher tax rates on themselves to provide more educational opportunity for others. In some communities wealthier neighborhoods may even seek to incorporate independent school districts to dispose of responsibilities they already share. This tactic has taken on special significance as the courts have ordered opportunities to be equalized within, but not across, school districts.

To some extent, state and federal governments attempt to equalize the educational inequalities between richer and poorer communities. The Elementary and Secondary Education Act of 1965 is an example of such an attempt. Under this act the federal government distributes $2-3 billion a year to the poorest schools, but even this infusion of funds is inadequate. Only two-thirds of the students eligible to receive aid from Title I of the Elementary and Secondary Education Act are actually served. This reflects a number of problems, including inadequate funding, poor selection procedures, and the lack of Title I programs at certain grade levels. Even those served by Title I programs only receive an additional $400-500 in educational services per year.[10] The most absurd and distressing statistic of all is, perhaps, this: The wealthiest schools are more likely

---

[10]U.S. Commission on Civil Rights, *Statement on the Fiscal Year 1984 Education Budget* (Washington, DC, July 1983).

than the poorest schools to have subsidized milk or food programs. Many poor schools are denied such benefits because they cannot afford cafeterias, extra personnel, or their share of total costs. While the federal government is spending $2-3 billion in special aid, over $150 billion is being spent on education, with the biggest share still going to wealthier communities.

The subject of school financing highlights several important dimensions of the educational opportunity issue. The localized nature of school financing, for example, provides an independent motive for segregation. Even persons who harbor few racial prejudices are not immune to self-interest. On the contrary, most people seek to minimize their tax burden while providing well for their own children. Thus, they seek to exclude poor children, many of whom are black, from their school systems. This exclusionist tendency illuminates again the close ties of racial and class discrimination.

The class discrimination inherent in existing patterns of school financing has recently become a major judicial issue. In August 1971 the California Supreme Court acknowledged that fiscal disparities between school districts "makes the quality of a child's education a function of the wealth of his parents and neighbors." Ruling that such discriminatory treatment violated the Fourteenth Amendment of the U.S. Constitution, the Court declared the state's entire system of financing public schools to be unconstitutional. However, the U.S. Supreme Court effectively overturned that decision in 1973 in a similar case originating in San Antonio, Texas. In its decision the Supreme Court admitted that the present basis for financing schools was "imperfect," but argued that it did not have the prerogative to interfere with the function of the legislative branch and overturn the wisdom and experience of state legislatures and educational administrators. Solutions to the inherent inequalities of school finance, the Court suggested, should be sought in state legislatures, not the courts.

Compensatory Education

An approach to equal education opportunity that has aroused relatively little hostility is compensatory education, the provision of added educational resources to children from poor or minority homes. Indeed, most of the federal money spent on elementary and secondary education is distributed to the lower-income school districts, either by federal statute (Title I of the Elementary and Secondary Education Act) or by allocation decisions made by the states that receive federal grants. The unspoken objective of these efforts is to improve the resources available to poor and minority groups without sharing those (via racial or class integration) available to upper-income groups. As we noted earlier, however, the total federal effort is small in relation to the size of the educational system.

Perhaps the most important form of compensatory education has been the preschool program, particularly Head Start. As the designers of Head Start observed:

> . . . the early years of childhood are a most critical point in the poverty cycle. During these years, the creation of learning patterns, emotional development and the formation of individual expectations and aspirations take place at a very rapid pace. For the child of poverty, there are clearly observable deficiencies in these processes, which lay the foundation for a pattern of failure, and thus a pattern of poverty, throughout the child's entire life.

To help such children get a more equal start in the education system, Head Start was created to provide educational, health, nutritional, and social services to disadvantaged children in their preschool years. Since its creation in 1964, over 8 million children have participated in Head Start.

Evaluations of Head Start have consistently documented its success in raising preschool children's capabilities, interest, and aspirations. At the same time, however, observers noted that the program's impact tended to be short-lived: After a year or two in their regular school systems Head Start children performed no better than their similarly disadvantaged classmates.[11] Critics of the program were quick to cite this as evidence of the basic genetic or cultural deficiencies of minority children. More sympathetic observers argued, however, that ghetto schools operated as levelers, that the higher motivation and aspirations of Head Start children were not being reinforced by their regular schools. Indeed, the realities of ghetto schools, combined with the increased awareness and ambition fostered by Head Start, might well inculcate an irrevocable sense of defeat. Accordingly, the Follow-Through program was created in 1967 to provide continuing services to Head Start children as they progress from kindergarten to the third grade. Unfortunately, the resources of the program have not been large enough to provide services to all needy Head Start graduates.

College Admissions

One very clear implication of our review of (un)equal opportunity in the preschool, elementary, and secondary school systems is that minority groups will be less prepared than others to enter colleges and universities. Because they are not provided full and equal opportunities to develop their skills earlier, they will not exhibit the required skills at the time of admission to higher education.

---

[11]For a review of the Head Start evidence, see Burt S. Barnow and Glen G. Cain, "A Reanalysis of the Effect of Head Start on Cognitive Development: Methodology and Empirical Findings," *Journal of Human Resources*, Spring 1977.

This will be manifest not only in grade records, but even more clearly in standardized college entrance exams (the SAT, for example) that are a major screening mechanism for admissions applicants. Accordingly, if all college applicants were treated equally, we would expect a much lower proportion of blacks and other minorities to gain entrance to higher education. The effect of such an "equal opportunity" policy would be to widen educational disparities between whites and blacks (and thus, as we shall note in the next chapter, to increase income inequalities as well).

The vestiges of prior discrimination thus raise very serious policy questions about our concept of equality and the appropriate role of educational institutions in fulfilling equal opportunity goals. On the one hand, it can be (and is) argued that equal treatment is the only objective of policy and that schools should not be expected to exceed that mandate. From this point of view, the overriding goal of higher education is to enhance society's productivity by concentrating resources on the most able. So long as all applicants are treated equally, then the goals of efficiency and equality are both fulfilled.[12]

As we have noted, however, this kind of admissions policy effectively "writes off" the talents of individuals who have been discriminated against in the earlier components of the school system. Hence, an alternative viewpoint stresses the importance of achieving equality of status between whites and blacks, while suggesting that black applicants will prove their worth (demonstrate their latent abilities) once they have an opportunity to catch up. Thus, it is argued, blacks and other minorities should be admitted to college and professional schools on a preferential basis (with lower test scores and grade-point averages), a policy that will not only hasten the achievement of status quality, but will ultimately fulfill our goals of efficiency as well.

Clearly, there is considerable merit to the above argument, particularly if the preferentially admitted students do indeed catch up. But the merits of the case are not likely to impress those who end up paying the costs of such a policy—in particular, those white applicants who are denied admission to make room for minority groups. Such students have worked hard to meet college admission standards and are naturally resentful when others with fewer "qualifications" take their place. Indeed, such students argue that they themselves are being denied equal opportunity—are the victims of "reverse discrimination"—and have sought appropriate relief from the courts. In one of the most publicized cases to date, a rejected applicant (Marco DeFunis) of the University of Washington Law School sued to gain admission on the grounds that he had outscored a number of admitted black and Spanish-speaking students on the Law School Admissions Test. The case ultimately reached the U.S. Supreme Court in the spring of 1974. Unfortunately, the Court was able to declare the case moot

[12]For a fuller discussion of this viewpoint see the symposium "On Equality" in *The Public Interest*, Fall 1972; or Arthur Okun, *Equality vs. Efficiency: The Big Trade-Off* (Washington, DC: The Brookings Institution, 1975).

because DeFunis had been admitted on a provisional basis while his case was working its way through the courts and actually was graduating when his case reached the Supreme Court.

A more recent case concerns a rejected applicant to the University of California's Medical School at Davis (*Regents of the University of California* v. *Alan Bakke*). Under a special admissions program, sixteen of that school's one hundred admissions are set aside for minorities, a policy that has been attacked on the same "reverse discrimination" basis. A superior court judge in the county ruled that the program did violate the equal protection clause of the U.S. Constitution, the corresponding provision of the California constitution, and Title VI of the U.S. Civil Rights Act of 1964. In June 1978, the U.S. Supreme Court agreed with Bakke. The Court noted that race could be considered as one factor in the admissions process, but ruled that rigid quotas based on race were too discriminatory.

There is no simple way to resolve these competing claims for educational resources; there is clearly some degree of merit to each argument. Only by making admission available to everybody (a policy initiated at City University of New York) can everyone's claim to admission be satisfied. But such a policy not only arouses serious concern for the quality of higher education, but puts severe pressure on school budgets. In the absence of open admissions, a delicate compromise must be struck between those claims to admission based on achievement and those based on denied opportunity (and thus potential achievement).

SUMMARY

Equal opportunity policies can help eliminate poverty in two ways: They may provide access to educational credentials; and they may dismantle artificial barriers between people and jobs. Access to educational credentials is important to the extent that it opens new employment opportunities or redistributes existing ones.

The federal government's effort to create equal opportunity in employment has not met with much success. Black workers continue to suffer inordinate levels of unemployment and to be relegated to undesirable jobs. A major reason for this continuing discrimination lies in the nature of government efforts. For decades the federal government has had the power only to exhort employers to create equal employment opportunities. It was not until the early 1960s that the government acquired some meaningful powers to enforce its proclamations. The Office of Federal Contract Compliance Programs may terminate contracts of discriminatory employers, while the Equal Employment Opportunity Commission may facilitate legal action. Those powers have been used rarely, however, and then mostly as a threat. Political, bureaucratic, and economic interests continue to impede the attainment of equal employment opportunity; what progress has been achieved is largely the result of private legal action, building on public legislation.

In the educational system, equal opportunity has been just as elusive. Local and state governments have not demonstrated a consuming ambition to open school doors to all. On the contrary, they have often employed a variety of manipulative techniques to forestall school integration for as long as possible. The localized nature of school financing also creates a tremendous incentive for wealthier and whiter communities to exclude poorer and blacker children from their schools. Federal authority to alter the pattern of segregation resides primarily in the power to bestow or withdraw funds under the Elementary and Secondary Education Act. But the amount of funds involved is relatively small and the political pressure to maintain their flow great.

FURTHER READING

AYRES, Q. WHITFIELD. "Desegregating Higher Education," *The Public Interest*, Fall 1982.

CONGRESSIONAL BUDGET OFFICE. *Inequalities in the Educational Experiences of Black and White Americans.* Washington, DC: Government Printing Office, September 1977.

JENCKS, CHRISTOPHER, et al. *Inequality.* New York: Basic Books, Inc., 1972.

MOSTELLER, FREDERICK, and DANIEL P. MOYNIHAN, eds. *On Equality of Educational Opportunity.* New York: Random House, Inc., 1972.

NEWMAN, DOROTHY K., et al. *Protest, Politics, and Prosperity: Black Americans and White Institutions, 1940–1975.* New York: Pantheon Books, 1978.

SOWELL, THOMAS. *Race and Economics.* New York: David McKay Co., Inc., 1975, Chs. 7–9.

U.S. COMMISSION ON CIVIL RIGHTS. *With All Deliberate Speed: 1954–19??* Washington, DC: Government Printing Office, 1981.

_____. *Affirmative Action in the 1980s: Dismantling the Process of Discrimination.* Washington, DC: Government Printing Office, 1981.

U.S. EQUAL EMPLOYMENT OPPORTUNITY COMMISSION. *Annual Reports.* Washington, DC: Government Printing Office.

Directions and Prospects

According to official estimates, over 30 million Americans remain in poverty. Although these estimates are exaggerated by the neglect of in-kind transfers, it is evident that millions of Americans are poor, either because their standard of living is below "minimally adequate" standards or because they depend primarily on public assistance (welfare) to maintain that poverty standard. Recognition of such widespread poverty has led to two simple questions: (1) Why are so many Americans poor? and (2) What policies will eliminate their poverty? The preceding chapters have provided much of the background material necessary to resolve these questions. This concluding chapter attempts to summarize the salient impressions of our inquiry and offer policy suggestions.

THE CAUSES OF POVERTY

The most popular diagnoses of poverty focus on the personal characteristics of those who are poor. The poor are viewed as less able, less motivated, overly reproductive, too aged or sick, or otherwise handicapped. By inference or declaration, they are thus assumed to be responsible for their own impoverishment. This Flawed Character view of poverty, as we have called it, is reinforced by conventional statistical profiles of the poverty population. Very high percentages of the poor *are* in families that are aged, or female-headed, or large, or prone to sickness and disability.

There are two critical weaknesses in these demographic theories of poverty, however. Not all of the poor fit one or another of the various categories of misfits. Indeed, the largest single demographic group among the poor consists of traditional male-headed families, most with a father working full-time all year round. But the weakness of demographic theories involves more than just narrow horizons; these theories also suffer from shortsightedness. Even those poor families who manifest distinctive demographic traits, such as broken homes, are not necessarily poor because of those traits. On the contrary, for the most part the aged poor were poor before they were aged, broken poor families were poor before they split up, large poor families were poor when they were smaller, and sick poor families were poor even when they were well. Thus, theories of poverty causation that are based only on observations at a single point in time fail to perceive the dynamics of impoverishment. They confuse association with causality.

A broader, more dynamic perspective on poverty is achieved by focusing on the relationship of people to the labor market. For the most part, it is a person's relationship to the market that determines his economic, and even social, status. One immediate advantage of this perspective is that it draws attention to two critical questions: (1) What forces determine how many good income earning opportunities are available? and (2) What forces determine who will obtain those opportunities? The myopic perspective of demographic theories of poverty encompasses only the second question. It assumes that good jobs are always available in sufficient quantity. But they are not, as history has repeatedly shown, and as we have again witnessed in the escalating unemployment rates of the early 1980s. To understand why so much poverty exists at any point in time, we must consider and resolve the first question. The answer to the second question tells us primarily how that poverty will be distributed.

In seeking to resolve the first question, we have put a heavy stress on the importance of aggregate economic policies in determining the extent of poverty. The number of available jobs is a phenomenon over which individual members of society have very little control. Similarly, they have little control over what kinds of jobs will be available or where they will be located. These decisions are made, instead, by the interplay of labor market forces, among which government fiscal and monetary decisions are often the most decisive. Accordingly, we conclude that collective social decisions in the area of economic policy—especially those concerning the extent and structure of the demand for labor—are responsible for much poverty.

We should not conclude, however, that all available income-earning opportunities are taken. Even in relatively prosperous times, some families will break up, others will become sick or disabled, and some may even choose not to work. Hence, even with prolonged full employment, not all families will participate fully in the economy. Some disequilibria between the number of available jobs and potential workers do arise from demographic forces, and we must include them as independent causes of poverty where appropriate. Family breakup and single parenthood rate high among these factors, with age and disability slightly less important.

The third general set of causes are those related to discrimination, both in the schools and in the labor market. Minority groups, the offspring of the poor, and women are deprived of an equal chance to acquire productive skills and use those skills in the labor market. Hence, racial, class, and sex discrimination have significant impact on both the distribution and extent of poverty. As long as discrimination persists, we may predict that the children of the poor, blacks, and female-headed families will dominate the ranks of the poverty population. Even in a relatively prosperous economy, discrimination tends to create artificial barriers between workers and jobs, leaving some individuals poor.

Finally, we have recognized that government efforts to assist the poor may also play a role in perpetuating poverty. Income transfers diminish both the need to work and the financial incentives to work. In extreme cases a job would actually reduce the income of a welfare recipient. These dimensions of the welfare system create an added barrier between people and jobs.

In assessing the causes of poverty, then, we may make the following generalizations: (1) labor market forces are primarily responsible for the extent of poverty, with demographic handicaps and discrimination of secondary importance; and (2) the distribution of poverty is determined by patterns of discrimination and demographic characteristics. Public programs to alleviate poverty and discrimination, while successful in many respects, also contribute to the problem by distorting work incentives. This is a reflection of the goal conflicts inherent in all such programs. Because available knowledge and statistics about poverty and discrimination are not complete, there is room for argument on the precise dimensions of each relationship. Nevertheless, the broad outlines of causality are clear enough to provide the necessary perspective for public policy approaches.

POLICY DIRECTIONS

An understanding of the causes of poverty gives clear direction to the formulation of required public policy. To eliminate poverty, we must first expand the number of decent job opportunities and their availability. Harry Johnson of the University of Chicago summarized the point well: ". . . in the absence of a policy of raising the demand for labor to the stretching point, ad hoc policies for remedying poverty by piecemeal assaults on particular poverty-associated characteristics are likely to prove both ineffective and expensive. The most effective way to attack poverty is to attack unemployment, not the symptoms of it."[1]

To reduce unemployment and poverty, the government has several options available. First and foremost, it must seek to maintain a high level of aggregate

---

[1] Harry G. Johnson, "Poverty and Unemployment," in Burton Weisbrod, ed., *The Economics of Poverty* (Englewood Cliffs, NJ: Prentice-Hall, Inc., 1965), p. 170.

demand by the judicious use of fiscal and monetary tools. In addition, it must give special consideration to the structure of demand those tools stimulate. Aggregate economic policies have identifiable impact on different areas, industries, and labor market groups. Accordingly, it is the responsibility of government policymakers to select that mix of public actions that maximizes impact on the unemployed and poor, while minimizing dislocations, such as inflation, elsewhere.

Aggregate economic policies must also incorporate clear supply-side incentives for employment and training of the poor. Tax, spending, or regulatory policies that raise the cost of hiring the poor will not reduce poverty. In developing macroeconomic policies, these potential supply-side effects must be addressed as well.

In addition to seeking full employment, government agencies must make a determined effort to equalize educational and employment opportunity. This will not only further reduce poverty and inequity, it will also make the attainment of full employment easier and less expensive.

Finally, the public must assume responsibility for those who are temporarily or permanently unable to participate in the labor market. Adequate income support must be available, both to alleviate hardship and to reduce intergenerational deprivation. Greatest priority should be placed, however, on reducing the need for public assistance to a minimum.

Viewed against this policy framework, recent public antipoverty activities do not appear well directed. Only rarely has there been a sustained and determined effort to reach full employment, and even at those times, policy decisions stopped short of considering the structure of aggregate demand thereby created. Instead, public antipoverty activity has, for the most part, been a bread and circus kind of affair. We have allotted—grudgingly, to be sure—huge sums of money to feed, clothe, and house the poor, in the hope, perhaps, of achieving social tranquility. At the same time, we have subjected the poor to a kaleidoscope of training and education activities, holding out false promises of job opportunity. Yet we have done close to nothing to create the job opportunities that are our most pressing need. Some recent experiences are worth reflection.

Welfare Reform

At the end of 1982 there were nearly 15 million individuals receiving, in the aggregate, nearly $50 billion of public assistance (cash and in-kind). Translated into tax dollars, this means that the average nonpoor individual in the United States contributed over $250 in 1982 to provide the poor with income maintenance. While these amounts are a small fraction (under 10 percent) of all government expenditures, they are large enough to stir public anguish. Indeed, the cry for welfare reform has been strident.

In Chapter 12, we reviewed the character of recent welfare reforms. The Reagan reforms of 1981 significantly altered the conditions of welfare receipt. Smaller income guarantees and mandatory work provisions are the central features of this "workfare" approach. Like earlier reforms, the Reagan program is subject to two general criticisms. Workfare, like other reforms, has been depicted as a "solution" to our welfare problems. It is not, nor could it be. At best, welfare reform can achieve a more equitable or efficient compromise between the conflicting goals of income adequacy, work incentives, and cost efficiency. The basic conflict between these goals will remain, keeping a final "solution" to welfare beyond our grasp.[2]

The second problem with welfare reform is that it tends to exhaust all antipoverty efforts. Because "welfare reform" is such an enticing prospect, it tends to receive high policy priority. The problem with welfare reform's high priority is that it threatens to impede more meaningful and permanent poverty remedies. Public interest in poverty issues dissipates easily. Welfare reform thus threatens to satisfy the need for action, to divert our attention away from more fundamental causes of poverty and inequality. There is grave danger that welfare reform will be regarded as a solution to the problem of poverty and that other remedies will be neglected.

Education and Training

Perhaps the second ranking area of public concern is the field of education and training. Administrative and Congressional spokespersons continue to exhort the young to stay in school and the unemployed—especially those on welfare—to undertake further training. Appropriations to expand government training programs are rarely denied, and political support for educational outlays is easy to muster.

No general case against educational and training expenditures has been presented here. Again, the focus is only on the appropriateness of those expenditures as antipoverty tools. The issue is important because educational and training programs gather much of their support on the basis of their reputed antipoverty effectiveness. What we have sought to demonstrate is that this belief bears very little resemblance to the causal roots of poverty. Lack of training or education, by itself, is not a very significant cause of poverty. Thus, programs to provide more education and training are not particularly well suited to reduce the incidence of poverty. What impact they have is dependent on manpower policies generally. The limited potential of educational advancement to eliminate poverty has been underscored by a recent report of the U.S. Commission on Human Resources and Advanced Education: The Commission found that 25 percent of all college graduates are already overtrained for the jobs available.

[2]For a review and critique of other recent welfare reforms and experiments, see Bradley R. Schiller, "Welfare: Reforming Our Expectations," *The Public Interest*, Winter 1981.

Training and education programs can still be improved, of course. Of particular interest is the potential to target training services more directly on the poor. CETA did this by focusing almost exclusively on the disadvantaged. Targeted tax credits attempt to do the same thing in the private sector by subsidizing the wages of selected low-income groups. Despite their good intentions, however, all such efforts will remain captive to macroeconomic policies. In the absence of full employment, the primary effect of such programs is to redistribute unemployment, not eliminate it.

Macroeconomic Policy

Recent public actions in the area of manpower policy best illustrate the mistaken direction of current antipoverty efforts. The single most important observation of this book is the causal significance of aggregate demand policies for the incidence of poverty. High unemployment and sluggish economic growth are the most certain and forceful agents in perpetuating poverty. Nevertheless, public policy in the mid-1970s and early 1980s can be characterized as a deliberate return to the slower growth and higher unemployment rates that characterized much of the 1950s. Recent decisions illustrate the direction of public policy.

From the first day in office, the Nixon Administration expressed grave concern for the movement of prices and the threat of accelerating inflation. To restore price stability, the Administration curtailed growth in government expenditures and increased the cost of borrowing. The effects of these actions were soon felt. Unemployment rates jumped from a low of 3.5 percent in early 1969 to over 6 percent in 1971. The number of persons in poverty increased at the same time. The Ford Administration contributed to this trend by declaring inflation to be "public enemy number one" and forsaking expansionary policies. As a result, unemployment rates continued to climb, reaching a peak of 9.0 percent in May 1975. At the same time, an additional 2 million Americans fell into poverty.

The Carter Administration initiated a much more expansionary policy. President Carter elevated the goal of full employment to highest priority and began in 1977 to stimulate aggregate demand. Unemployment rates fell steadily for two years, and the number of poor persons declined. In 1978–79, however, inflation accelerated, and the Administration's priorities switched from expanding employment to fighting inflation. Once again, the poor and unemployed were sacrificed to price stability, with relatively little consideration of alternative policies.

President Reagan decried the high unemployment rates and slow growth produced by Carter's policies but nonetheless increased the pressure of antiinflationary policies. In the process the United States experienced back-to-back recessions and its highest unemployment rates since the 1930s. Another 4 million Americans were pushed into poverty.

The lesson of these repeated experiences is clear: Fighting inflation is politically more important than fighting poverty. Whenever a trade-off between full employment and inflation is apparent or imagined, our employment goals are quickly abandoned. This forestalls any real prospect of eliminating poverty.

Equal Opportunity

Recent activity in the area of civil rights has largely been a question of the courts leading and the executive branch timidly enforcing. The Reagan Administration, for example, did not file any school desegregation suits for two-and-a-half years. Its first suit was filed in July 1983 against the state of Alabama for allegedly maintaining a "dual system of public higher education based on race." The suit charged that the state's college system denied black applicants admission to traditionally white schools, excluded blacks from the faculty and staff of those schools, and allocated disproportionate resources to the white schools. Critics welcomed the Administration's action, but questioned whether the Reagan Administration would pursue the case vigorously or initiate similar ones. In other instances (e.g., North Carolina state colleges) the Administration had elected to avoid litigation in favor of negotiated settlements.

It is important to realize that even complete enforcement of civil rights legislation will not lead to equal status for whites and blacks. Even if all racially based barriers to achievement fell tomorrow, blacks would continue to be handicapped by past discrimination. Black school children would still be far behind their white peers in educational attainments. Equal opportunity to attend college would thus still exclude most blacks. In the labor market, too, the enforcement of nondiscrimination would be of relatively little use to a person who has been denied twenty years of training and experience. The elimination of racial discrimination would narrow racial differences in education and income, but the process would be excruciatingly slow.

To achieve equal economic status between whites and blacks, we must do more than enforce equal opportunity; we must also compensate for the heritage of previous discrimination. This means providing compensatory education and training. It also means providing preferential opportunities. Black school children with fewer attainments will have to receive special consideration, while job requirements, in terms of qualifications, experience, and credentials, will have to be set aside for many black workers. As we noted in Chapter 14, such extreme "affirmative action" inevitably conflicts with the claims of those whites who feel they have "earned" admission to desired schools or jobs and thus necessitates difficult and delicate compromises. But to forsake any such action is to perpetuate discriminatory status.

CAUSES, ATTITUDES, AND POLICY

While present policy directions are not well suited to achieve equality or eliminate poverty, there is some prospect for future change. Both the nonpoor and the poor are becoming increasingly frustrated with policies that provide more income maintenance and fewer opportunities. A Harris poll taken in 1976 showed that 80 percent of the American public regards our welfare problem as "very serious." They want more jobs provided for poor persons, and less welfare. If required, the necessary jobs should be guaranteed by the government.

Although public demands for less welfare and more jobs are persistent, an undercurrent of hostility and distrust remains. Over 80 percent of the public agrees that "too many people on welfare could be working" and that "too many people on welfare cheat by getting money they are not entitled to."[3] With respect to minority concerns, 41 percent of white America believes that black unemployment rates are high because blacks don't want jobs.[4] In addition, one out of four whites believes blacks have less native intelligence. Only 4 percent of all whites believe that job discrimination is a major barrier to black employment. White perceptions of Spanish-speaking minorities are comparable.[5] Finally, a majority of Americans opposes preferential access to jobs or schools for either poor people or minorities, preferring to let "merit" determine access to schools and jobs.

These perceptions of poverty and discrimination are major determinants of public policy. If we are going to eliminate either poverty or discrimination, public perceptions must reflect reality more closely. Then those perceptions must be reflected in public policy.

[3]Louis Harris survey of June 1976.
[4]CBS/New York Times poll of October 1977.
[5]Louis Harris and Associates, *A Study of Attitudes toward Racial and Religious Minorities and toward Women* (New York: National Conference of Christians and Jews, 1978).

INDEX